Please return/renew this item by the last date shown
HEREFORD AND WORCESTER COUNTY LIBRARIES

TIME AND THE
PRIESTLEYS
THE STORY OF A FRIENDSHIP

Jack and Jacquetta, summer 1967 (photograph by Mrs Gabriel Karminski)

TIME AND THE
PRIESTLEYS
THE STORY OF A FRIENDSHIP

DIANA COLLINS

FOREWORD BY IRIS MURDOCH

ALAN SUTTON PUBLISHING LIMITED

First published in the United Kingdom in 1994
Alan Sutton Publishing Limited
Phoenix Mill · Far Thrupp · Stroud · Gloucestershire

First published in the United States of America in 1994
Alan Sutton Publishing Inc
83 Washington Street · Dover · NH 03820

British Library Cataloguing-in-Publication Data

A catalogue record for this book is available from the British Library.

ISBN 0-7509-0828-9

Library of Congress Cataloging-in-Publication Data applied for

Typeset in 10/13 Bembo.
Typesetting and origination by
Alan Sutton Publishing Limited.
Printed in Great Britain by
Butler and Tanner, Frome, Somerset.

CONTENTS

Foreword *by Iris Murdoch*   vii

Preface   xi

Acknowledgements   xiii

  1 *A Public Man*   1

PART I MEETING THE PRIESTLEYS
  2 *First Encounters*   11
  3 *Feminine Values*   17
  4 *Eros Ascendant*   24

PART II JACK
  5 *The Early Years*   37
  6 *The Middle Years*   49
  7 *Life and the Theatre*   68
  8 *Theatre, War and Politics*   82
  9 *Active Politics, 1945 and After*   92

PART III JACQUETTA
 10 *Early Days*   105
 11 *Growing Up*   115
 12 *Archaeology and Marriage*   124
 13 *Marriage, Archaeology and Love*   134
 14 *Love and the Civil Servant*   145

PART IV JACK AND JACQUETTA
 15 *The Course of True Love*   159
 16 *Growing Together*   170
 17 *Divorce and Marriage*   180
 18 *Creative Happiness*   188
 19 *Sunlight over Alveston*   203
 20 *The Sunset Years*   219

 21 *Time to Go On*   239

Index   249

FOREWORD

Jack Priestley covered the century. Diana Collins here presents a splendid, detailed and affectionate account of Jack's life: his childhood in Bradford, his marriages, his versatile talents as novelist, playwright, essayist, philosopher, politician, and great human being. How he fought in the First World War and how, in the Second, his frequent broadcasts, uttered in his rich Yorkshire voice, were a constant inspiration. Also he was a painter! He found his perfect partner in his third wife, Jacquetta, a distinguished archaeologist, and herself a brilliant and original writer. Diana Collins gives an account of Jacquetta's very different early life in Cambridge, her first marriage to the archaeologist Christopher Hawkes, her love affairs, and her wartime work in the Civil Service.

There were many sides to this remarkable man, J.B. Priestley. He studied Gurdjieff, Ouspensky, Dunne, Jung, sometimes making use of this in his plays. Both he and Jacquetta claimed not to be Christians, yet they are both in a deep sense spiritual, even, in Jack's case, in some way mystical. His works remain memorable, his novels ever rereadable, from *The Good Companions* and *Angel Pavement* (early) to *Lost Empires* and *The Image Men* (late), while his plays are continually performed all over the world. As I write, *An Inspector Calls* is running in the West End. He loved actors: actors loved him. He was also a generous friend to writers and was (for instance) an early discoverer of John Cowper Powys.

He was a very surprising man, and to be kept in a state of surprise by him was one of the charms of his company. He was a very kind man and possessed a unique mixture of robustness and delicacy. He would tell you about some comic thing which had happened to him – and nobody was a better raconteur than Jack on the subject of life's little absurdities – and then you would find him saying the most penetrating things about Degas or Homer or contemporary poetry. But even when he was most fascinating he never just 'held forth' to you – he wanted to know what you thought yourself. He seemed to understand at once, for he was as full of intuition as of sympathy. John

Bayley (my husband) and I knew Jack for many years and always delighted in our meetings. In the Isle of Wight, where he and Jacquetta were then living, we would walk along the cliffs to a little village and have what he taught me to call a 'Dog's Nose' – gin in a half of bitter – before going home for lunch. Often Jack was at work with his pictures, and would show us the results.

Later, at Kissing Tree House near Stratford-on-Avon, he and Jacquetta would dispense the same wonderful hospitality. Sometimes we were taken to a Shakespeare play at the nearby theatre. Once it was *The Merchant of Venice*, and afterwards Jack remarked that he thought he could have managed the fifth act better than the Bard! He said this of course with a twinkle, but the detailed comments and criticisms he then went on to make showed that there might have been something in it! With another twinkle he suddenly observed, 'The quality of Meursault is not strained', as he poured out some very delicious white burgundy. John was so amused by this spontaneous jest that he has been repeating it ever since!

When I, incited by various people to turn my novel *A Severed Head* into a play, wrote a script which I was not happy with, I took it to Jack, who said, 'This won't do, Duckie!' Considerably altered and improved by Jack, we put it on together and it ran for a long time. Also I learnt many things. Jack had such a wonderful instinct for what could make people laugh (as well, incidentally, as for what stirs their deepest feelings and makes them cry). When the hero of the play went to see a psychiatrist, who was carrying off his wife, and I hadn't been able to find an apt expression for the tension between the two men, Jack solved the problem. He made the psychiatrist say after a tense pause, 'Did you find a parking space?' Of course the audience dissolved in mirth.

Jack made good use of his interest in Jung, and his Time Plays show how much he had thought about the nature of the strange medium we live in, and how a drama can illustrate its workings, in something like the same way that Proust did in the course of his great novel. Jack's *Literature and Western Man*, a brilliant and scholarly survey, shows his remarkable ability to feel, think and demonstrate as effortlessly and as sharply as a critic as he does in his novels and plays. Although I could not follow, I was always enchanted to listen to what he said about the unconscious, and about the borderlands between myth and being. His delight in his own experiences, and the interest in them which he gave his listeners, was extraordinarily infectious. He had such a vivid and enthralled sense of things – a vision that often recalled Blake or D.H. Lawrence. Like Shakespeare's Falstaff, he was the reason why wit was in others, and was certainly a great cause of joy and pleasure in others. His own pleasure in living and his appetite for life was so great. I remember his saying that sometimes in the morning he was conscious of a great blue ball of promise and happiness, like a shining soap bubble, above his head – and whether its promise was fulfilled that day or not, it was a great thing to know it had been there.

Diana Collins has written a book that not only conveys so much of what Jack's friends felt about him, but a great deal about the permanent essence of his genius as a human being and a writer. Her book is immensely enjoyable, and its calm modesty of tone does not conceal what a great man Priestley was, and how that impression of greatness remains with those who knew him. Diana and her husband Canon John Collins were of course close to Jack and Jacquetta, not only as friends but as colleagues in the Campaign for Nuclear Disarmament. Jack shared that mission with them, just as he shared all his ideas and projects with his wife Jacquetta, and entered so much and so helpfully into all of hers. All his friends miss him. I miss him very much.

Iris Murdoch
February 1994

PREFACE

This, as the sub-title indicates, is a personal book. Jack and Jacquetta Priestley were our close and dear friends for more than thirty-five years. An unlikely friendship as people might, and some did, say – just as the marriage of Jack and Jacquetta might well have seemed improbable, as did my own marriage to John Collins, eventually Canon Collins of St Paul's Cathedral. Both marriages were deeply happy and, in very different ways, creative.

I have written of how the understanding and knowledge of two people develops, by working together in a common cause, staying in each other's homes, holidaying together, getting to know their friends and their families and hence gaining a knowledge of their respective backgrounds. Two biographical sections are therefore included, one of Jack and one of Jacquetta.

My discussion of their writings reflects my own reading and reactions. I write of their intentions and ideas after much fascinating talk with them, both together and separately.

As far as facts are concerned, I have been as scrupulous as possible. I have had long sessions with their children, relatives, friends and colleagues – I have fabricated nothing and I have concealed nothing essential. In my view a biographer is not entitled to pass moral judgements either by way of excuse or censure – the facts must be ascertained and presented in as honest and unbiased a manner as is humanly possible. This I have tried to do.

As for the rest, it is simply my experience and knowledge of two wonderful and generous friends. They say that love is blind; leaving aside perhaps the first overwhelming onslaughts of a sexual love, I believe the contrary – it is love that truly sees.

The fact that on 13 September this year Jack would have been one hundred years old made this seem the appropiate time to celebrate two remarkable and gifted individuals.

ACKNOWLEDGEMENTS

My debts are many. First to Jacquetta Priestley, without whose patient co-operation, encouragement and generosity this book would not have been possible.

Then a very special thank you to Iris Murdoch for her lovely foreword. Also for a very nice lunch and much lively Priestley-talk with Iris and her husband, John Bayley.

Jack's children, Barbara Wykeham, Sylvia Goaman, Mary Priestley, Rachel Littlewood and Tom Priestley have all given me time and shown me family letters and photographs, as have Jacquetta's nephew, Richard Holmes, and his wife Priscilla. Jacquetta's son, Nicolas Hawkes, has done the same.

I have spent happy hours with Miss Ann Puddock, the Priestleys' housekeeper for some fifty years. Christopher Hawkes' cousin, Joan Lampen, has filled in much of the Hawkeses' family background.

I am indebted to many of the Priestleys' friends: Denis Forman, Peggy Lamert, Robert Robinson, Stephen and Amy Pratt, Michael Denison and his wife Dulcie Gray, Richard Pascoe and his wife Barbara Leigh-Hunt, and to Lady Richardson, widow of that great actor, Ralph Richardson. Charles Pick, Jack's friend and long-time publisher, has given me helpful information and advice.

I am indebted to Diana Webster, Christopher Hawkes's biographer, who has given me permission to use and quote from her book *Hawkesye*. I also thank Christopher's widow, Sonia Chadwick Hawkes, who, in a perhaps uneasy situation, has been open and helpful and allowed me to quote from family letters.

Wayne McKenna has kindly and helpfully allowed me to quote from his biography of W.J. Turner, and Mrs S.A.C. Hamilton, who inherits the copyright, has given me permission to quote from Turner's poetry and writings.

Peters, Fraser and Dunlop, J.B. Priestley's agents, have kindly given me permission, on behalf of the estate, to quote from the play *Dragon's Mouth*. The Society of Antiquities kindly sent me copies of Jacquetta's reviews and articles with permission to quote from them.

Jacquetta's first publisher, the Cresset Press, no longer exists, and I have no knowledge of copyright other than that of the author herself. Acknowledgement is made to Chatto & Windus for the use of quotations from *A Quest of Love*.

Messrs Heinemann have given me permission to use lengthy quotations from the many works of J.B. Priestley.

Finally, I must express much gratitude to Robin Denniston for agreeing to act as my agent, and for all the hard work he has put into *Time and the Priestleys*; an act of true friendship.

If I have overlooked any copyright, or helpers, I sincerely apologize. I have tried to cover everything in the book.

ONE

A PUBLIC MAN

It was in the summer of 1940 when my husband John and I, along with thousands of others, first became conscious of J.B. Priestley as a public figure. He was already among the popular novelists and playwrights of the thirties, but in 1940 it was Winston Churchill and J.B. Priestley to whom the world listened.

By May 1940 the position of Britain appeared dire, with virtually the whole of Europe in the grip of the Nazi terror, France on the point of collapse, and the British Expeditionary Force in the greatest danger. On 10 May Churchill made his first speech as prime minister to the House of Commons and to us all, 'I have nothing to offer you but blood, toil, tears and sweat.' By 26 May the evacuation of the BEF from Dunkirk had begun. There were influential people who felt and said to each other that the British position was well-nigh hopeless, weak, isolated and alone: how could Britain possibly withstand the onslaught of the mighty German army and air force? Italy was still neutral, and Mussolini had offered to mediate and secure the best possible terms. Should we not take up this offer and try to save something from the wreckage?

The War Cabinet met; passionately Churchill urged that Britain should fight on, if necessary alone. He was supported by the two Labour members, Clement Attlee and Arthur Greenwood, but opposed by Lord Halifax and Neville Chamberlain. It was a majority vote, three to two; and so the war went on. Once this decision had been taken it had to be presented to the people. With the threat, and already on the Continent the fearsome reality, of aerial bombardment, this would be a people's war, with the so-called civilians in the front line along with the fighting forces. On 4 June Churchill delivered a long and brilliant speech to the House of Commons. It had been feared that only some twenty to thirty thousand men could be saved from Dunkirk. In the event, although an enormous amount of equipment was lost, over 338,000 allied troops were brought safely to England. 'This struggle was protracted and fierce,' Churchill reported. 'Suddenly the scene has cleared, the crash and thunder has, for the moment – but only for the moment – died away. A miracle of deliverance, achieved by valour, by perseverance, by perfect discipline, by faultless service, by resource, by skill, by unconquerable fidelity is manifest to us all.' He ended his speech with the words that rang round the world:

> We shall not flag nor fail. We shall go on to the end. We shall fight in France, we shall fight on the seas and oceans, we shall fight with growing confidence and growing strength in the air, we shall defend our Island whatever the cost may be, we shall fight on the beaches, we shall fight on the landing grounds, we shall fight in the fields and in the streets, we shall fight in the hills; we shall never surrender. . . .

It was a magnificent, oratorical *tour de force*. Churchill, though he certainly possessed the common touch, was an aristocrat, born of a long line of public servants, soldiers, and ministers of the Crown; the history of England was in his bones. He had a resonant, growling voice which a slight impediment made immediately recognizable, as did his dogged determination to continue to mispronounce the word 'Nazis' as 'Nazzees'. He was also, and this was surpremely important, a master of the English language. With his fine, rallying, rhetorical phrases, stirring and inspiring, summoning to combat and to courage, he led and carried us through what may still be called 'our finest hour'. But something more was needed, and it was a brilliant idea to call upon another, quite different master of the English language.

J.B. Priestley was a man of the people. He too had a highly individual voice, rich, warm and seductive, and still carrying echoes of his Yorkshire youth; he was also an experienced and skilful broadcaster. He was the perfect complement to Churchill.

Priestley spoke to us of England, the England that he deeply loved and deeply understood. 'I am as English as steak and kidney pudding,' he said of himself. His talks were intimate, confidential and easy, he was travelling with us, sharing the everyday details, the domestic problems, the dangers, the doubts and hopes, and all the conflicting emotions of that perilous period. He celebrated the way of life, the countryside, the cities and the qualities of the people of Britain.

On 5 June, the day after Churchill's great speech, Priestley gave his first broadcast. John and I, newly married, listened with pleasure, and then with hope.

'I wonder how many of you feel as I do', he began, 'about this great Battle and evacuation of Dunkirk. . . . What strikes me about it is how typically English it is. Nothing, I feel, could be more English than this Battle of Dunkirk, both in its beginning and its end, its folly and its grandeur. . . . very English (and when I say 'English' I really mean British) in the way in which, when apparently all was lost, so much was gloriously retrieved.' He reflected on the part played by the little ships, and in particular by the little pleasure steamers:

> They liked to call themselves 'Queens' and 'Belles'. . . . They seemed to belong to the same ridiculous holiday world as pierrots and piers, sand castles, ham-and-egg teas, palmists, automatic machines and crowded sweating promenades. But these 'Brighton Belles' and 'Brighton Queens' left that innocent foolish world of theirs – to sail into the inferno, to defy bombs, shells, magnetic mines, torpedoes, machine-gun fire – to rescue our soldiers. Some of them – alas – will never return. Among those was one that I knew well, for it was the pride of our ferry service to the Isle of Wight – none other than the good ship *Gracie Fields*. I tell you, we were proud of the *Gracie Fields*, for she was the glittering queen of our local line, and instead of taking an hour over her voyage, used to do it, churning like mad, in forty-five minutes. . . . She has paddled and churned away – for ever. But now – look – this little steamer, like all her brave and battered sisters, is immortal. She'll go sailing proudly down the years in the epic of Dunkirk. And our great grand-children when they learn how we began this War by snatching glory out of defeat, and then swept on to victory, may also learn how the little holiday steamers made an excursion to hell and came back glorious.

From then on, Priestley's broadcasts were the postscripts following the nine o'clock news on Sunday evenings. For the next two or three weeks, John and I were in Hampshire; we had gone to attend a friend's wedding, and stayed on for a short holiday together before John became an RAF chaplain. The poet in Priestley often found its way into his prose, as it did when he spoke of the loveliness of that exceptionally sunlit spring, and he would often quote from the English poets that he loved.

We listened to his account of a night out with the Home Guard. England by then was preparing seriously for invasion – our airmen could watch the enemy forces massing along the Continental Channel

Jack delivering one of his famous 'postscripts' at the BBC in the 1940s (BBC)

ports. Bombs had begun to fall, and we were warned about the descent of German parachute troops. They might be disguised, we were told; nuns and priests, for some extraordinary reason, seemed to be the preferred camouflage. Signposts all over the country had been removed, so that it was impossible for us, as well as for the enemy, to find our way anywhere. So there was Priestley on top of a hill at night. 'I felt', he said, 'a powerful and rewarding sense of community; and with it too a feeling of deep continuity. There we were, ploughman and parson, shepherd and clerk, turning out at night, as our forefathers had often done before us, to keep watch and ward over the sleeping English hills and fields and homesteads.' He reflected on earlier invasion threats. He felt, he said, 'that all this raiding and threat of invasion, though menacing and dangerous, was not some horror big enough to split the world – but merely our particular testing time; what *we* must face, as our forefathers faced such things, in order to enjoy our own again. It would come down upon us; it would be terrible; but it would pass. You remember Hardy's song, "In Time of The Breaking of Nations":

> Only a man harrowing clods
> In a slow silent walk,
> With an old horse that stumbles and nods,
> Half asleep as they stalk.
>
> Only thin smoke without flame
> From the heaps of couch-grass:
> Yet this will go onward the same
> Though Dynasties pass.
>
> Yonder a maid and her wight
> Come whispering by;
> War's annals will fade into night
> Ere their story die.'

There in the depths of the Hampshire countryside the emotions that Priestley touched were the same reassuring emotions that John and I too felt that night.

Priestley often hung his talks on some familiar everyday object or incident: a brood of ducklings on a Hampstead pond at night, 'a tiny feathered flotilla – just squeaking specks of yellow fluff', that somehow or other attracted a ring of spectators whose eyes, ears and imaginations 'were caught and held by those triumphant little parcels of life'; or the sight of a drunk man defying an air-raid and standing in the middle of the road singing 'Rule Britannia' at the top of his voice – 'He had the right idea,' said Priestley, though he did add that he didn't really wish to encourage such behaviour in the middle of an air-raid. Then there was that giant Yorkshire pie that Priestley saw in a shop-window when he visited Bradford after a particularly destructive air-raid. Somehow the proprietor had preserved it and brought it out still magically steaming and smelling as all good Yorkshire pies should. Priestley defended himself for 'yapping on about pies and nonsense' at such a time by saying, 'We must keep burnished the bright little thread of our common humanity that still runs through these iron days and black nights, and that we are fighting to preserve. And indeed I hope to enlarge that private all-important little world of our own reminiscence, humour and homely poetry in which a pie that steamed for forty-five years and successfully defied an air-raid to steam again, has its own proper place.'

As, thanks to the RAF, the threat of invasion receded, we had the London Blitz, which John and I briefly experienced. Priestley spoke to us again. 'On these recent nights, when I have gone up on to high roofs, and have seen the fires like open wounds on the vast body of the city, I've realized, like many another settler here, how deeply I've come to love London, with its misty twilit charm, its hidden cosiness and companionship, its smoky magic. The other night when a few fires were burning so fiercely that half the sky was aglow, and the tall terraces around Portland Place were like pink palaces in the Arabian nights, I saw the dome and cross of St Paul's silhouetted in sharpest black against the red flames and orange flames, and it looked like an enduring symbol of reason and Christian ethics seen against the crimson glare of unreason and savagery. "Though the great rains put out the sun, here stand I for a sign."' John loved St Paul's; before the war he had spent several happy years there as a Minor Canon. The vision of the majestic cathedral sailing serenely through the flames meant a great deal to him.

There is one more quotation – indeed there are many – that I find hard to resist. Here it is:

It's often been said . . . that we Islanders are a cold-hearted and unimaginative folk, and it's a thundering lie, for we have some of the most glorious witnesses to our warmth and heart, and height of imagination, from Shakespeare onwards, that the world can know. Always, when we've spoken or acted, as a people, and not when we've gone to sleep . . . that lift of the heart, that touch of the imagination, have been suddenly discovered in our speech and our affairs, giving our history a strange glow, the light that never was on sea or land. . . . No burden, it seems, is too great for the people. Then there can't be too rich and great a reward for the people.

The Priestley postscripts were required listening every Sunday in homes, in schools, in pubs, in places of work all over the land, they must have been heard by millions of people. The result was that wherever Priestley was recognized – his voice usually gave him away – people would come up and shake his hand, and tell him how much hope and encouragement he had given them; some just wanted to touch him. He had a hugh mailbag of appreciative letters. All this adulation embarrassed him – he felt he was grossly overpraised for these short pieces, hastily tapped out on his typewriter. Much later he wrote:

> They were nothing more than spoken essays designed to have a very broad and classless appeal. I meant what I said in them, of course; a man is a fool if he tries to cheat the microphone. I didn't see then, and I don't see now what all the fuss was about. To this day middle-aged and elderly men shake my hand and tell me what a ten-minute talk about ducks on a pond or a pie in a shop-window meant to them, as if I had given them the *Eroica* or *King Lear*. I have found myself tied like a man to a gigantic balloon, to one of those bogus reputations that only the mass media know how to inflict.

There was no false modesty in this; that was never part of his make-up. If he was satisfied with anything he had written he was quite happy to say so.

Priestley never wanted the postscripts to be published, but had, in the end, to agree. In a preface he said, 'What really holds the attention of most decent folk is a genuine sharing of feelings and views on the part of the broadcaster. He must talk as if he were among serious friends, and not as if he had suddenly been appointed head of an infants' school.' And he reflected on 'those strange months, when first the world wondered if each week would see the end of us, and then afterwards drew a long breath of relief and admiration as the common folk of this island rose to meet the challenge, and not only saved what we have that is good, but began to dream of something much better.'

Reading through these postscripts, it is apparent that Priestley's emphasis does gradually change; he talks more and more about the better world for which we were fighting. There was nothing particularly subversive about that – didn't we all want something better? Even those who had grown up in the interwar years were aware of how sadly the promise of 'a land fit for heroes' had been betrayed. We had seen the ravages of unemployment and the hunger marches of the thirties, and Priestley had written about these. And when in 1939 families were evacuated from the big cities, we had been shocked by the arrival of children who had clearly never sat down to a proper meal, who were ill-clothed, ill-fed and lice-ridden. Comfortable Britain had suddenly woken up to the state of its inner cities.

As Priestley's insistence on a fairer and better social order after the war developed, authority began to get nervous. On Sunday 10 October 1940 he delivered his last postscript. Although he said then that 'The decision was mine, in no way forced on me by the BBC,' it was widely believed that his talks were considered too radical and too left-wing, although he firmly and truthfully denied any particular party allegiance. Years later he wrote: 'I received two letters – one was from the Ministry of Information telling me that the BBC was responsible for taking me off the air, and the other was from the BBC saying that a directive had come from the Ministry of Information to end my broadcasts.' Whatever the truth may be, many people believe, and I certainly do, that in 1940 the will of the British people to fight on alone in an apparently hopeless situation, was roused and sustained by the power of the spoken word, brilliantly conveyed by two great masters of the English language, Winston Churchill and J.B. Priestley.

PART I
MEETING THE PRIESTLEYS

TWO

FIRST ENCOUNTERS

It was towards the end of 1957 that John and I first met Jack and Jacquetta Priestley. We had considerable reservations about each other. Neither Jack nor Jacquetta would have had much, if any, experience of ecclesiastics. Jack had been brought up in the strict Sabbatarian atmosphere of a Baptist chapel, against which he quickly rebelled. Jacquetta's background was academic, scientific and non-religious. To those who did not know John, he could have appeared as a publicity-seeking 'political' priest, neglecting his proper duties for the seductions of the media. Those who disapproved of his activities were quick to propagate this unflattering image.

Our reservations were largely a result of the bad publicity surrounding the respective Priestley/Hawkes divorces. Jacquetta had elected to be cited as the co-respondent, but this honest decision landed them in trouble. The judge in his summing up had delivered himself of a thoroughly unjust attack on Priestley's behaviour, without regard to inadequate evidence before the court, and without any knowledge of the complicated background to this divorce. It was only later that we learned the true version of all this sorry business.

Jack was, it is true, a famous grumbler, and, in some quarters, had a reputation for being difficult and grumpy. I once chaired a meeting of the Campaign for the Abolition of Capital Punishment, and Jack was one of the speakers. On that occasion he did appear thoroughly out of humour, and took not the slightest notice of me. 'Priestley's a surly fellow,' commented Victor Gollancz as we had supper together after the meeting. Victor and Priestley, though often in political agreement, disliked each other.

The occasion of our meeting with Jack and Jacquetta was the beginning of the Campaign for Nuclear Disarmament. Public anxiety about British nuclear policy had been growing steadily since the Conservative government had decided that Britain needed to manufacture its own H-bombs. Duncan Sandys' elucidation of our 'defence' policy was hardly reassuring. 'We have taken a very bold step', he explained, 'in deciding not to do the impossible. We have decided not to defend the whole country, but to defend only our bomber bases.' This was, to say the least, an extraordinary kind of new non-defence policy, about which the undefended public had never been consulted – they just had to pay up.

Anxieties about health hazards from atmospheric testings increased with the 1957 series of British tests on that Pacific island so inaptly named Christmas Island. Government ministers kept declaring blandly that the tests would harm nobody, but scientists knew better, and some were beginning to speak. There were a number of burgeoning anti-nuclear groups, but they were uncoordinated. The most significant of these was the National Campaign against Nuclear Weapons Tests, based in Hampstead, which had Lord Russell as president, Arthur Goss, a Quaker, as chairman, and that seasoned and redoubtable campaigner, Peggy Duff, as secretary. It also had a panel of eminent supporters, including reputable scientists.

Then, on 2 November, an article 'Britain and the Nuclear Bombs' by J.B. Priestley appeared in the *New Statesman*. Before he began to write, Priestley had asked the magazine to supply him with all the arguments it could muster in favour of the bombs. He then sat down at his typewriter to demolish them. He was, as always, immensely readable, humorous and moral, tapping out one memorable phrase after another. His attack was on the so-called 'realistic' arguments, and the folly of refusing to face realistically the real position of Britain in the world. To the argument that no men in their right minds would let loose such powers of destruction, he replied: 'Surely it is the wildest idealism, at the furthest remove from sober realism, to assume that men will always behave reasonably and in line with their best interests.' He was not arguing for pacifism: 'There is no suggestion here of abandoning the immediate defence of this island. Indeed, it might well be considerably strengthened. . . .' To the suggestion that as an independent nuclear power Britain might be in a position to mediate between America and the Soviet Union, he pointed out that we could not afford to continue competing in the nuclear race, 'an insane regress of ultimate weapons that are not ultimate. . . . We cannot at one and the same time be both an independent power bargaining on equal terms, and a minor ally or satellite.' These were prophetic words: we were soon having to buy large slices of our nuclear arsenal from America, and American bases under American control became part of the British countryside. 'Our "hard-headed realism,"' he concluded, 'is neither hard-headed nor realistic just because it insists on our behaving in a new world as if we were still living in an old world, the one that has been replaced.'

There remained the moral dimension: 'We ended the war high in the world's regard. We could have taken over its moral leadership, spoken and acted for what remained of its conscience; but we chose to act otherwise – with obvious and melancholy consequences. . . .' His points were carefully argued and spelled out and he ended his article with a plea: 'Alone, we defied Hitler; and alone we can defy this nuclear madness into which the spirit of Hitler seems to have passed, to poison the world. There may be other chain reactions besides those leading to destruction; and we might start one. . . . This might well be a declaration to the world that after a certain date one power able to engage in nuclear warfare will reject the evil thing for ever.'

This was the catalyst; the article chimed with everything that John and I felt and thought about the nuclear issue, and we were by no means alone. Letters in support of Priestley poured into the *New Statesman* office, and a second article produced a further deluge. The editor, Kingsley Martin, and his office were quite unable to deal with this inundation. They sent the letters to the Hampstead group. It was already considering becoming an all-out anti-nuclear campaign, and had asked its eminent supporters for their views.

Events moved quickly. Kingsley Martin had been ambivalent over the nuclear issue; now he felt he must go with his readership. He

Jack and Jacquetta with Kingsley Martin (far left), the editor of the *New Statesman*, and Julian and Juliette Huxley in the late 1950s

called a meeting in his flat; this included Jack and Jacquetta Priestley, Commander Sir Stephen King-Hall, Professor Blackett and George Kennan, who had just delivered the 1957 Reith Lectures, 'Russia, the Atom and the West', in which he had questioned the whole nuclear strategy. They decided that the time had come to launch a national campaign. Kingsley indicated that the Hampstead committee was ready to sink its identity in a larger movement, and would hand over its bank balance, its new office off Fleet Street, and its February booking of the Central Hall, Westminster. Peggy Duff was ready to offer her services. When a sizeable and centrally situated place was needed for a larger meeting of interested people, it was Peggy who suggested 2 Amen Court, John's official home as a canon of St Paul's. His name as a possible chairman was raised, and, since the Priestleys were uncertain about this turbulent priest, Peggy was deputed to take him along to their flat in Albany to be introduced.

John came back from the meeting in high spirits. He was really impressed by Priestley: he seemed a delightful man, they had got on well together, and they had similar views about an anti-nuclear campaign; reservations had melted easily away. As for Jacquetta, no normal male, especially one susceptible to female charms, could fail to be dazzled by her. Now it was my turn: the Priestleys wanted us to join them for dinner, but John could not manage the only date they could find, so I was to go alone.

I went with some apprehension. In many ways I felt positive about J.B. Priestley. I remembered the famous postscripts, and while still at school, an aspiring student of English literature, I had read, with pleasure, *The Good Companions*, and its successors, *Angel Pavement* and *They Walk in the City*. We had known little about Jacquetta, except that she was an archaeologist, and had recently published a highly praised book called *A Land*. I was eager to meet them both, and the slight aura of wickedness that hung about them was undeniably intriguing.

The entrance to Albany was itself somewhat awesome. I was met by an immensely tall and splendidly uniformed doorman – he had once been a regimental sergeant-major. He directed me to staircase 'B', on the left of a long straight passageway known as 'the rope walk'. High, dark buildings on either side contained the apartments, many of them with those blue plaques on their walls bearing the names of the famous people who had once lived within. All was silent and cold, severely classical and dimly lit, rather grand and gloomy. I climbed the wide stone staircase to a thick wooden door with 'J.B. Priestley' on its large brass door-plate.

Once inside there was warmth and light and welcome, though I was a little overawed by Jacquetta, who looked so elegant in her long evening dress, and who had a slight air of formality that made you wonder what lay behind. I had not understood this as a dinner party, more of an anti-nuclear get-together, so I had put on a short woollen dress. The only other guest was Laurens van der Post's wife, Ingaret, whom I already knew and liked – nothing alarming about Ingaret, she was kind and cheerful, and often funny without meaning to be. Of course I was struck by Jacquetta's appearance, tall, dark-haired and with a beautifully curved cheek line. Her eyes were grey with a hint of greenish blue, they had a Mona Lisa look, neither cold nor lacking in kindness, just mysterious. Her fascinatingly lovely smile quickly dissipated any faintly chilling formality. Jack, on the other hand, could certainly not have been described as handsome. He was not particularly tall, was thick-set and a bit fat, with a high-domed forehead and head that was losing hair on top. His mouth was rather heavily sensual, and there was a knowing twinkle in his eyes. He immediately put me at ease by explaining how happy he was to be dining with three women; he preferred their company to that of men – they were usually much more interesting. It was a happy, easy

Jack selecting one of his many pipes at his apartment in Albany, Piccadilly (Reuter Photos)

evening, and I felt greatly drawn to both of them. There was no call for party manners, nor social small talk. In so far as anyone can, I had only to be myself. I quickly discerned that no kind of personal falsity could long flourish here. How mischievous, malicious and false are those sedulously propagated public images.

These instant friendships are some of the delights and mysteries of life. They are often unexpected, as was John's and mine with Jack and Jacquetta. I wonder what it is that so immediately draws people together, before you have had any chance of getting to know one another, and when you may only have exchanged a few words. Sometimes, not always, there may be a hidden sexual element – people talk in a reductionist manner about 'the chemistry' – but I think it is always very much more: psychological in the deepest sense, almost as if there are people whom your true inner self instantly recognizes. When that happens you soon discover that you have not been mistaken.

Two meetings of what are called 'the great and the good' soon took place in John's large study. The Campaign for Nuclear Disarmament was founded. Lord Russell became its president, J.B. Priestley the vice-president, and John was asked to be chairman. Ritchie Calder was vice-chairman, an imposing executive was elected, and Peggy Duff became the miraculously energetic and experienced organizing secretary. So now there were comings and goings in 2 Amen Court, and meetings of the executive to hammer out a policy, to plan the February launching and to work out a further plan of campaign. Soon after our dinner in Albany Jack must have been attending one of these meetings, and I remember seeing him out of the front door. He gave me a friendly kiss and said, 'We rather took to you. Did you take to us?' Of course he was expecting the affirmative answer that he got.

THREE

FEMININE VALUES

On 17 February 1958, at the Central Hall, Westminster, CND was publicly launched. The hall was packed, as were the five extra halls that Peggy Duff had optimistically booked for overflows. Some of the best public speakers in Britain spoke on CND platforms. That night they included Michael Foot, A.J.P. Taylor and J.B. Priestley, who proved himself once again a real spell-binder. The national press completely ignored this remarkable and, as it was to prove, significant and influential meeting. The publicity breakthrough came later, with the Aldermaston marches.

Meanwhile Jacquetta had decided to get together a group of women, all rather distinguished and high-powered. Among them were Dr Antoinette Pirie, a reader in opthalmology at Oxford University, Marghanita Laski, Margaret Lane, Storm Jameson and Dr Janet Aitken. I, the only undistinguished one, was happy to be invited to join them.

Jack and Jacquetta were much influenced by the ideas of the great psychologist, Carl Gustav Jung. They believed with him that a proper balance of the masculine and feminine principles was essential for the health of the human psyche and therefore of human societies. Society in Britain, and even more so in America, was dangerously unbalanced by too much of the masculine and insufficient of the feminine.

One of Jack's many beguiling essays is called 'Eros and Logos'. True he indulged himself, as he liked to do, in 'large, loose, wild generalizations,' but wrapped in his captivating and highly individual style was wisdom and humanity. 'What I am suggesting', he wrote, 'is that we should begin substituting in our scheme of life the values of the female principle, Eros-Yin, for those of the masculine principle, Logos-Yang.' These, he pointed out, were not identical with male and female − 'I am myself a fairly robust male, but I am devoted to Eros,' while numbers of women including the most aggressive feminists have been captured by Logos. He considered America: 'American society does not show us Eros triumphant. Its chief values are masculine values. The restlessness, ruthless ambition, emphasis on change, inventions, gadgets, mechanical progress, rather pedantic idealism, the idolatry of business are all masculine, Yang stuff.' Of course, he argued, it was not possible to exclude Eros, but it arrived 'in an inferior form – crude sex, hard liquor, sex without personal realationship, drink as a short cut to unconsciousness' – a wild generalization, yes, but he did acknowledge another more feminine America, not quite driven away by Logos-Yang. So to the USSR: 'The essential Russian character, as displayed by its great literature, belongs more to Eros than to Logos, though it has always been haunted by a kind of wild Logos. . . . Russian Communism is Logos gone mad. . . . A state that ignores the claims, which ought to be primary, of lovers, husbands and wives, parents and children, represents Logos at work without any check from Eros. It destroys private happiness, all those relationships and styles of life that are at the heart of Eros, for the sake of a theory, or mere power, or some vague dream of happiness that has never been realized yet. That such societies should be piling up atom bombs, should surprise nobody. This is Logos on the spree.' To be fair, Jack did write that, 'a society entirely dominated by Eros would sink into stagnation and sloth, and, oddly enough, I suspect, would begin to develop its own cruelties, Yin being as cruel, in her own way, as Yang can be in his.' Jack had more hope for Britain: 'There is in British life still a suggestion that Yin is with us . . . we should have formed a neutral block, wearing the colours of the Yin, under the banner of Eros, who has not yet been completely banished from Western Europe.'

CND was undoubtedly well-leavened by Eros – one reason, perhaps, why it had the support of so many creative people from the world of the arts. Its members hoped for great things from the influence of women, and they did play a huge part in the work of CND, toiling away at all hours in all the local and specialist groups. There were women's anti-nuclear groups overseas as well, 'Voice of Women' in Canada and 'Women Strike for Peace' ('strike' in its dual sense) in America, and CND women were soon in touch with these. On a less philosophical level, women were concerned that their children, grandchildren and future descendants should live, and live without the threat of radioactive poisoning. This, rather than the success or failure of competing ideologies, was primary.

Jacquetta shared Jack's ideas, and was herself an imaginative writer, but, as an archaeologist and a prehistorian, she had something else. She was aware, more than most, of the long, slow climb of humanity from the simplest possible forms of life, existing only in mud and water, to the slow dawning of human consciousness, through millennia of struggle to

survive, and the earliest civilizations, up to the pesent day. A willingness
to put a catastrophic end to this immensely long and amazing story, to
poison the lands and waters that had nurtured and made it all possible,
was something that could not be tolerated; no ideology, no religion
could ever justify such an Armageddon.

So the women's group met in Albany – now, for me, one of the
friendliest of places – and we discussed what we should do. First, it
was essential to counter the government's dishonest reassurances about
nuclear tests. This, with the help of our scientists, we proceeded to
do. *Tomorrow's Children*, written by Dr Antoinette Pirie, was a
straightforward, factual warning of the nature of nuclear poisons from
fall-out and the ways in which they could affect future generations.

Jacquetta next put forward the idea of an all-women public meeting –
only women speakers, only women to be admitted. Speakers would
have ten minutes each on different aspects – I inevitably got
'morality'. In addition we would introduce semi-dramatic interludes.
We would collect quotations that would illustrate some of the dottier
ideas about nuclear defence. This was not difficult; indeed, it turned
into an indulgence in a kind of macabre black humour. Many of the
crazier quotations came from America. We had, of course, no access
to anything the Russians might be saying – perhaps they were not
allowed to say anything. A heated debate was taking place in America
as to whether you might be justified in shooting your neighbours if
too many wanted to crowd into your shelter. The consensus seemed
to be that you would be justified, and you were advised to keep a gun
ready. Market forces were quick to arrive on the scene, and we
collected a number of advertisements for so-called survival kits,
odourless toilets, various forms of super shelters, all duly priced – one
was advertising 'seven years to pay'. Rather more sober and horrifying
were extracts from the Hollifield Report, the result of Senate hearings
from expert scientists. The quotations were read alternately in dead-
pan voices by two actresses; they were horribly effective. We ended
on a note that was tragic and emotional, readings from letters written
by a young Japanese woman, a survivor of Hiroshima, who had to
watch her husband dying in slow agony from radiation sickness.

It was Jacquetta who spoke for us all. Of the arms race, she said:
'Scores of scientists, political dons and politicians here and in the US
build exquisite pagodas of logic about so-called arms control and the
credibility of the Deterrent. Yet it is all nonsense, because if the great
powers confronting one another behaved as reasonably as that,
accepted the rules of zones of influence, and the finer points of

credibility, then, of course, they could have stopped the race long ago. . . . The arms race, of course, is the material expression of something in the human mind, and it is there – in the human mind – that it has got to be stopped.' Looking back over our long history, she pointed to irreversible changes in the structures of our social conduct. Cannibalism, human sacrifice, slavery had all been abandoned, not because we could not still practise them if we so wished, but because in our developing minds they had become intolerable and impossible. Another great change was taking place in western societies' conduct towards women. Why should it not be women who might be able to bring about the final and effective revolt against war? 'I am not usually a feminist,' she said. 'I think man and woman together make the complete human being. But in this one thing I feel differently. Men have the instinct to fighting and to war – we have not. . . . We have come into our strength at the very moment that war has left the battlefields and come into the homes. . . . It might be that we should still be living in caves if it were not for masculine genius. . . . But now masculinity is running amok, and we have to come to the rescue . . . to push humanity along the road that it has already started to tread . . . to that longed for moment when war becomes impossible in the human mind.'

One woman was so moved by the meeting that at the end she rushed up to Jacquetta and insisted on giving her a gold watch to be sold for CND – she would not take 'no' for an answer. I have become something of a connoisseur of public meetings; this one, beautifully produced and stage-managed, was quite exceptional. But although a number of excellent women journalists and reporters attended, once more the meeting went unnoticed by the national media.

The women's group went on with its work. We lobbied Members of Parliament, we lobbied delegates to the Geneva Disarmament Conference, we held another meeting, Jacquetta and I attended conferences abroad. We even organized a 'Women's Day', taking over the streets of London to the considerable annoyance of the traffic and the police, though pedestrians clearly enjoyed it all. We made floats, we staged small dramas, there was singing and dancing, everything we could think of. I found Jack sitting gloomily in Albany surrounded by balloons, bits of costume, cardboard cut-outs for scenic effects. 'I wish you'd all stop,' he said in a weary and melancholy voice.

The big success of the women's group was a deputation to Prime Minister Harold Macmillan. So far he had refused all CND overtures, but he could not very well refuse us. The group was joined by Iris Murdoch, Dame Peggy Ashcroft, and the Nobel prizewinners,

Professor Dorothy Hodgkin and Dame Kathleen Lonsdale. Dame Alix Meynell, who had just retired from a distinguished career in the Civil Service, was our leader. Harold Macmillan is on record as saying how impressed he was by the women, by their courtesy, their knowledge and the way in which they presented their case. He also admitted that the force of their arguments and the strength of CND had helped him in his successful efforts to secure a test-ban treaty.

CND itself attracted wide support, and soon gained wide publicity. Jacquetta joined Jack as a member of the executive, and was a loyal and conscientious member, and a great support to John. The original executive saw the campaign as a means of influencing the political parties to accept the logic of their case. This was to be achieved by conventional democratic means, writing, speaking, lobbying and peacefully demonstrating. To some of the many young people who flocked to the campaign, this was tame stuff; they wanted action and excitement, such as that provided by civil disobedience.

The Aldermaston marches were at first a splendid and impressive outlet for all supporters. Jack was not in favour of the marches, but

Jacquetta, Richard Calder and my husband Canon John Collins at the head of the Aldermaston to London march, 1962 (The Hulton Deutsch Collection)

when he saw the publicity he acknowledged that he had been mistaken. For himself he had had more than enough of marching in the First World War. But Jacquetta and I slogged along the roads together, defying wind and rain and blistered feet. Jacquetta strode along with her fellow executives at the head of the march, always wearing her Venetian gondolier's hat, wide-brimmed and scarlet, as familiar to the marchers and the press as John's beret and cassock.

Jack worked hard for CND. To the inevitable clamour for action he wrote: 'People cannot understand that to an author writing is doing, that when he has written, he has taken action. Beyond the printed page is another world that most writers — and I am certainly one of them — enter without confidence and probably with loathing. It is a world of meetings, from intrigues in a smoke-room corner to committees talking on and on long after the last oxygen has gone.' So Jack wrote articles and made speeches on behalf of the movement, but he was suspicious of his own skills. He wrote of 'the dubious little art of oratory — so much ego-swelling ham theatre', and he was always suspicious of the crowd, and of those demagogues who sought power through manipulation of the crowd. With his gift of words and his dramatic instinct, Jack knew that he possessed such powers, but he used them with care and integrity and only for things in which he believed.

There were real conflicts in Jack between the creative artist and the concerned and compassionate citizen. 'What is a writer to do?' he asked. 'If he shuts his mind and heart in order to concentrate on his own work, he cannot help feeling a self-centred and callous exquisite, fiddling while Rome burns. If he opens his heart and mind to the daily tidings of woe, to all the stress and strain of the world, he finds it almost impossible to work properly.' Somehow or other, with his almost superhuman energy, Jack did manage to produce a huge amount of work — essays, articles, novels, plays, autobiographical writings, books of literary criticism — while answering as best he could the calls of his compassionate heart. He described himself as a naturally indolent fellow!

Meanwhile, he laboured on for CND. He organized a splendid fund-raising event at the Festival Hall, rallying his many theatrical and other contacts. He called the show *Stars in your Eyes* — he was exceptionally good at titles. It was a great success. He wrote a television play, *Doomsday for Dyson*, which was duly screened. Many producers in the BBC and ITV were sympathetic to CND, but the government had its eyes on them. Jack's play got by, as did *The Off-*

Shore Island by Marghanita Laski. Perhaps they were sufficiently imaginative, but when it came to the factually based programme *The War Game*, this was banned, and could only be shown privately to small groups.

Some years later, I read a novel which Jack had written in 1937, called *The Doomsday Men*. It was a romantic thriller in which three fanatics – a millionaire, a physicist and a cult leader – plan to blow up this irredemably evil world. The day of the apocalypse arrives. The cult followers gather in the desert; they are credulous, brain-washed and presumably eager for mass suicide. Dawn is the appointed hour – a wonderful desert dawn, for the last day of the world. Mercifully the physicist has miscalculated, and only the crazy fanatics get blown up.

If this sounds something of a send-up, the book is, of course, beautifully written, with some wonderful descriptions of the desert, lively and convincing characters, and a really exciting story. I drew Jack's attention to it. 'Yes,' he said, 'we creative chaps can sometimes be quite prophetic.' Jack was a profoundly intuitive man – a manifestation of Eros? – intuitive about people and their feelings, intuitive about wider issues, about, for lack of a better word, the *Zeitgeist*.

The story of CND has been told elsewhere and I shall not pursue it here. Jack found the introduction of democracy into the campaign a trial and a bore, with its unwieldy executive meetings, all day AGMs, and too many politicians *manqués* leaping to their feet with points of order, talking, talking and talking. Jack was fond of John and always a loyal supporter, but thought him much too gentle and patient a chairman. Jack prided himself on being a tough no-nonsense kind of chairman, racing through the business. After the split over civil disobedience with Lord Russell and his resignation as president, Jack resigned as vice-president, on the grounds that you couldn't have a vice without a president. He was, as Jacquetta said, a great resigner. I think he was thankful to have an excuse to get away from all those boring meetings. Jacquetta nobly soldiered on to the end.

Working together in a cause in which you all deeply believe is an excellent way of getting to know people, but it is no substitute for spending leisuretime with them, for staying as friends in each other's homes, for holidays together. That is the world of Eros in which true and permanent friendships happily flourish.

EROS ASCENDANT

In those early years of our friendship Jack and Jacquetta were living on the Isle of Wight; Albany was for their London activities. We first went to visit them in their real home in April 1968. This meant driving to Lymington, leaving the car, and crossing the sea to Yarmouth, in an updated version of the immortal *Gracie Fields*. Here Jack arranged for a car to meet his guests and take them up to Brooke Hill. It really was up: the car soon began to climb and we entered a long drive with a wood on the right (a home for badgers and the original surviving red squirrels) and on the left a little gate leading into a garden. We arrived at the top and there, large and imposing, stood Brooke Hill. Its position was superb, with views from every quarter, across woods and hills to the sea, dazzling and sparkling in the bright spring sunlight. This was an augury: 'Collins weather' became what Jack called 'a running gag'; every time we stayed with the Priestleys, and visits were quite frequent, we had glorious weather. Over so many years I can only remember one or two really unsettled weekends.

We were greeted in a large entrance hall, with stairs leading up to a gallery on one side, a large grand piano in one corner and huge windows some 15 ft in height opposite the gallery. It was ideal for the musical festivals that Jack used to arrange for the pleasure of people who lived locally. The great windows could be covered with thick teak shutters, excellent sounding-boards for the music. Jack was a great music lover, and would tinkle happily on the piano. The rooms were large, the drawing-room with its fine view to the west, and on the right of the hall what was known as the music room, where Jack kept a pianola and his painting gear. Jack possessed a multitude of talents and in middle age he had taken up painting – he experimented with oils and watercolour, but his most successful paintings were gouaches. He liked mountain scenery and skyscapes of broken cloud and was especially good at skies, often using his thumb for the cloud effects. The dining-room seemed the only relatively small room. It looked out on a pleasant little terrace, a perfect place for a summer evening dinner, with lobster from Yarmouth freshly caught and excellent white wine. Outside and below the house were banks of rhododendrons and a garden of azaleas in glorious bloom on that blue spring day. Jacquetta explained that the little garden we had noticed on the way up was on their only piece of clay soil, and here they had a rose garden and grew all their own vegetables.

The Priestleys were generous hosts. 'We don't invite weekend visitors for work or business,' Jack said. 'We like just to have our friends.' Weekends were for relaxation; during the week they had a working routine – writing in the mornings, walking or pottering in the afternoons, working again between tea and dinner, then a bath and change, one of Jack's excellent dry Martinis, dinner and a pleasant evening. It struck me how sensible an arrangement this was; in households where you didn't change for dinner, drinking often started around six o'clock, so by the time you got to food you would have had more than enough to drink, and a good dinner was really less enjoyable.

The Priestleys were fortunate in having Miss Pudduck and Gertrude, who ran the house with occasional help from the gardener's wife. Miss Pudduck was an exceptionally good cook and an efficient housekeeper, and Gertrude, who had once been nursery maid to the

An aerial view of Brooke Hill, the Priestleys' home on the Isle of Wight, during the 1950s (Skyfotos)

young Priestleys, did everything else. A secretary came in by day for typing and letters; it was an ideal life for two authors.

Brooke Hill with its surrounding woods and hills was a fine place for walks. One of the favourites was over the downs to Freshwater Bay. Here, in the local pub, Jack introduced us to 'Dog's Nose', beer laced with gin. Though not, I'm afraid, appreciated by me, as I am not a beer drinker, John found it pleasant as well as mildly and happily intoxicating. After the pub session no one felt much like toiling back over the downs, more up than down in that direction, so Jack ordered a car to drive us back to the house for lunch.

We walked and talked and ate and drank together. The Priestleys were a fascinatingly balanced couple: Jack's wide-ranging mind with its constant flow of ideas, its breadth of knowledge and reading, and Jacquetta's, equally interesting and imaginative, more scholarly and academic. Jack, in his dealings with people and with the world, was an extrovert; Jacquetta is an introvert. 'She needs me to warm her, and bring her out to people,' Jack said. I dislike labelling people, as if that could explain a unique human being, but labels are sometimes a convenient shorthand. The result of their different personalities was that Jack was a happy and easy host, though not always as easy a guest. Jacquetta says of herself that she is not a good hostess. That is not so; she is thoughtful and considerate about the needs and pleasures of her guests and of her friends. What she does perhaps lack is the immediate, intuitive perception of other people's feelings, something that Jack instinctively had.

At the end of the weekend, they gave us a joint present, *Journey Down a Rainbow*, a collaborative work investigating past and present societies in New Mexico and Texas. It is inscribed a little formally, 'For Diana and John Collins, with the Priestleys' good wishes'. Later books, always given generously, came 'with love'. *Journey Down a Rainbow* is dedicated, incidentally, to 'Carl Gustav Jung, the wise old man'.

In this book Jack and Jacquetta separately investigate two contrasting societies. Jack goes to Texas, land of the oil millionaires, which exhibits the most up-to-date social and cultural patterns of the twentieth century. Jacquetta visits neighbouring New Mexico, where the Pueblo Indians still live on or near their ancestral homes, and still preserve much of their ancient culture. The letters which they write to each other make up the book. They offer entertaining and illuminating accounts of both societies, and include social criticism, philosophizing and reflection. Because they are personal letters they reveal much of the thinking and character of each of the writers. They are a perfect introduction to the Priestleys.

Jacquetta seems to have had the better time; she was involved in something that deeply interested her, and with which she had an instinctive sympathy. Jack, on the other hand, moved through a society with which he was not greatly in accord, though he paid ample tribute, as did Jacquetta, to the kindness and generous hospitality of the Americans. Jacquetta's journey begins in Albuquerque, where she meets a number of men and women who are refugees from the American way of life. She is soon taken to see examples of Indian culture, and these make her

> increasingly aware of the tremendous creative force of these ancient peoples . . . upon their American conquerors. Because their culture had grown slowly from the land and the imagination, they created patterns, shapes, combinations of colours, which can be distinguished as belonging to them and them alone in all time and space. The Americans, who, in spite of their marvellous feats of engineering and engineered architecture, have never, so far as I know, produced so much as a formal moulding peculiarly their own, are most strongly attracted towards the arts and traditions of these poor and materially powerless people.

Jacquetta has a highly developed visual sense; she enables a reader to share her delight in the artefacts that capture her imaginative interest, and also in the mountains, deserts and forests of New Mexico.

Jack meanwhile is bemoaning too much noise, too much bad food, too much socializing, too little, or, sometimes, owing to the peculiar Texan licensing laws, too much, drink, not enough good talk, and, worst of all, 'a society entirely dominated by the masculine principle'. 'I am convinced', he writes, 'that good talk cannot flourish where there is a wide gulf between the sexes, where the men are altogether too masculine, too hearty, too bluff and booming, where the women are too feminine, at once both too arch and too anxious. . . . It is the society that these men have created, are still creating, that does not know what it wants, that is lunatic. . . . It is', he concluded gloomily, 'the society of the hydrogen bomb.'

Jack's analysis of the imbalance of masculine and feminine principles in American society was rather beyond some of the local newspaper reporters. In Houston, he was horrified by a headline purporting to come from an interview with him (though, in fact, one had never been given), which read: 'Says all Texan men are bores'. 'If I had believed this, I would never have had the hardihood to declare it on the spot, though I will put on record here that several Houston women, after hearing my disclaimer, told me they were disappointed, and that I ought to have said it.' In his journeyings Jack came across other examples of baffled disappointment and dissatisfaction in some of the wealthiest of American women. Women always found they could talk easily to Jack.

Jack did suffer in the cause. Here he is at the Foreign Affairs Association of Dallas, waiting to hear an address from a well-known general: 'half-fed on nursery mush, icily sober, my chilled stomach appalled, every cell of my famished brain signalling distress, I was compelled to listen to after-dinner speeches . . . I seemed to cross bare-footed all the frozen tundras of Siberia while the retiring president, the new president, the secretary, the treasurer, the chairman went on and on and on.' The general's address was at least 'lucid and not unreasonable', but it was not encouraging, 'clearly based on the belief that no co-existence with Communism was possible: we were already at war.'

Meanwhile Jacquetta writes happily about the homes (pueblos) of the Indians: 'I don't want to sentimentalize these pueblos – they must be uncomfortable and mildly unhealthy – but I do like them so much. I suppose it is partly because they are true villages . . . places where people live because their parents and grandparents did, because their sacred buildings are at the heart of them and their fields and orchards spread round about, and because all their tales concern the neighbouring rivers, mesas and mountains.' Is that sentimental? Isn't it rather the lament of many deracinated people inextricably trapped in the noise and ugliness of the modern world? It is also, and one finds this in the writings of both the Priestleys, a lament for a lost sense of the sacredness of life, and, in Jack's case particularly, a lament for the lost magic of religious symbols that no longer work in human consciousness.

Jacquetta enjoys herself, and invites the reader to do likewise, with the pottery, painting and weaving of those ancient peoples: 'It is astonishing what vigour they have. A fine Pueblo pot brings more life to a room than a fire or flowers. I am becoming more and more excited as I discover how these things can annihilate all the expensive machine products of our age.' Perhaps most astonishing are the long, fringed and beautifully patterned sashes made by the basket-maker

Indians from the white, brown and blackish hairs of their domesticated dogs. 'The making of patterns is a thing we take for granted, yet surely it represents one of the least explicable urges of our kind . . . where did the patterns come from, charged with emotional force to make a woman living as humbly as a badger give hours to their expression? . . . We still understand so little about their origin. . . .' And then comes the lament: 'On every hand the development of the imagination is threatened by mass production at its most corrupt. . . . Sometimes I fear that life on the imaginative level may be slowly stifled. Already in our Western civilization poetry, once open to all, has become inaccessible to most people. Will it soon be dead and the other arts dying?'

Jacquetta is alert to the beauties of the natural world; she has had since childhood a deep sense of 'participation mystique'. She has a sharp eye for detail: 'the fine colours of the flicker woodpeckers glowed through the dark pine needles'. She catches the last brilliant colours of the wonderful American fall, and she delights in 'the odd yet inevitable communities of plants and creatures' in Arizona, especially 'the Suguaro, those giant and noble vegetables, where two kinds of flickers cut their nesting holes in the cactus, and the diminutive elf owl continues to nest on the spring summit. How delicious to be an owl with a nest on the top of a slender column, held up twenty or thirty feet towards the stars, able to slip off and go hawking the great fat-bodied moths that fly around your tower.'

Jack, in his passage through the urban jungle, assembles his thoughts:

I have coined some new names. . . . First then *Admass*. This is the name for the whole system of increasing productivity, plus inflation, plus a rising standard of material living, plus high pressure advertising and salesmanship, plus cultural democracy and the creation of the mass mind, the mass man. (Behind the Iron Curtain they have *Propmass*, official propaganda taking the place of advertising, but all with the same aims and objects.) . . . It is better to live in Admass than have no job, no prospects of one . . . But that is about all that can be said in favour of it. All the rest is swindle. . . . In this empire are many kingdoms . . . *Nomadmass* . . . the land of the new nomads, dominated by the internal combustion engine. To enjoy it you must never want to get out of your car . . . 'drive-in' everything . . . *Hashadmass* . . . everything turned into a tasteless hash . . . Spanish, French, Italian restaurants that have long ceased to be Spanish, French or Italian . . . We have it, of course, in England now; it arrives with Admass. Probably most of the money earned in Hashadmass – the big money I mean – is spent in the smaller but richer kingdom of Luxad . . . Gracious living, casual living . . . any other kind of living dreamt up by the copy-writers. In Luxad you see yourself doing what you have been told is the latest thing to do . . . Admass, Nomadmass, Hashadmass, Luxad . . . They have almost a Biblical ring these names, but those raging old intuitives, the Hebrew Prophets, would have made short work of them – Woe! Woe! Woe!

When Marghanita Laski worked on the updated version of the *Oxford English Dictionary*, she insisted on including Admass, which is now permanently in the English language.

Jacquetta is particularly delighted by being able to watch two Indian ritual dances. At the first she is carried away by 'the all in-ness, the pervading unity' of the November ritual. She writes: 'the dance expresses in the language of poetry the truth of man's unity with nature, the truth that science represents to us, curing our delusions of grandeur. Yet because of their poetry they offer us visions for which science has no eyes.' Jacquetta herself is both a scientific observer and a poet. A more important dance is the Shalaka, for which there is long and earnest preparation, which lasts all night, and in which is symbolized the ritual descent of the gods. She finds herself even more caught up 'in the divine purpose of the dancers'. 'It is a night . . . of the blessings of new houses and of village shrines, it is a night seeking fertility – good hunting – health. Perhaps it is best to say that the Shalaka is to secure universal wellbeing – wellbeing that spreads out to the four quarters of the earth from Zuni, its most sacred centre.'

The only kind of ritual that Jack is able to recount is a football match at Fort Worth. Jack enjoyed playing and watching games, but, alas, Admass had taken over American football. 'The great bowl, brimmed with anticipation, was humming away, already tuning up for its symphony of howls and roars. . . stirring up and heating up a dark excitement released from the mysterious recesses of our being. However familiar it may be it is still frightening, monstrous.' He reflects upon the Roman blood sports in the Colosseum, and continues: 'I have sometimes been tormented by the fancy that if the future should prolong the lives of the present, if civilization should mean organization and not values, if sensation should become more and more blunted and some release had to be found for the dumb drilled mob, then the bloodstained games might once more affront the sun . . . and this time to be relayed on colour television for invalids, stay-at-homes and children.' This was 1953, before colour had arrived on our TV screens, before actual and imaginary violence was explicitly, and increasingly, offered to us.

While Jack looks to the future with foreboding, Jacquetta gazes into the past with a sadness for so much that has been lost. She gives us a great deal of fascinating information about the Indians, their lives, their rituals, and their 'essential chthonic religion': 'The ideal of behaviour was good humour and conformity at home and peace abroad. The Pueblos claim never to have made war, but only to have defended themselves. . . . In spite of their simplicity and naturally poetic outlook, good sense and sincerity are respected among the Indians.' She concludes: 'the integrity of their whole existence is the inner power that has enabled the Pueblos to hold out against all the forces of alien religions, commerce and wars.'

What does Jack in Texas discover about religion? He notices the numbers of strange sects, little chapels among the filling stations, and all along the highways posters bearing Biblical texts, 'competing not too hopefully with advertisements for gasoline and breakfast foods'. It is on one long stretch of *Nomadmass* lined with advertising hoardings that Jack's attention is finally concentrated by a particularly large hoarding, announcing that 'The Wages of Sin is Death, but the Gift of God is Eternal Life.' That set Jack thinking, and thinking set him writing 'a lay sermon to Nomadmass':

Let nobody imagine that I have quoted that text in order to jeer at it. I believe it to be true; though the largest and most astonishing claim made along that shouting highway, it was the only one that I believed to be strictly true. . . . Eternal life is not just time going on and on; the text relates to the present, no will be or shall be about it. God is not about to intervene to punish or reward. His gift simply is; we receive it by recognizing it for what it is. . . . Eternal life is always a new and heightened experience of the Here and Now . . . all moments of noble living, the ecstasy of love, the compassion and understanding that enter into every genuine personal relationship, the creation and rapt appreciation of great art, the adventures of mind among significant ideas, even an amazed wondering about ourselves, all demand this unknown dimension, this timeless being. Every greatly heightened state of consciousness involves eternity.

As for the sin that brings death, that is 'the narrowing and blunting of consciousness', the acquiescence in automatic reactions. 'Those who respond less and less to life, behaving more like automata than living spirits are dying every day. . . . It is useless putting up such reminders of ancient wisdom unless they are accompanied by warnings against Nomadmass and Admass. . . time is the master of Nomadmass and Admass. The timeless soul has no status there.' To all of this John and I could only say 'Amen'. It is a fine sermon.

Jack is hilariously funny in his various tribulations, usually at the expense of Admass, but he grows tired: 'When I was younger I liked to travel alone . . . then there was always the chance – though God knows the odds were against it – of meeting at last somewhere far away that strange beautiful woman, not Greta Garbo, but her younger sister perhaps, whose image, which is a part of their own anima, haunts all young men about to travel.' But now he says, at the age of sixty: 'I have met that woman, I know now who she is, when I can return to her.'

Jack and Jacquetta are reunited in Santa Fé:

The air up there was wonderful, mountain-fresh, warm in the sun, but with a hint of the cold night and all the snow to come to the North; I greeted my wife in my favourite weather. . . . We arrived at what was virtually a place of our own, which might almost have been a warm cave. There we talked and talked, ate the dinner and talked. Afterwards we went out to find the icy breath of night on our cheeks, to see the huge glitter of stars, from the familiar blaze of constellations to the silver dust that was a vista of illimitable worlds. They regarded us for once without irony – I forebore, for once, to make my speech about higher levels of being. It was a night when a man could believe there was a good life up there, a good life down here, and perhaps some possible connection between them, without saying too much about it.

There was a good life being lived at Brooke Hill. Happiness is contagious, and houses catch an atmosphere from the people who live in them; this was a home of deep happiness. It was all set for good talk too. Jack maintained that the balance between himself and Jacquetta was just right, with all his robust and active heterosexuality he had a strongly intuitive feminine side, and Jacquetta with her mysterious feminine beauty had a corresponding masculine side to her nature.

We paid three more visits to Brooke Hill. The next time was in autumn, when there were mushrooms to be gathered on the downs, and fine sunsets to admire. On one occasion we were treated to a brilliant conflagration, cloudy and wild, flaring and flaming all round the skies. Nobody wanted to talk, so we just sat with awe and wonder in a companionable silence. Then there was winter, with brisk walks in the pinewoods; and finally the blaze of high summer, when Jack and I tried unsuccessfully to play tennis, and Jack took us up on to the flat roof of the house for an enlarged vision of all their magnificent views. That was our last visit, as Jack and Jacquetta had decided that they must move nearer London, and were beginning to house-hunt on the mainland. It seemed sensible to move, but Brooke Hill had a romance about it that I look back on with a special, slightly nostalgic, pleasure.

So you get to know your friends, then you meet their friends, who often become your friends too. The Priestleys were generous with their friends, not jealously guarding them, but cheerfully mixing them. And then, as you come closer, you get to know their relatives and their children. You are glad and eager to learn more about those who have captured your interest and your affection. So this seems the moment to delve a little into the earlier lives of Jack and Jacquetta.

PART II
JACK

FIVE

THE EARLY YEARS

'I did not discover the proletariat at Oxford or Cambridge, for the West Riding working class was in my blood and bones.' Jack was proud of his Yorkshire background. He was grateful for it and for the years in Bradford in which he grew to manhood. One way and another Bradford and the Yorkshire moors and dales found their way into many of his books.

Bradford was a thriving wool city, and Jack's forebears worked in the mills. Necessity sent his Priestley grandfather out at an early age, and before there was any compulsory education he was, and, as far as we know, he remained illiterate. But his eldest son, Jonathan, was able to benefit from the new state education, and was bright and clever. Somehow money was found to send him to a teacher-training college. His father had other children, and could not have earned more than 30s a week, so how this was managed is a mystery. Perhaps there were scholarships, or perhaps the Baptist chapel helped, for the Priestleys were conscientious Baptists. Jonathan returned to Bradford with a passionate belief in the importance and value of education, the golden key that was to unlock a better future for everyone. He was a dedicated teacher, and went on to become a headmaster, a well-known, solid and respected citizen.

In 1891 Jonathan married Emma Holt, at first sight an unlikely choice. He had, Jack suggests, 'plucked her from the clogs and shawls back at t'mill, a free and easy rather raffish kind of working-class life, where in the grim little back-to-back houses they shouted and screamed, laughed and cried, and sent out a jug for more beer.' Holt was an Irish name, and Bradford was full of impoverished and hungry Irish labourers who had come to the city to find work. Emma must have been at least half, if not wholly, Irish. She was high-spirited and witty, much given to frequenting music-halls (a taste enthusiastically shared by her son); there wasn't much of the strict Baptist about Emma. Perhaps it was the Celtic Scot blood that Jonathan inherited from his mother that drew him to such a lively personality. The expression on Emma's photographed face is jaunty, intelligent and has a kind of mischievous humour about it. Jack, christened John –

Jack's parents, Jonathan and Emma Priestley. The photograph was taken in Blackpool
and may well have been taken during their honeymoon in 1891

Boynton was added later – was born on 13 September 1894. His
mother died when he was two years old, so he had no memories of
her, and his father never spoke about her. Only two stories have come
down to us. One tells how, when Emma grew tired of a meeting,
probably of educationalists, that her husband was holding in their
front parlour, she took advantage of the high window by fixing a hat
on a broom handle, and marching round and round in front of the

window in an attempt to break up the solemn male conclave. She is also reported as having once been turned out of a theatre for laughing too loudly and too inappropriately; Jack liked that. Those stories somehow fit the face that gazes out of that faded old photograph. We would have liked to know more about Emma Priestley.

In 1898 Jonathan married Amy Fletcher, who now took charge of the household. 'I had a stepmother', wrote Jack, 'who defied tradition by being always kind, gentle and loving. . . . I was happy at home. Yes, I was happy there, so wherever my desire to write came from it certainly did not come out of any frustrated, neglected childhood. I was outside the fashionable literary movement before I even began.' A few years later, in 1903, Jack's half-sister Winifred was born, rather young to be much of a youthful companion for the growing boy. As Jonathan Priestley progressed in the world he moved up from Mannheim Road, where he had begun his married life, to 5 Saltburn Place, in a new suburb being built on the edge of the city. With the open moors just beyond, it was almost in the country. This was to be Jack's home until after the First World War.

The house had two rooms on each floor. Up at the top, under the sloping roof, was an attic room that was Jack's own. The rest of the family fitted in on the floor below, and on the ground floor were the two important living rooms, a kitchen dining-room at the back, and in the front the parlour. In the semi-basement was another kitchen and a room with a sink and a mangle for the family laundry. Steps led out of here up to the backyard, where the washing was hung out to dry. There were two temperamental coal-fired ranges that had to be lit every day. It must have been hard work for Jack's good-natured stepmother. Not only was all the washing and ironing done at home – no machines, no drip-dries – but also all the baking, including the bread. Thursday was baking day, and on Sundays – a special treat – they had cream. 'We were always good eaters at our house,' said sister Winnie proudly. There wasn't much room in the kitchen – one large pan was usually placed in the middle of the table – but there was a lot of fun there, all kinds of Priestley in-jokes. Jack kept them constantly amused, and their father was able to relax too, able to 'let go of his dignity and be a clown . . . never artfully funny, just downright silly, like a boy among boys'.

Many years later, at the age of fifty-five, J.B. Priestley, the established writer, produced an enchanting little book called *Delight*. He called it his grumblers' apology, his bit of penitence for all the times when his 'glowering pudding face' and his grumblings had upset his family and friends. 'So now', he wrote, 'my long-suffering kinsfolk, my patient friends, may a glimmer of that delight which has so often possessed me, but perhaps too frequently in secret, now reach you from these pages.' And here is the earliest of those delights:

I can remember, as if it happened last week, more than half a century ago, when I must have been about four, and on fine summer mornings would sit in a field adjoining the house. What gave me delight then was a mysterious notion, for which I could certainly not have found words, of a Treasure. It was waiting for me either in the earth, just below the buttercups and daisies, or in the golden air. I had formed no idea of what this Treasure would consist of, and nobody had ever talked to me about it. But morning after morning would be radiant with its promise. Somewhere, not far out out of reach, it was waiting for me, at any moment I might roll over and put a hand on it. I suspect now that the Treasure was Earth itself and the light and warmth of its sunbeams, yet sometimes I fancy that I have been searching for it ever since.

I like to believe that the treasure that stirred the imagination of this talented child was an intimation of his own creative gift, that was to grow and flower, and bring delight to many people; perhaps it was a part of the magic that he searched for all his life, slowly understanding that 'What is truly magical rises from your own depths.'

The little dreamer grew into a fine, broad-shouldered healthy lad, and a keen games player. At first there were the childhood games, Tin-can-Squat, which I and my children and grandchildren know as 'Kick the Bucket', the old favourite, Prisoner's Base, and others with strange names and stranger rules. Soon there was football, a great favourite with Jack, cricket for the summer, and long walks, sometimes twenty miles a day over the moors. There was all the indoor fun as well, for 5 Saltburn Place was a hospitable house. Christmas seems to have been one long party celebrated in clouds of pipe and cigar smoke, with hot toddy and even more good food than usual, and there were numerous Christmas games, especially charades, in which Jack soon took an active part. But in all this normal extroverted life, he kept his secret dreams.

Jack loved and admired his father, whose only real fault seemed to be his sudden explosions of violent temper, sometimes accompanied by hurling china about and throwing suitcases down the stairs – departures on holiday were frequent signals for such tempers. Jack observed this and thought to himself that he would never allow his own temper to erupt in such a wild manner – and he never did. But Jonathan Priestley never sulked, and once the storm had blown over he was his cheerful and friendly self. When they did all get off on their yearly seaside holiday – they travelled by night, with packets of sandwiches as it was cheaper – then Jonathan would chat to everyone they met on the way and find out all about their lives and interests. His father, Jack wrote, 'was unselfish, brave, honourable and public-spirited . . . he wanted to teach, to counsel, to guide, but not to gather or use power. He was a most loveable man.'

Jack's kindly stepmother was also a woman of character, and was especially indulgent to Jack, whom she considered a budding genius. She had had little education, but was determined to keep up with the Priestleys and to educate herself. She read Dostoevsky and Tolstoy as well as the English classics, though how she found the time is a mystery. Although naturally timid, she took herself off alone to a season of Greek drama at one of the local theatres. She was dreadfully shocked by *Oedipus Rex*.

His Bradford home was a good atmosphere for Jack. He lived among people who read a great deal and were interested in the arts. Bradford had two theatres, two music-halls, and a great deal of first-class music. There was an Arts Club and a Playgoers Society. Jonathan Priestley was a very good play reader, and could have been a good actor. Jack could act as well; one of his minor dramatic accomplishments was a series of public 'turns' with a ventriloquist's doll that he had acquired. 'Oh! he could be so funny,' said Winnie.

Jack heard plenty of discussion and argument about education – with which he got bored – and also about politics, with voices getting louder and louder as the disagreements grew fiercer. Many local people had a tendency to shout, often because they or their parents had worked in the mill and were used to competing with the noise of the looms. Like most, though not all, of his friends, Jack's father was an old-fashioned non-Marxist socialist, holding to 'The looser and warmer tradition of English socialism', as Jack described it some fifty-eight years later: 'It may have moved towards an impossible goal, but on the way it could do more good than harm. . . . I grew up in this English socialist tradition, and at heart I still believe in it. Liberalism is modern man's nearest approach to real civilization; as soon as most of it was sneered away, the power men took over, the secret police arrived, torture came back. This old-fashioned English Left was Liberalism with the starch out of it. It was life-seeking, life-enhancing, a protest perhaps too late on behalf of the feminine principle.'

Jack soon had his own friends with whom he argued for hours and hours in pubs and cafés, and on long walks over the moors. As he grew into his teens, he transformed his little attic into a bed-sitting-room, hung reproductions of his favourite pictures round the walls, and made bookcases out of old orange boxes. He was immensely proud of it. Soon he could entertain his friends up there – boys of course, no girls allowed. Jonathan was a straight-laced Baptist about sex. And in whatever time there was, young Jack was up in his attic hopefully scribbling away.

Sixteen was the age to leave school. Jack told his father that he didn't want to try for a scholarship to Cambridge, though he might easily have been successful. He was bored with school, and unattracted by ancient traditions, 'so much English hocus-pocus'. It was life, real life that was beckoning. Jonathan, however, was not going to have his son lounging about at home, trying this and that, scribbling away; he must earn his keep. He suggested that Jack should go into the wool trade. Jack was astonished by such a proposal coming from his socialist father, but as he had no other plans, he agreed, and became a very junior clerk with Helm & Company, Swan Arcade, Bradford.

The hours were long, and the pay far from wonderful, but Jack managed to eke out his pennies, to buy books at 2*d* each, and to frequent the theatre, the music-halls and the concert chambers. He read and read and wrote and wrote. Looking back on some of these early efforts, Jack later declared that he could find no glimmer of talent in them, but he still struggled on. And soon there were girls to distract and delight him, and some were sufficiently charmed by this youth with what he described as his 'innocent pudding face' that they volunteered to type his articles, stories and verses for him. They only got paid in kisses; Jack had no spare cash.

During this rebellious and argumentative teenage period, Jonathan was disappointed in his son, whom he knew to be clever, but who now appeared something of an 'idle, smoking, drinking, girl-chasing, verse-writing, floppy-tie wearing "young dandy"': he saw no sign of him developing into a sound West Riding citizen. He was not really reconciled until Jack had an article published for which he was paid one whole guinea. From then on Jack began to have pieces published regularly in the local press, and some further afield, and his father was suitably proud. It was sad that he did not live long enough to see his son's later and spectacular success.

In the course of his work, Jack was able to travel abroad: he visited Denmark, Sweden, Holland, Belgium and Germany, but his heart remained in Bradford. He had no idea of ever going to live in London. His only vague dream of a future was to be able to rent a cottage for about 9d a week somewhere on the edge of the moors, and about a 2d bus ride from the centre of town. Here he would settle down and write; he reckoned he could live easily and happily on £1 a week. 'Bradford', he said, 'seemed to offer me all I wanted from a town, and already I had a deep affection for the surrounding countryside . . . a part of me is still in Bradford, and can never leave it.'

As well as his essays, sketches and stories, Jack wrote poetry. He wanted, perhaps more than anything else, to be able to write poetry. He believed that 'poets are the best, the real top people', the true purveyors of magic. Jack never had any illusions about his own capabilities; he saw clearly what he could and could not do, and in the end he accepted sadly that, though he could write good verse, he would never be a true poet. After a lifetime's reading and familiarity with all the great poets, Jack reflected:

> Let us be clear about poetry and poets. . . . It is true to say that young Jack Priestley will never write poetry. It is not true to say there is no poetry in him . . . to write poetry as distinct from mere verse, a man must be able to go mad, while still keeping himself saner than most men; there must in fact be a certain relation between his conscious mind and his unconscious. . . . Young Jack P. does not possess this sort of mind, a very rare sort, and can never acquire it. But in the larger non-literary sense of the term, he is full of poetry, being ardent and generous minded, unashamed of his emotions, imaginative, and so I declare firmly he will remain.

Once, in an idle moment, I asked Jacquetta what special gift she would have asked from a fairy godmother; although she had had one small book of poetry, real poetry, published, she replied unhesitatingly, 'the gift of poetry'. I too would have asked for that.

In his later teens Jack had a poet friend now long since forgotten, James A. Mackereth. He was, Jack said, a true if not distinguished poet. He had given up everything to live simply with his wife out on the moors, so that he could dedicate himself to poetry. Though Jack was very much younger, he visited this poet regularly. They would sit out in his garden, and later in his study, they ate cake, drank tea, and smoked together, and Mackereth would read his poetry to his young acolyte. Around midnight Jack would walk home, his mind open to 'unlimited possibilities, both in this life and some other', and in

> that blessed mood,
> In which the burthen of the mystery
> In which the heavy and the weary weight
> Of all this unintelligible world is lightened.

'I was luckier than most', Jack wrote, 'having found a poet, ampler and finer in his talk than in his writing, to receive me in his garden and take me into his lamplit study. There certain not ignoble expectations, which youth brings with it to the common scene, knew some degree of satisfaction. I believe such expectations, a feeling that life should have warmth, generosity, nobility, arrive with each generation; they are not taught but somehow inherited.'

Meanwhile, Jack, now in his late teens, continued to enjoy his life and his many interests . . . 'a robust lad, a loud and emphatic talker, a notable clown at parties'. But he was still a junior clerk at Helm & Company, and although the dream of a cottage on the moors seemed to be fading, there was nothing beyond the determination to be a writer to take its place. 'I have never been much of a planner, but at this time I was not visited by even the ghost of a plan.' This state of mind continued until after that glorious summer of 1914. In June he took himself off for a European holiday: Amsterdam for the pictures, a walking tour down the Rhine and back by Brussels, and a performance of *Der Rosenkavalier*. He had 'a roaring good time . . . I believe I did nothing but enjoy what could be enjoyed, because we were soon to be at war. Consciously, of course, we never entertained a thought of it, but deep in the unconscious, which has its own time and a wider *now* than consciousness knows, already the war was on, a world ending.'

Early in September, a week or so before his twentieth birthday, Jack enlisted as an infantryman in the Duke of Wellington's West Riding Regiment. Looking back, he has speculated on what drove him so quickly and unexpectedly into the Army:

There came out of the unclouded blue of that summer a challenge that was almost like a conscription of the spirit, little to do really with King and Country and flag-waving and hip-hip-hurrah, a challenge to what we felt was our untested manhood. Other men, who had not lived as easily as we had, had drilled and marched and borne arms – couldn't we? Yes, we too could leave home and soft

This photograph of himself in uniform was used by Jack as a postcard to his family when he joined up in 1914: 'I hear now that we are going out in a month. We leave here on Monday'

beds and the girls to soldier for a spell, if there was some excuse for it, something at least to be defended. And here it was.

When I asked Jack about the war, he said, 'I spent the first year trying to be a hero, and the rest of the time trying to stay alive.' He was three times wounded, the second quite seriously, and after that he decided to apply for a commission, which he quickly got. He found to his surprise that he could lead and organize other men: 'I had let loose a part of myself I did not even know was there. I played the man of action.'

It was during the war that Jack encountered for the first time the English upper classes. Of course, Bradford had had a modest and rather innocent social hierarchy, though Jack had never thought about it, but he had no conception of the complexities of the English class structure, of its rituals and its absurdities, and was amazed by it:

The British Army never saw itself as a citizen's army. It behaved as if a small gentlemanly officer class still had to make soldiers out of under-gardeners, runaway sons, and slum lads known to the police. These fellows had to be kept up to scratch. Let 'em get slack, they'd soon be a rabble again. All the armies in that idiot war shovelled divisions into attacks, just as if healthy young men had begun to seem hateful in the sight of Europe, but the British

Command specialized in throwing men away for nothing. . . . I came out of that war with a chip on my shoulder . . . a big heavy chip, probably some friend's thigh bone.

After the war Jack found that he could get an educational grant, and so he applied, after all, to Cambridge, and was accepted to read modern history and political science at Trinity Hall. He had done little writing during the war, mostly poetry and short stories, but now he felt unable to tackle the whole vast subject of the war, as many of his fellow writers did – Edmund Blunden, Robert Graves, Siegfried Sassoon and others. It was many years before Jack could bring himself to write directly about his experiences, as he did in *Margin Released* in 1962, but that was not the war book that he might have written. 'Unlike most of my contemporaries who wrote so well about the war,' he said, 'I was deeply divided between the tragedy and the comedy of it. I was as much aware as they were, and as other people born later can never be, of its tragic aspect. I felt, as indeed I still feel today and must go on feeling until I die, the open wound never to be healed, of my generation's fate, the best sorted out and then slaughtered, not by hard necessity but mainly by huge murderous folly.' (Virtually all Jack's boyhood friends died in the Battle of the Somme.) 'On the other hand,' he continued, 'military life itself, the whole Army "carry on" as we used to say, observed closely, seemed to me essentially comic, the most expensive farce ever contrived. To a man of my temperament, it was almost slapstick, so much gigantically solemn, dressed up, bemedalled, custard-pie work, with tragedy, death, the deep unhealing wound, there in the middle of it.' He could not do it, he wanted to get on with his life, to look forward, not to look so painfully back. So with his meagre grant, he went off to Cambridge.

As well as Cambridge and writing, Jack had something else on his mind. Among the girls with whom he had dallied and who had typed for him, there was one who did not forget and who was not forgotten. This was Emily Jane Tempest, always called Pat, whose family lived opposite the Priestleys. Pat was two years younger than Jack and was very pretty. As well as typing, she played the violin with Winnie or Jack as her accompanist. All through the war she had written regularly to Jack, and when he was wounded and in hospital, she had visited him. By the time he returned home she was working in the Bradford Reference Library, where Jack did much of his reading.

After a spell of sharing a room in college, which Jack didn't much enjoy, he looked around Cambridge and found a little house to rent;

Jack at Cambridge, with his gown over his uniform, shortly after the war

renting was easy in those far-off days. So in June 1921 Jack and Pat were married in the Westgate Baptist Chapel in Bradford. Winnie and her mother were against the marriage. They didn't like Pat, they thought she was scatter-brained, wouldn't be able to run a house properly, wouldn't be able to keep up with Jack, wasn't in fact good enough for 'our Jack'. Jonathan Priestley was perhaps wiser; he understood that his son, now in the vigour of his early manhood, needed to get married.

Though Jack never really took to academic life, he and Pat were happy together in Cambridge. They had plenty of friends; one of Jack's closest and most long-lasting was the poet Edward Davison, at that time editing the *Cambridge Review*. Jack took his degree in two years, and was put out by achieving only a 2.1; he knew that he should have got a first. The education grant ran for another year, so he and Pat stayed in Cambridge, and he supplemented the family budget by lecturing, coaching, reviewing and writing.

One of Jack's earliest books, *Brief Diversions, Tales, Travesties and Epigrams*, was published in 1922. He called it 'a little book of undergraduate odds and ends'. It had marvellous reviews, not just locally in Cambridge, but from leading reviewers like Edmund Gosse and J.C. Squire in the London papers. Hopefully, expectantly, Jack waited, but nothing happened; no editors or publishers wrote to this promising, highly praised young man. 'My career', he said, 'began with an enormous anti-climax.' All the same, he was in print, he had been noticed, and the connection with Squire was to prove especially helpful.

Jack was never deterred by what might have looked like adversity. He went doggedly on, putting together sketches and essays, many of which he had contributed over the years to various journals, and this collection was published as *Papers from Lilliput*. He dedicated it to his father. Here we see, though sometimes a little stiff and creaky, and occasionally repetitive, unquestionably the writer who was to become such a lively, imaginative, original and delightful essayist, one of the best, and probably the last of the great English essay-writers.

As the third university year ended, Jack looked rather anxiously around at his prospects. Pat, I believe, would have followed him anywhere, but the academic world of far-off lectureships and foreign professorships held nothing that attracted him. Pat was pregnant, and money was in short supply. Jack had managed to save a small capital of around £50. He decided to risk everything and to freelance in London – 'a decision received with bitter incredulity at home in Bradford'.

SIX

THE MIDDLE YEARS

Jack was now twenty-seven, and his intuition, even in the face of sober common sense, was right; London was the best place for any talented young writer, and the best place for Jack. He and Pat found a large ground-floor flat, and since the rent was rather more than they could manage, Edward Davison moved in to share expenses.

J.C. Squire, who edited the *London Mercury*, now came to Jack's help and invited him to contribute essays and criticism. Squire recommended him to John Lane of the Bodley Head, who took him on as a reader. Jack was pleased to remember that he recommended the first novels of Graham Greene and C.S. Forester. In yet another good turn, Squire introduced Jack to Robert Lynd, literary editor of the *Daily News*, who gave him work as a reviewer. All this provided Jack with a steady income, and was good practice in the craft of writing; it also brought him into London literary circles. He was particularly happy in his friendship with Robert Lynd, and at literary parties in the Lynds' hospitable home he met most of the well-known writers of the day. Another specially valued friendship was with the poet, Walter de la Mare; Jack described him and Robert Lynd as 'the most delightful characters and companions'.

Life for Jack involved a lot of hard work, but that never daunted him; and all seemed to be going well. His first child, Barbara, was born on 4 March 1923. There is a photograph of him nervously holding the baby at arms' length as if she might break. But while Jack's literary career was expanding and moving forward, life for Pat was becoming less easy. Barbara's birth had been difficult, and Pat was beginning to feel unwell; by October she was once more pregnant. It was harder for her to share in Jack's life as she had done in Cambridge. At the literary parties that Jack enjoyed, he was the gifted up-and-coming young writer, the bluff Yorkshireman whose loud and emphatic voice, lively talk and talent to entertain made him an amusing and interesting character. Pat was a woman of intelligence and character, but was inevitably seen as Jack's provincial and adoring wife. In any case she was soon tied to her babies and her home, and her health continued to decline.

J.C. Squire, the editor of the *London Mercury* who helped Jack in establishing his literary career, was a member, along with Jack (seated, centre), of this team for a charitable cricket match, *c.* 1934, and is seated to Jack's left. Other friends include Ivor Brown (top right), R.C. Sherriff (third from the right on the back row), A.J. Cronin (bottom left) and Arthur Bliss (to Jack's right) (New Pagemoy Photos)

On 30 April 1924 a second daughter, Sylvia, was born, two months prematurely. Pat had been very ill and had had to be taken to Guy's Hospital, where she had a Cæsarean section. It was then that a fatal bladder cancer was discovered. The baby, as well as her mother, needed special care, and extra nursing at home, but Sylvia flourished amazingly, and was known as 'the miracle baby'. Jack, hoping that clean country air might benefit Pat, moved his family out to Chinnor Hill in Buckinghamshire. This was not, for Jack, a complete literary exile: their next-door neighbour was Gerald Bullett, a literary friend from Cambridge, and his wife Rosemary, and not far off was another congenial companion, Frank Kendon, a young poet. Pat must have suffered a great deal of pain, and was soon having to spend time back in Guy's Hospital for exhausting and unavailing treatment. They engaged a cook-housekeeper, and Pat's mother often came to help with the children. Granny Tempest was the perfect grandmother, small in stature but large in comfort and love. If the children were frightened in the night they could creep into her bed. At mealtimes they were never

'Granny Tempest' with Barbara,
Chinnor, 1924

Sylvia and nurse, Chinnor, 1924

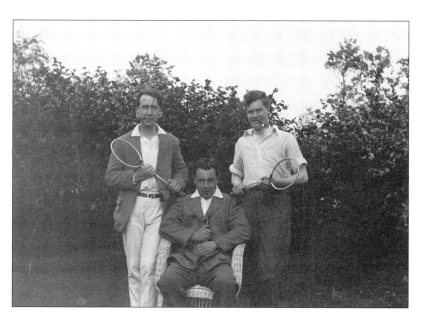

Jack, seated, with friends, Teddy Davison (to his left) and Gerald Bullett (to his right)
at Chinnor, 1924

Jack with his first wife, Pat, in the garden of their home at Chinnor Hill,
Buckinghamshire, in 1924

forced to eat things they didn't like, nor to sit up at the table until their elders had finished – life for them was relaxed and comforting. The children, especially Barbara, adored their grandmother.

There is a 1924 photograph of Jack and Pat standing beneath a parasol in the summer garden at Chinnor. Pat is of medium height and very slim, her straight dark hair frames a thin though still well-featured face; she looks older than her years. She had been young and pretty; now she is a mature and suffering woman. She must have already known that she was dying. Her expression is calm, with the faintest suggestion of a smile; there is a strength and a kind of remote beauty about her.

As can be imagined, the bills were piling up, with hospital and medical fees and extra help in the house to pay for. Jack worked literally day and night to keep the family afloat and to provide the best that he could for his wife. Two letters written around this time by Pat to her mother in Bradford show nothing but concern for Jack and his extra burdens, commenting on how hard he is working, and how worried he is about paying the bills. She understood only too well the crippling effects of her illness, and she ended one letter sadly, 'In fact it is quite difficult to die.'

Jack visited Pat regularly when she was in hospital, sometimes returning late to Chinnor, sometimes stopping in London. When he could he continued with his London life, and at one of the literary parties he met Jane Wyndham-Lewis, an attractive, clever and talented woman. Jane had a four-year-old daughter Angela, but she was in the process of divorcing her husband Bevan. She was immediately fascinated by Jack, and at first, unaware that he was already married, she announced to a friend, 'That is an extraordinary man. I am going to marry him.' She became Jack's mistress and by June 1924 she was pregnant. Their daughter, Mary, was born on 4 March 1925.

Jack's life was now complicated as well as tragic. A further sorrow in June 1924 was the death, at the early age of fifty-six, of his much-loved and admired father. The burden that Jack carried would have crushed a lesser man. He wrote of a late afternoon when he returned to Chinnor after visiting Pat in hospital, 'so deep in despair I did not know what to do with myself. I was nearly out of my mind with misery. Finally, just to pass the time while I was at the bottom of this pit, I decided to write something – anything – a few pages to be torn up after I felt less wretched. On my desk was a rough list of chapters for the Meredith book [commissioned by Macmillan as part of 'The English Men of Letters' series]. I chose one of the chapters, not the first, and slowly, painfully set to work on it. In an hour I was writing freely and well. It is in fact one of the best chapters in the book. And I wrote myself out of

Jack at Chinnor, 1924

my misery, and followed a trail of thought and words into the daylight.'

Jack was always a brilliant and perceptive critic; in *George Meredith* he was particularly good on Meredith and the comic spirit, and in his examination of Meredith's poetry and of his fiction, but the chapter that, in my view, is the finest in the book is the third, 'His Attitude: Nature – Man – Earth', though it might be thought of as the most difficult, dealing as it does with Meredith's philosophy of life and his attitude to religion. Jack saw Meredith as untouched by the controversy between religion and science, creation and evolution, that induced a sense of strain in so many Victorian writers. He viewed Meredith as a true pagan who rejected 'the old war between the spirit and the flesh . . . He sees that animal life is not something to be gradually eliminated but the broad foundation of our spiritual life . . . the body must be disciplined but not subdued, for brain and soul, its leaders and not its enemies will have need of its vital energy.' So, instead of strain, he found in Meredith 'a splendid buoyancy and completeness'. Meredith for Jack was not simply a poet of nature, but *the* poet of nature, more truly than Wordsworth, who was always wanting nature to be leading to something more, some kind of mystical and spiritual vision. For Meredith nature simply is, and he rejoices in her. Nor was Meredith a pantheist, for, as Jack rightly observed, 'If everything is God, then nothing is God. . . . Pantheism is neither a religion nor a philosophy, but a certain poetical state of mind.' All his life Jack remained fascinated by the great mysteries of life and death, now weighing so heavily upon him. He was in sympathy with Meredith's philosophy, but he detected a weakness in his attitude to death. 'We feel that he is deliberately shutting off his imagination . . . he has not compared it with his real experience, the actual stuff of life. . . . There are moments when the fragrant drift of smoke through which we have caught so many memorable utterances thins away from the face of the oracle and we catch sight of nothing but a gilded mask, whose moving lips frame for us resounding but idle words.' In the spirit of praise Jack concluded, 'This weakness must not blind us to the real force and splendour of Meredith's attitude. Sometimes there may be nothing but the gilded mask, but more often than not there is the sensitive and ardent face, glowing with real thought and emotion.' It is a magnificent piece of writing, and might well have carried Jack through his dark night of grief.

As Pat grew worse, and had to spend more and more time in hospital, they decided to move back to London and found 5 Scarsdale Villas to rent. Edward Davison had married and gone to America, so Jack was wholly responsible for all expenses. An old friend from Cambridge, now a doctor, and Barbara's godmother, arranged for Pat to be transferred to a side ward in the Royal Free Hospital, and here she received excellent nursing, and no further painful and useless treatment. However much Pat suffered, and she must often have been in agony, she never complained. Right up to the end she remained brave and unselfish, her concern being entirely for those she was leaving, and most especially for her husband Jack. At last, on 15 November 1925, she died. Her death certificate records the cause of her death as: 1) Sarcoma of the pelvic floor; 2) Exhaustion. Pat had been the love of Jack's youth; with her death and the death of his father, his own youth was buried.

Jack took himself off, possibly with Jane, for a much-needed holiday. He returned to sort out his family responsibilities – something he never shirked. He prided himself on being a 'good provider', and as well as looking after his wife and children he was generous to other relatives. Jack and Jane had spent a considerable time apart, but now there were together. Jack needed Jane and relied on her. At the time of Mary's birth, Jane's divorce had not yet been finalized, and Mary had been registered in the name of Wyndham-Lewis, though she was always called Priestley. It was now clear that

Jane Wyndham–Lewis, Jack's
second wife

once Jane was finally divorced, after a decent interval she and Jack would get married. Jack would take on Jane's daughter Angela, and Jane would take on Jack's two small daughters. This meant a household of six, at first with just one mother's help. Later there came a succession of nannies. Jack rented College House at Church Harborough, near Oxford, which was large enough to contain them all, and had a coach-house opposite the main building, where Jack could work in peace in the upper room. The children were immensely impressed and excited when he kicked a football right over the coach-house.

Now, at last, there was peace and order in Jack's life and in September 1926 he and Jane married quietly in the registry office at Witney. Jane's mother was Welsh, and the family lived in Cardiff; her father, originally from Devon, was a marine surveyor. Jane was a pretty and attractive woman, with dark curly hair and a sparkling smile. She was naturally musical and had a beautiful speaking voice. She was a good linguist and had gained a degree in Latin and French at Bedford College, London. She was three months older than Jack, a sophisticated woman of the world, a good hostess, a good organizer, interested in food and knowledgeable about French cookery, quite capable of managing a large household with any amount of entertaining of famous and well-known personalities; she had drive and ambition. There was no doubt about Jack and Jane's mutual attraction, and their shared interests.

Once all was settled Granny Tempest brought three-year-old Barbara and two-year-old Sylvia to College House – a new home, a new stepmother, and two new sisters. It was a difficult and bewildering time for the two little girls. While it was fine for Jack to play the role of the bluff Yorkshireman, Jane did not want the children to grow up with Yorkshire accents and easy Yorkshire manners: Barbara and Sylvia had to be taught to speak properly and to behave in the approved middle-class fashion. So, after two days, Granny Tempest returned to Bradford, and her grandchildren never saw her again. This was a special grief to Barbara, for her Granny had been a stable figure in a childhood in which homes changed and people kept appearing and disappearing.

After two years the family moved back to London, and lived in Hampstead. Throughout this disturbed and difficult time in Jack's life, his literary output had steadily increased. As well as essays, reviews and books of criticism, he began to try his hand at novel writing. Although he did not consider himself a born novelist he was fascinated by any new challenge, and in quick succession he produced *Adam in Moonshine* – 'All fine writing and nonsense, a little coloured balloon' – and *Benighted* – 'written late at night – an attempt to transmute the thriller into symbolic fiction with some psychological depths'. Most of the 'fine writing' in *Adam in Moonshine* is in Jack's evocation of the Yorkshire Dales of his boyhood, and he does delightfully convey the magic of that uniquely beautiful piece of the English countryside.

Although he did not possess what he called 'the mark of the true novelist, the trick of maintaining an even flow of narrative', he was still determined to try, and just to make things difficult for himself he was contemplating a long picaresque novel – two of his favourite books were *Don Quixote* and *Tom Jones*. But he still had to earn money for his expanding family and here friendship came once more to the rescue.

Hugh Walpole was ten years older than Jack, an established and successful popular novelist. Though he is now almost forgotten, I remember reading his books, the 'Herries' series and the 'Jeremy' books, with enormous pleasure. He and Jack had met soon after Jack's arrival on the London literary scene, and in September 1925 Jack had been to stay with Walpole in his home in the Lake District. Luckily for posterity Walpole kept a diary and on 20 September it records:

Jack with Hugh Walpole in the garden of Walpole's Lake District home during their collaboration on *Farthing Hall*

'Arrived Priestley – a north-country – no nonsense about me – I know my mind – kind of little man' (Walpole was tall); and the following day: 'I find Priestley very agreeable. He is cocksure and determined, but has a great sense of humour about himself.'

The friendship developed happily, and Walpole suggested to Jack that they might collaborate on a novel, *Farthing Hall*, to be told in an exchange of letters between a middle-aged scholar and an enthusiastic young man. Perhaps Jack had had enough of enthusiastic young men with his moon-dazed Adam, so he chose the middle-aged scholar. Thanks to Walpole's popularity as a novelist, Jack's share of the advance and the royalties would be substantial enough to keep him and his family going while he worked on his long novel. The collaboration was happy, a tribute to both men. Walpole's diary records: 'I certainly find Priestley an enchanting companion. I've never had a writing man for a friend before who has been so close a companion. Henry James was too old, Conrad too mysterious, Swinnerton too untrustworthy, Bennett too egoist – all good friends, but none of them with the sweetness and humour that Priestley has.'

When Jack finally produced his lengthy manuscript, his publisher was against it: too long; too unfashionable; a hopeless title; times were bad; it would never sell. Jack stuck to his novel and to his title. It was, of course, *The Good Companions*, appropriately dedicated to Hugh Walpole. The runaway success of this book was to make Jack a rich man, and transformed his style of living – a style that Jane was well able to cope with and which she partly dictated. I need hardly say that it was only the style that changed: in success or in failure – and he experienced both – Jack remained always and unaffectedly, Jack.

He never forgot a kindness, and publicly as well as privately expressed his gratitude to those who had helped him. He wrote a fine tribute to Walpole's generosity and to his innumerable and untrumpeted kindnesses, especially to struggling young writers. Nor was Walpole in the least envious of the huge success that he had helped to make possible for Jack. Here is an extract from Walpole's diary after one of Jack's visits in 1939:

Strange man – so sensitive and vain, so sure of his uniqueness, his power, his wisdom, yet with a marvellous control of his real nature (he is peevish and complaining, but I have never known him once in all these years lose his temper), so pessimistic, but with such a gorgeous sense of humour – so penurious about little things, and yet so generous-minded. He is so gruff, ill-mannered,

On the back of this photograph Jack has written: 'In the study [at Well Walk] where I finished *The Good Companions* – taken 1930' (Photopress)

and yet how sweet he was to Mrs Brown on Sunday. He can be an admirable critic. But through all and everything there is a deep sweetness that pervades his whole nature, which is why I love him.

It was that 'deep sweetness' that John and I so soon discovered in Jack, and which was one of the many reasons why we too loved him.

Jack always felt that the huge success of *The Good Companions* did him a disservice. Among intellectual young critics something that was so widely read and enjoyed could not be real literature, whatever that may be, and Jack was liable to be dismissed as a 'lowbrow', 'popular' writer – perjorative terms in literary circles. I met this very early when I was around thirteen – was it a condemnation of the book that a schoolgirl could read it with pleasure? My headmistress thought so.

The Good Companions is a fine and enjoyable book – exhilarating, exciting, humorous, tender. It is a story of three people – Bradford-born Jess Oakroyd, the young, dreamy, musical Inigo Jollifant (both of whom are trapped in frustrating situations) and Miss Trant, a middle-aged spinster who is comfortable, secure and dull. All of them cut

A window display for *The Good Companions* (Sims & Co.)

their roots, embrace risk and uncertainty and set out on a search. For what? Adventure? A dream of magical romance? Their true selves?

On their travels alone and finally together as part of a musical troupe, 'The Good Companions', they tour England. We have a great panorama of English life and characters. Perhaps only Miss Trant finds true happiness, though the other two come close. Jess Oakroyd does get to Canada to live near his beloved daughter Lily, but only after he has been summoned back to Bradford to his wife's deathbed. There was little love lost between them, but she was his wife and the mother of his children. Her death and burial are told with a perfect economy of language that make it profoundly moving. I commented on this to Jack. 'It is good, isn't it?' he said, and added, 'Somehow it doesn't quite belong in that book.' Yet in a way, I think it does.

Jack wrote *The Good Companions* as what he called 'a holiday of the spirit' following Pat's illness and death and all the associated anxiety and strain. He was temperamentally opposed to the use of direct personal experience in creative work, and for the most part his deeply distressing personal experiences had to wait until they could emerge, as they later did here and there in his work, in imaginatively realized characters, situations and symbols.

Jack followed *The Good Companions* with a very different novel, *Angel Pavement*, a London book. To read it now it seems extraordinarily

The striking dust-jacket design by Pinder Davis for *Angel Pavement*, Jack's second novel, published in 1930

topical. It is the story of a small family business that had been flourishing, but with the onset of the recession of the thirties finds its order-books shrinking and its employees beginning to fear unemployment. When a foreign stranger named Golspie arrives, with grandiose plans for expansion and an assurance of new orders, the worried owner believes him; before long the business is ruined, Golspie has absconded, and the axe of unemployment has fallen. The characters are marvellously alive, all quite ordinary and undistinguished people, created with so much sympathy and compassion. Interestingly, when all is lost, and their men appear ruined, it is the women who show spirit and courage and begin to pull them out of their slough of despond. A number of people consider *Angel Pavement* Jack's finest novel.

Jack once observed that there is always another character in any novel: society itself. This is certainly true of Jack's novels, as it is of many of those of Britain's greatest writers. It is this extra character that gives solidity and breadth to a novel. When society is too feeble or even lacking, however brilliant the writing, there seems, in the end, an unsatisfying thinness.

The family continued to expand. A fourth daughter, Rachel, was born in 1930, and two years later Tom arrived. Jack bought 3 The

Rachel's christening, 1930, with godparents Rose Macaulay and Hugh Walpole (top left) and daughters, Angela, Sylvia and Mary (left to right) (Pacific & Atlantic Photos)

Grove, Highgate, where Coleridge had once lived . . . a year or two later he bought Billingham Manor in the Isle of Wight as a holiday house. This latter became more of a home for the children: they kept their own ponies, there were woods and fields to play in, and the sea was not far away. Jane ran both houses admirably and was well able to manage large house-parties at weekends. She furnished and decorated the houses artistically, and once in the country she became a keen gardener, and turned herself into a highly professional ornithologist. Whatever Jane did, she did thoroughly. Jack had begun to make a lot of money, but didn't quite know what to do with it. Jane took over the financial management – she was clever with money and took an intelligent interest in the ups and down of the stock market. As royalties from *The Good Companions* poured in, Jane turned them into a trust to pay for the education of the four girls and to ensure their future. This probably helped Jack with his increasingly large tax bills. He deeply and rather unreasonably resented the amount of tax he now had to pay.

While material circumstances and surroundings seemed as good as possible, all was not, however, well with the marriage, nor with the older children. Jack was not a sexually faithful husband – could he ever have been at this stage in his life? His enormous energy included an abounding sexual energy. 'I was always looking for something,' he said, and added, 'I never found it.' All the same in these, his promiscuous days, he admitted that he 'had a lot of fun with a lot of nice women.' Jack was a deeply sensual man, always gentle and personal. 'Sex', he would say, 'is a psychological act.' He rejoiced in a richly seductive voice: 'I believe you could talk a woman into bed,' I once said to him; he agreed, rather pleased. So Jane had problems, as well as temperamental problems of her own, and when things got too tense she was apt to take to her bed with what we would now call psychosomatic illnesses.

Barbara and Sylvia had an unhappy childhood; although they could not remember their mother, Jane was not a substitute. At first it was Mary, pretty, clever and talented who was the centre of Jane's attention. Sylvia, so close in age, felt particularly left out in the cold, and would stand outside crying, with no one to play with, while Jane was shut away amusing Mary. In defiance of much psychology, Barbara and Sylvia have nevertheless grown up into splendidly balanced and kind, as well as artistically gifted, adults, who have both made happy and lasting marriages.

Despite his infidelities, Jack was in fact very much a family man. He was wonderful with small children, and loved playing with them and

This still from a family home movie shows Jack in the garden of 3 The Grove, Highgate, in the early 1930s

making them laugh. He bought them presents, taught them conjuring tricks and invented all kinds of games. As they grew older he played tennis and croquet and other outdoor games with them all. There is a little piece in *Delight* called 'Family Silliness – Domestic Clowning', in which Jack recalled all the family fun, usually at the Sunday family dinner:

> To a sensitive outsider the scene would bring no delight at all. . . . But then it is not meant for outsiders, sensitive or otherwise. . . . You have to be thoroughly in it and of it to appreciate its quality. Somewhere below this rowdy monkey business are deep hidden roots, and somewhere above are invisible blossoms. Without a happy togetherness, the little farce would never have begun. And it is scenes like these, without dignity, real wit or beauty, made up of screeching and bellowing and fourth rate jokes about treacle pudding or castor oil, that a man who feels his life ebbing out may recall with an anguish of regret and tenderness, remembering as if it were a lost bright kingdom, the family all at home and being silly.

That was Jack at home with all his children, and with him there were no favourites: all were treated equally, including, of course, his step-daughter Angela. He wasn't so good when it came to the troublesome teens, but while they were small he could make life magical. Mary later observed that it was round the table, sharing good food, that the family seemed most united.

In spite of Jack's family and his real affection for Jane and reliance upon her, the marriage nearly broke when he fell passionately in love with the twenty-three-year-old Peggy Ashcroft. Peggy was a beautiful young woman, and an immensely talented actress. She was generous and warm-hearted, her personality as lovely as her face. In later years she supported all our good causes, and gave unstintingly of her time and her talents: you could always rely on Peggy. Jack's infatuation is easily understood, and yet there seems something about it that one can only call somewhat adolescent, not a matter of flesh and blood and everyday life, though clearly that is what Jack would have liked it to be. Later he referred to it as a huge 'anima projection', a new and temporarily overwhelming experience. Peggy insisted that it was never a fully consummated affair. In fact Peggy, with all her charm and talent, could not have been the kind of intellectual companion that Jack needed.

After Jack broke with Peggy and returned home, the children remember this as a bad period, full of tension, with banging of doors

Billingham Manor, Isle of Wight, where Jack did most of his work during the 1930s. The study, at the top of the house, has since been demolished (Farmers Press Agency)

and icy silences. Jack was moody and grumpy, Jane distraught and difficult; nobody was happy. Baby Tom arrived as something of a little peacemaker, a role he has continued to play in the family. He was an enchantingly attractive small boy, and Jack loved to play with him. Tom was very close to his mother, who had always wanted a son, and was perhaps rather spoiled by her, but the sweetness of his nature prevented any real spoiling of his character. As he grew older, he found his father difficult and lacking in understanding of or sympathy with the problems of adolescence. Tom remained always an affectionate and admiring son.

So gradually the family settled down, and Jack threw himself into his work. He had published two highly successful novels, and he did not abandon the novel form, but he was ready for a new challenge. He began to write for the theatre – something which had always fascinated him and which opened a whole new and exciting stage in his life.

SEVEN

LIFE AND THE THEATRE

Jack did not turn to the theatre until he was assured of an income sufficient to meet the needs of his growing family, but the theatre must always have been there, at the back of his mind, waiting for him. There was a challenge in it too, since it had been said that novelists could not write plays. So Jack sat down and wrote *Dangerous Corner* in a week.

On the face of it, the play is a whodunit, with some psychological and character interest thrown in. The characters are not explored in any depth, and the work is not capable of endless interpretations and reinterpretations, but the clues to the outcome are cleverly, though not too obviously, planted, and the mystery is maintained until the final and unexpected dénouement. 'Priestley is certainly a very clever man,' commented one critic, but Jack was never content just to be 'clever'. There are interesting suggestions about the connection between lies and the real nature of truth, and a time trick at the end, though it can, on the surface, be seen as a dramatist's clever idea, suggests the mystery of the nature of time with which Jack was becoming more and more concerned. The play opened in May 1932. After five days, and a few dismissive criticisms, the management thought it was bound to fail. Jack personally subsidized it until it began to pay and it then had a successful run. Somewhere, all around the world, either professionally, or in small amateur groups, *Dangerous Corner* is still being performed. As always, however, Jack mistrusted his own facility; he got bored with anything that came too easily, he wanted new challenges, he wanted to experiment, and never to go on repeating himself. So he was inclined to dismiss *Dangerous Corner* as nothing more than 'a box of tricks', definitely not one of his favourite plays. The work nevertheless illustrated Jack's instinct for what audiences wanted, and he found that not only could he write easily for the theatre, but that this was the form of writing that he most enjoyed.

Jack was drawn to the theatre for many reasons; in his Bradford youth he had been a passionate playgoer, and had once thought of himself as a budding actor. Writing is a solitary profession, shut up on your own for hours on end, and Jack was a convivial man. So he enjoyed the contact with actors and actresses and directors; he enjoyed the dramas, even the difficulties, and, of course, the rewards of working together in a common enterprise. He disliked, and would have nothing to do with, all the razzmatazz, the false glamour, the smart hangers-on; it was the good solid working theatre of the professionals that he wanted. Naturally he liked success, but that was not the prime object. He was in search of something deeper.

Jack's feet were firmly planted on the ground; nobody could have enjoyed, nor tasted more fully of all that life has to offer. He had had, he said, 'a rich, thick slab of experience', a real Yorkshire plum-pudding of a life. At the same time he was haunted by the feeling that there was something more than all the fascinating, beautiful, enthralling, and often tragic panorama on offer, and in which everyone played a part; and that was something so deep and mysterious that it could only be fully expressed in symbol and myth. There is plenty of underlying symbolism in Jack's work, but for him it was the theatre, the medium itself that was symbolic. As a symbolic figure, the actor's 'sharply-coloured ironic life is a parody of all our lives . . . where there is self-consciousness there – you may say – is the theatre . . . We all play character parts. . . . There is more in "All the world's a stage" than meets the eye. Perhaps even the balance that all good drama must maintain between illusion and reality, between the dream-life of the play, and the real life in the play's presentation is a reflection of our own strange existence.' Jack was drawn by 'the ancient witchery of the work, the eternal fascination of the theatre, the theatre that in the ancient world was a religious institution'. 'I am not sure', he wrote, 'that the link between the Theatre and Religion has been broken for ever . . . with intelligence and sincere emotion behind it, a theatrical production, that mimics a piece of life, is a very rich four-dimensional creation, a tiny epitome of the universal drama of creation. . . . God', Jack announced, 'is a dramatist.'

Jack said that he planned *Laburnum Grove*, his next play, when he was in a nursing home, and wrote it rapidly during convalescence. 'In the theatre', he commented, 'either everything goes right, or everything goes wrong, irrespective of the merits of the play itself.' This time everything went right, and the play was a success. He called it 'an immoral comedy', and, like *Dangerous Corner*, it had a clever surprise ending. The 'immorality' allowed for plenty of the dramatic irony that Jack enjoyed. The play was a mild satire on people's attitude to money, so often our Achilles' heel, and also on the English financial system. Jack was moving into the most political period of his life.

In 1934, however, a different kind of play arrived, one for which Jack always held a special affection. For many years Anton Chekov had been one of his favourite writers, both as a man and as a dramatist, and *The Cherry Orchard*, his favourite play. It was the sense of the tragi-comedy of human beings and of their lives, of their pathetic attempts to live by their illusions, of the continuing ironies of experience, of the atmosphere of 'laughter-through-tears' that Chekhov so brilliantly created, to which Jack's temperament immediately responded. Jack wrote a short book on Chekov, where he described *The Cherry Orchard* as a 'a play about time and change and folly and regret and vanished happiness and hope for the future'. Of Chekhov's attitude to his characters he wrote: 'He is revealing them to us in a strange light, infinitely tender and compassionate.' This kind of tender compassion was also Jack's, and his too was a phrase I have always cherished – a 'tenderness for life'. Jack was with the Chekhov who said that, 'Man will only become better when you make him see what he is like,' as he was with the Chekhov who wrote: 'When one listens to music, all this (that is the whole panorama of life) . . . is no longer meaningless, since in nature everything has a meaning. And everything is forgiven, and it would be strange not to forgive.'

And so to *Eden End*. 'I brooded for a long time over the people of this play and their lives, and then wrote it quickly and easily, and to my mind that is the way that plays ought to be written. The long brooding brings depth and richness, the quick writing compels the whole mind, and not merely the front half of it, to work at the job.' *Eden End* (note the symbolism in the title) might well be described as a play 'about time and change and folly and regret and of vanished happiness and hope for the future', but personally I think it is more interesting to look at the differences rather than the similarities between it and *The Cherry Orchard*. There is, for instance, a peculiarly English, and not at all Russian, sense of resignation, an acceptance of the hands that fate has dealt, a willingness to accept the second best and to go on trying. And there is hope, that Stella Kirby's marriage may more or less work, that her younger brother and sister may find something better; and for Sarah, the devoted and loving old nurse, there is a different kind of hope. When Stella, her pet, comes to say goodbye, and fears that she may not see her dear old nurse again, Sarah replies, 'Oh, I'll see you sometime. There's a better place than this, love.' The play did well, and has had numerous revivals.

In the midst of his theatre work, and of the novels and essays that he was still writing, Jack made and wrote his *English Journey* – to the

A scene from *Eden End* in a revival by the company Jack founded, the London Mask Theatre, featuring Brian Nissen, Dorothy Dewhurst, Angela Baddeley and Jessica Spencer (photograph by Angus McBean)

south-west, then up to the north, including his own West Riding, and back down the east side of England. His account of where he went and of what he saw is brought to life not only by his own descriptions but also by all the varied people with whom he talked and whose lives he touched during his travels. Gazing across Southampton Water at the Isle of Wight, he encounters 'the landscape of Tennyson's poetry: sunset and the Needles, rooks in the old elms, and the Spring bright with daffodils that has always haunted English poetry'. As he crosses the downs approaching Salisbury he sees 'far away in a luminous haze the spire of Salisbury Cathedral . . . a noble view of England, and Constable himself could not have contrived a better view of it. You have before you a Shakespearean landscape.' But on entering the city he notices the labour exchange, and outside it 'as pitiful a little crowd of unemployed as ever I have seen. No building cathedrals for them, poor devils; they would think themselves lucky if they were given a job helping to build rabbit hutches.' As Jack travels he muses on the state of England: '. . . the machine itself, I said, was not at fault, being merely our dumb slave, but the shoddy, greedy, profit-grabbing, joint-stock-company

71

industrial system we had allowed to dominate us, there was the real villain'. And again: 'One of the dreadful ironies of our time, when there were never more men doing nothing and there never was before so much to do.' Does history, as some people think, just go round in a circle?

As he moves northwards, things, of course, get worse. In the Black Country, in West Bromwich, Jack visits Rusty Lane, 'surrounded for miles by all the grim paraphernalia of industrialism . . . I have never seen such a picture of grimy desolation as that street offered me. . . . There ought to be no more of those lunches and dinners, at which political and financial and industrial gentlemen congratulate one another, until something is done about Rusty Lanes – while they exist in their foul shape, it is idle to congratulate ourselves on anything.' Jack has much good to say, though, of the many people of all varieties that he meets. He finds nothing wrong with the British people: 'they are much better than their ordinary life allows them to be'. And wherever Jack meets something good and hopeful, something he can admire, he celebrates it.

And so to the West Riding and to Bradford, his old home. He has come partly to attend a reunion dinner of those who were left from his old wartime battalion, and it cannot help reviving memories of the terrible losses of what used to be called the Great War. Jack and

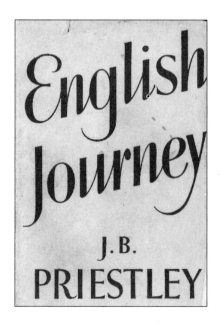

The dust-jacket of the first edition of *English Journey*, published in 1934

several others had arranged that the men who could not afford the rather high price of the dinner would be provided with free tickets. But there were still those among them who were given tickets and yet did not appear. Jack learned that, even so, they felt they could not attend as they had no decent clothes. Jack was very much distressed. 'They ought to have known they would be welcome in the sorriest rags, but their pride would not allow them to come . . . we could drink to the tragedy of the dead, but we could only stare at one another, in pitiful embarrassment over this tragi-comedy of the living, who fought for a world that did not want them, who had come back to exchange their uniforms for rags. . . . I have many vivid dreams, and the dead move casually through them; they pass and smile, the children of the sword.' A day out in the Dales is a happy interlude - 'I know of no country that offers us such enchanting variety' – and Jack is able to rejoice in the marvellous brilliance of this coloured autumn day. But before he leaves, he meets an old acquaintance, an elderly unmarried woman, who has just retired after working for fifty years as a weaver in the same mill:

A brief childhood at one end, and a few sinking weary years at the other end; she has a pension of 5/- a week from the mill and 10/- a week from the State, and an invalid sister to support. She never asks herself, as she stirs in the dark mornings when she hears the hooter blowing . . . whether mills were created for men and women, or men and women for the mills. She does not complain much, perhaps because she realizes, like all the protesting gentlemen who lounge before large club fireplaces, that if, during and after her fifty years of toil, she had been treated with any more consideration it would have meant the ruin of a great country. And, not being a literary sentimentalist, she does not say that a country in these years has no title to greatness, had better face and risk ruin if it still allows its people to suffer such damnable injustice.

Of course, things are better now – comparatively – but perhaps we should look again at *English Journey*. 'Unemployment is a price worth paying. The adoption of the European Social Chapter would be the ruin of British industry.' I wonder. And it is an alarming thought that when, in 1939, we had gone to war, and become occupied day and night preparing to kill or to be killed, there was work for everyone to do; and money to pay for it all.

Perhaps it was Jack's enormous reserves of energy that enabled him to persist in describing himself as indolent and mentally lazy. He wrote a piece about himself smoking a morning pipe, and lolling in a large hot bath while the rest of the family were up and about attending to the chores of the day, and there was he, 'a pampered slug'. Maybe this unappealing epithet was a reflection of Jane's comfortable and well-ordered household. Billingham Manor had another aid to creative writing; a great new study had been built for Jack up at the top of the house: 'The best workroom I have ever had', he wrote, 'and probably the best I shall ever have.' It had large windows all round, two of them curved at each end, so that it felt like the bridge of a ship. Not only was it safely away from a rowdy young family, but there was plenty of room for Jack to pace up and down, and gaze at the great sweeping views of at least a quarter of the island.

Jack had dedicated his favourite play *Eden End* to Jane, and the dedication of *English Journey* reads: 'To Jane who has shared so much of this England with me, and to Thomas whose England this is, for better or worse, with the author's love'. Jack honestly intended to do his best to make his marriage work. But while there was peace in the household, there may still have been tensions between husband and wife. It would have been surprising if there had not been, and Jane continued to suffer from unexplained illnesses. Whatever the reasons, doctors suggested that it might be better for Jane to spend winters out of England, so in 1936–7 Jack took his entire family off to spend the winter on a ranch in Arizona. This was a happy period for the family, and wonderful for the children. Friends came to stay, including a prolonged visit from Edward and Natalie Davison. Jane gave lessons to the older children, but there was plenty of time to play, to ride, to explore and to picnic, and in the evenings there were games with the cowboys. Jack wrote with pride that his family were described as 'the best and liveliest bunch' they had ever had on the ranch. And outside he had a little hut 'put up' for himself where he could retire and work in peace.

Jack had gone first to New York to supervise a production of *Eden End*, while the family found their way down to the south. In spite of his meticulous care in the rehearsing, the play was a failure, and he received gloomy telegrams informing him of the fact while en route to the family in Arizona. Back in his little hut, he found himself 'motionless and alone with the immense vanity, which is the scribbler's curse, raging now like a fever; the children of my tenderest fancy had just been massacred by halfwits; my most intimate confidences had been answered by yawns; eyes glazed with boredom

Jack at Wickenbury, Arizona, where he wrote *Midnight on the Desert*, photographed
c. 1936

had stared contemptuously at scenes dear to me.' In all his long life,
Jack did a great deal of reviewing, but he never dealt out to others the
kind of wounds that he himself sometimes received. His criticism was
perceptive and constructive, and if he thought really badly of any
book or play he refused to write about it at all. Quite soon Jack
stopped 'travelling in the dreary circle of self-interest' and got on
cheerfully with the next piece of work.

Two years later he returned again to Arizona with his family. These
winters produced, among other ventures, two chapters of auto-

A rare photograph of the whole of the Priestley family, taken during their holiday in Arizona in 1936 and sent as a New Year's card by Jane Priestley. Left to right: standing: Sylvia, Barbara, Jane, Angela Wyndham-Lewis, Mary; seated: Tom, Jack, Rachel

biography, *Midnight on the Desert* and *Rain Upon Godshill*. In these two books Jack reflects upon the world, upon politics, upon the nature of man, upon the problems of consciousness, time, mortality and his own special brand of a limited survival after death. There is so much of interest, and so much of Jack himself in these two books, that it is almost impossible to select from the eminently quotable pieces which appear on every page. Jack used to say that he feared that people were inclined to think of him just as an entertainer – and he certainly did produce a great deal to entertain a great many people. But he felt that his serious ideas, as well as his critique of so much in the modern world, were neglected. So it is upon these that I will concentrate.

On this journey to Arizona Jack had read a number of books purporting to describe humanity in the light of modern scientific and psychological discoveries – a number of 'man is nothing but . . .' treatises, with comments such as, 'Life is simply an affair of radio-electric cells, the difference between the amoeba and man being that the amoeba is a comparatively simple arrangement of cells, whereas man is a large and complicated one' – 'the fashionable trick', said Jack, 'of trying to explain a thing by its roots and not its fruits'. Another characteristic offering was that the explanation of, and the trouble with, Jesus, was that 'he was a severe sufferer from the Oedipus complex'. Jack commented: 'We should not shoo a cat out

Midnight on the Desert: A Chapter of Autobiography, the outcome of the Priestleys' stay in Arizona, was published in 1937

of the room on such evidence as this.' Jack did add: 'I cannot call myself a Christian, for much of the doctrine bewilders me, and some of it definitely repels, and I have long felt it was a mistake to pile Greek philosophy and Roman Imperial organization on top of the essential personal teaching of this supreme religious genius.' But fascinated as Jack was by the discoveries of the physicists, especially by their cosmological theories, they were not enough for him. They stopped at the point at which he wanted to go on; either they were certain that their explanations were comprehensive, or they thought it was not their business to draw conclusions for the lives of men. 'But,' wrote Jack, 'if there is no invisible sphere, no great communion of mind, no shared adventures of the spirit, no reality unknown to outward sense, and all's plain sailing, why do we seem to move through a haunted world?' And again: 'There is more than sheer greed of experience in our hunger for immortality. There is something nobler than mere fear of death. We cannot help feeling that life is more than the sketchy improvisation we have given it.' So Jack turned his attention to the two mysteries that had always haunted him, human self-consciousness and time.

Jack had reviewed J.W. Dunne's book, *An Experiment in Time*, and was immediately excited by Dunne's theory of serialism, based partly on his experience of dreams, which seem to contain both past and future happenings. Dunne, who was a mathematician and an aeronautical engineer, postulated a series of different times, existing – if that is the word – in different dimensions, and ourselves as a series of observers able to move between these different dimensions. I cannot attempt to summarize this complex theory, but will quote Jack's conclusions: 'If time is illusory or multiple, our mode of apprehending a dimension of things we cannot grasp spatially, then there is nothing absurd or contradictory about immortality . . . and if we are in fact a series of observers existing in a series of times, then nothing is lost, and we are ourselves the products of our whole experience of life.' This immediately opened up a huge range of human meaning and possibilities.

The second book that Jack discovered almost coincidentally – books do seem to come into our hands at the moment when we need or are ready for them – was Ouspensky's *New Model of the Universe*. Ouspensky, 'that queer mixture of scientific rationality and esoteric dogmatism', was also a believer in different dimensions and different times. Jack was attracted by his third dimension, a line of the actualization of other possibilities contained in any moment but not actualized in time. That seemed to open a way of escape out of the dilemmas of free will and determinism in which Dunne appeared to leave the individual trapped. Ouspensky's final dimension is circular, which means that we go on living the same lives over and over again: we exit by the back door, only to re-enter immediately by the front – to my mind a very dreary idea, even if it can account for the queer sensation of *déjà vu* that most of us experience from time to time. Ouspensky does offer us some means of escape from this endless circling: there are points at which we can make a different choice and turn the circle into a spiral in order to progress to some better or higher existence.

Although Jack found a certain amount to criticize in these theories, they were immensely important to him. Once we escape from the strait-jacket of passing time human life achieves a meaning and a value that we intuitively believe that it must have. Survival after death is not a matter of any possible reward or punishment, it offers us a chance of change and development, even perhaps the righting of wrongs in some other dimension of time. That Jack was on the track of real and important truths must be evidenced by the discoveries of mathematical physicists. They assure us, on strict scientific and mathematical evidence, rather than on the intuitions of brilliant men, that our perception of time is illusory, relative only to our position in, and apprehension of, the natural world: time is not an absolute. This must, they tell us, be a universe of many dimensions; in fact the theoreticians who regard 'super-strings' as the basis of the universe seem to postulate an almost unlimited number of dimensions. These are dizzying speculations, and Jack would have been delighted by them.

In *Rain Upon Godshill*, written in Jack's splendid new study at Billingham Manor, Jack tried to spell out his beliefs, to spare a little time to think quietly and creatively. Despite his criticisms of the theories of Dunne and Ouspensky, he accepts happily their assertions of the illusion of passing time and their forays into different dimensions. He meditates on precognition, and on what is called coincidence, which is after all only a description, and not an explanation of something that most of us experience. That we live in an immensely mysterious and complicated universe he felt certain. As to the second mystery of human consciousness, of the individual self and the soul, Jack rejects the Christian conception of persons arriving in the world with new and individual souls – he suggests that it would be more reasonable to suppose that the immortal soul exists before birth, and that it has perhaps to be in time, linked to physical and mental characteristics, for purposes of its own. Jack considers

Jack looking out of the window
of his study at Billingham Manor
(*Daily Herald*)

reincarnation, which seems, on the surface, to explain a good deal about ourselves, but which, he says, 'has never really come home to me, never chimed with my own deepest experiences. The cosmos you discover in moments of profound feeling is the genuine one. Ecstasy follows the sudden unveiling of truth.'

It is this ecstasy, known to mystics, Christian and otherwise, which infused Jack's beliefs, or perhaps one should say his intuitions about life. He reflects in *Rain Upon Godshill* that it is in moments of such heightened consciousness that all feeling of separate individuality is lost. In fact, 'the deeper inward you go, the less you are separately yourself, but more a part of other selves', or even, though he would not put it that way – a part of some greater self. 'In black misery', he writes, 'you certainly feel a solid little lump of ego, but the further you move away from misery, the more the self seems to thin out, turning from a thick egoistic substance into a large fragile vessel.' Could this be something like what is meant by losing your life in order to find it?

That all this may sound vague and woolly Jack would be the first to agree. He approved of the woolly-minded, the open-ended, and deeply distrusted those who imagined they had everything securely buttoned up in some dogmatic strait-jacket. He was fond of quoting John Cowper Powys, whom he considered a neglected genius, to the

Jack at work in Billingham Manor

effect that a man 'should combine scepticism about everything with credulity about everything – the true Shakespearean way to take life'. That was Jack's way: 'A mind without credulity', he wrote, 'would never learn anything new, a man without scepticism would believe any nonsense . . . so long as a man guards against intolerance and anger, it is better to believe in too much than in too little.'

So Jack went on speculating, relying upon his intuitions, his experience and sometimes upon his dreams. Jack had an exceptionally vivid dream life, he felt that it was a whole world of experience. There were many different kinds of dream, more or less significant, some appearing almost more real than life. There was one such that he experienced around this period that affected his whole outlook.

He was standing alone on a high tower, and looking down upon myriads and myriads of birds of every variety, 'a vast aerial river of birds', all flying in one direction. Then suddenly the flight was speeded up, and he saw 'generations of birds flutter into life, weaken, falter and die', and the sight made him desperately unhappy. 'What was the use of all this blind struggle towards life?' Then flight was speeded up again, rushing by so fast that he could see no movement from the birds; it was 'an enormous plain sewn with feathers':

But then along this plain flickering through the birds themselves, there passed a sort of white flame, trembling, dancing, then hurrying on: and as soon as I saw it I knew that this white flame was life itself, the very quintessence of being: and then it came to me in a rocket burst of ecstasy that nothing mattered, nothing could ever matter, because nothing else was real, but this quivering and hurrying lambency of being. . . . It left nothing to mourn over behind it . . . for now all real feeling was caught and purified and danced on ecstatically with the white flame of life. I had never felt before such deep happiness as I knew at the end of my dream of the tower and the birds. . . . And as it was with the birds so it would be with men, if I had the strength and courage to dream it. There would be millions and millions of them, and some of them I would have known and loved; but again it would not matter, for the white flame, trembling, dancing, then hurrying through them was all knowledge and all love. . . .

EIGHT

THEATRE, WAR AND POLITICS

In *Rain Upon Godshill* Jack meditated around two fine reproductions of Pieter Brueghel the Elder's pictures, *The Peasants' Wedding* and *The Hunters in the Snow*. 'He is an artist from and to the people,' Jack wrote.

> We writers, if we do not wish, on the one hand, to whisper to a few, and on the other hand, merely to tickle the mob, could find in him an inspiration. . . . Then, as now, in man's spiritual life, the seas were dark and heavy, and the steering gear had nearly gone . . . there was still colour and gaiety in the foreground, but in the background . . . doomsday. . . . In this world Brueghel painted his peasants – humanity, all of us. . . . It is realistic . . . the seasonal atmosphere is terrific. . . . You are compelled to look *down* on the scenes . . . you now discover that a kind of magical element has found its way into this world . . . somewhere just round the corner is a fairy-tale country. This is not plain realism, but realism merging into the magical. And as you stare again, feeling a trifle haunted, the realistic–magical turns into the symbolic. . . . Many of the details, sharply observed and recorded, are comic – but the effect is beautiful and faintly tragic – which is how most of us should see life, and, if we are writers, record it.

That could be a description of what Jack was trying to do in his plays and in his novels, and what he often succeeded in doing. It is a fair description of that much misunderstood book, *The Good Companions*, as it is of the plays in which he often attempted what he called 'a stealthy edging away from naturalism'.

Jack could never resist haring after any new idea, and ideas kept bubbling up. He regularly discussed his work with Jane; she would read through what he had written, and he valued her comments. This time one of the most successful ideas came through her. In those far-off days, travel was by ship, and Jack quite often made the Atlantic crossing to New York. When on his own he was apt to regard sea

Jack with Basil Dean at a rehearsal for *When We Are Married*, 1938 (Planet News)

voyages as happy opportunities for sexual encounters, an activity in which he was by no means unusual. On this occasion, however, Jane was with him, and had picked up an amusing French novel, the story of a couple apparently securely married for many years who discovered that, owing to some technical irregularity, they had never been legally married. She thought it might appeal to Jack, who was delighted, and in next to no time there was *When We Are Married*, one of Jack's funniest and most enduringly popular comedies. It is the tale of three Yorkshire couples celebrating their silver weddings; they were married on the same day, by the same Baptist minister. The men are highly respectable citizens, an alderman, a local councillor, and a solicitor, all prominent members of the Baptist chapel. For such an auspicious occasion, the Press has been summoned, as well as a professional photographer. Jack has a great deal of fun with these characters, and so does his audience. Jack was a connoisseur of male vanity, his humorous self-knowledge kept his own well in check, and he was able to turn his observations upon the pomposities and hypocrisies of his fellow men, and upon the characters he created, as he does here, especially upon the self-satisfied males. A good deal of rather painful and very funny self-knowledge follows the awful revelation that, after all, they are not properly married. Jack has even more fun with the photographer, who arrives and remains thoroughly drunk; when the actor playing the part fell suddenly ill, and no replacement could be found, Jack at very short notice was prevailed upon to take his place, 'about which', said Jack, 'I have boasted ever since'. The play reached the West End in October 1938, and ran through 1939.

Around this time – in fact, a year or two earlier – Jack produced his experimental Time Plays. *Time and the Conways* is one of the best known, and probably the most often performed. Like *Eden End*, it is centred upon a family gathering, but here it is the leap forward into a sadly disillusioned future in the second act and the return to present time in the third that give the play its particular and ironic poignancy. Although in many ways a sad play, the final note of resignation and acceptance echoes that of *Eden End*.

Time and the Conways owes much to Dunne's time theories, but *I Have Been Here Before*, produced in 1937, is much closer to Ouspensky. Four characters meet apparently coincidentally at a Yorkshire pub. Three of them have vague feelings of 'having been there before'; the mysterious Dr Görtler, researcher into time theories, knows that they have – there is no coincidence. In the light of Ouspensky's theories, considerably adapted by Jack, the three work out their tangled emotions. The main and most interesting character, Osmund, makes a different choice, allowing them all to escape from the endlessly repetitive circle of their lives. Jack sustains the mystery and the excitement to the end, and, although he uses much of Ouspensky's theory, the magic, the dreams, the imagination and the drama are entirely Jack's.

Such was Jack's involvement with the theatre that he set up his own repertory company – The London Mask Theatre. In spite of dire warnings from so eminent and experienced a dramatist as Bernard Shaw, it was a success, and might have gone on being so, had it not been for the war. The company produced a number of distinguished and successful plays, and it was also, of course, a vehicle for Jack's own. Many of the leading actors and actresses of the period worked with the company, and appeared in Jack's plays, and Jack made a number of lasting friendships. Perhaps the friendship that meant most to him was that with Ralph Richardson and his wife. Jack and Richardson had mutual tastes outside the theatre. They worked together in five of Jack's productions and he wrote two plays specially for Richardson – *Cornelius*, about life in a city office, and *Johnson Over Jordan*. Jack had an enormous admiration for Richardson's talents: 'Just as I am not the plain down-to-earth writer that many people have called me, so Richardson is not, as I have often seen him described, the ordinary Englishman enlarged . . . he can be a bank clerk, an insurance agent, a dentist, but very soon mysterious lights and shadows, tones of anguish and ecstasy are discerned in banking, insurance and dentistry. . . .'

In *Johnson Over Jordan*, Jack said, 'I handed Richardson a packet. It made outrageous demands on his skill and endurance.' This was Jack's most ambitious play. 'I took', he said, 'such dramatic technique as I possessed as far as it would go, using the most objective form there is for material that is deeply subjective, trying to take my characters outside ordinary passing time altogether, to create, you might say, a four dimensional drama. . . .' To this end, Jack employed all the resources of the theatre, tricks of lighting, masks, ballet, and music specially composed by Benjamin Britten. Music plays an important part in a number of Jack's plays; for him it was the most magical and mysterious of the arts. The play begins immediately following the death of its main character, Robert Johnson (Ralph Richardson). It is not a play about life after death, but a play about life, with Robert Johnson the Everyman of our time. 'It is really', said Jack, 'a biographical-morality play in which the usual chronological treatment is abandoned for a timeless-dream examination of a man's life.'

'Twice and twice only', Jack later wrote, 'has a play of mine so wrung me I could no longer see.' One was a production of *Time and the Conways* in Vienna in 1946, when, for Jack, 'the play was stronger, more poignant, than ever before'. The other was the final performance of *Johnson Over Jordan* in 1939. The play might well have run longer, but, on the outbreak of war, all the London theatres were closed: they did reopen, and remained open for the duration, but it was too late for *Johnson Over Jordan*. Jack wrote of the final performance:

The end of the play, when Johnson said his farewells, and then turned to go towards the glitter of stars, the blue dark spaces, the unknown, while Britten's finale sounded from the orchestra pit, moved most people any and every night. But this was the last night, the last farewell, the last glimpse of Johnson against the starry sky, the last sound of Britten's triumphant crescendo – never, never again . . . and I might have been staring into the grave . . . Perhaps it is more sensible to write books and not plays, but it is not out of books that such moments arrive, beautiful and terrible.

The play had a mixed reception but was universally hailed as a triumph for Ralph Richardson. Older critics were hostile, perhaps disconcerted, though some of the younger ones were enthusiastic. Many people were fascinated, and Jack had three times as many letters of appreciation as for any of his other plays.

Other lifelong friends were Michael Denison and Dulcie Gray. Jack was a good talent-spotter. He gave Michael his first part in 1938, and engaged him, under contract, for the London Mask Theatre. Michael was paid £2 17s 6d a week, but he wanted to get married. Out of the blue he was offered a part in an Aberdeen repertory company at £9 per week. Dulcie Gray, to whom he was engaged, had just finished drama school as a star pupil, so the Aberdeen group were willing to take her on as a junior at £6 a week. This was wealth – they would be able to afford to get married, but Michael was under contract. Jack was on holiday, being motored around England; he was tracked down at the Welcombe Hotel, Stratford-on-Avon, and Michael's plight was explained to him. 'Ah well,' said Jack, ever warm-hearted and romantic, 'Let the lad go.'

Michael returned gratefully to play the poet in *Music at Night*, written for the Malvern Festival in 1938 and produced in London just after the outbreak of war. This was perhaps an even more difficult play than *Johnson Over Jordan*. Jack described it as 'an attempt to dramatize the mental adventures of a group of persons listening to the first performance of a piece of music'. The play moves from the surface of the mind to deeper and deeper levels of consciousness. 'The strange happenings in Act IV arise from my belief that, at these depths, we are not the separate beings we imagine ourselves to be.' Michael says that, such was Jack's technical skill, the play really did work on stage, though Jack himself felt that the last act failed.

The Denisons had considerable experience of working with Jack. 'He was', says Michael, 'that rare thing, a distinguished playwright who understood actors' problems, could communicate with us and even listen to us, and appeared to respect our contribution.' Jack did indeed respect the professional craft of acting, as he respected any genuine craftsmanship. 'He was a wonderful friend', said Dulcie, 'inventively funny, and his small shouts of laughter when he bared his teeth a little and slightly shook his shoulders, his brilliant mimicry of pretentious aquaintances, and his kindness to anyone in trouble, were totally endearing.'

This was a good time for the Priestley family, comfortably and happily divided between Highgate and the Isle of Wight. Jack worked in the mornings, and played rather athletic games with his children in the afternoons. There were often large weekend parties with writers

Jack with Tom in the garden of Billingham Manor (Photopress)

Jack enjoying a game of ludo with Tom, Rachel (left) and Mary at Billingham Manor during the war

Jack accompanying his daughter Mary, on the violin, at Billingham Manor, 1941

and publishers, sometimes musicians, and usually an ornithologist or two for Jane. Mary remembers how in the evenings she would hide behind the drawing-room sofa to listen to all the fascinating talk. Billingham Manor ran on oiled wheels, perhaps even more smoothly when Miss Ann Pudduck came as cook-housekeeper in 1938. She was already a well-trained cook, and Jane's knowledge of French cuisine added to her skills; she had not intended to stay long, but in fact she was with the family for fifty years, and for those of us who came later, it was impossible to imagine the Priestley household without her.

There may have been peace at home for Jack, but there was no peace in the world. He could never leave his own creative writing, but, as soon as war was declared, his attention was upon events and upon his hopes for a new and better England. When the famous postscripts came to an end, he continued nightly overseas broadcasts, mainly to America, where he was well known, and where his words had considerable impact. The war disrupted the lives of most British families, and it thoroughly disrupted the Priestleys. By September 1940 Jack was in London working on his broadcasts. The children were back at boarding school, except for Angela who had embarked on a stage career. So Jane and Miss Pudduck set off for Highgate. When they arrived at 3 The Grove, they found a telegram on the doormat inside announcing that the Army had taken over Billingham Manor. Before such high-handed commandeering, the army was supposed to give forty-eight hours' notice. Jane was allowed back to collect some clothes, and that was all. When the London Blitz began in earnest, a large land-mine exploded outside 3 The Grove, making it barely habitable. Jack and Jane rented a flat in Whitehall Court, and later moved to B3–4 Albany, where they stayed.

Now there was no family home, and for much of the time there was no family, and Jane wanted to do something useful. She was one of the pioneers of nursery schools, and as chairman of a group had been responsible for planning, equipping and engaging staff for a school in North St Pancras. Now she received a message from the Women's Voluntary Service to the effect that there was an urgent need for hostels in the country for mothers and babies and unattached under-fives from the main cities, so that they could be relatively safe from the bombing. It was to this enormous task that Jane devoted her formidable talents of organization. She found suitable houses in Herefordshire, not too far from where the children's schools had been evacuated. She cabled friends in America, and soon had a promise of £1,000 for initial expenses, and the rest of the money came out of Jack's pocket. Jane believed in going

Jack and Jane at the 'Priestley nursery', Broxwood Court, Herefordshire, during the war

straight to the top: she wrote to the Minister of Health, and received assurances of support. The main Herefordshire nursery was a large house, Broxwood Court, which became the headquarters; the work expanded quickly, and eventually there were seven flourishing 'Priestley nurseries'. All were properly equipped and staffed, with trained nurses and visiting doctors. Jane managed to find excellent helpers, and always received great loyalty from those she employed. At Broxwood Court she was much helped by Miss Puddock and by Gertrude, who had once been the children's nursery maid. In May 1941 Jane produced her first report on Broxwood Court. She wrote:

> Our head cook and caterer is Miss Ann Pudduck . . . everyone who visits the hall, as well as the permanent residents, are all impressed with the quite remarkably high standard of cooking. Miss Pudduck in peacetime could cook a seven-course dinner for twenty. Now she faces her very heavy day with a smile, and the highest degree of efficiency. We have two breakfasts, four lunches, two teas and one supper – some 70–80 people are catered for daily.

All of this in conditions of stringent wartime rationing was a remarkable achievement.

The first batch of children arrived bringing an epidemic of measles, and the next lot an epidemic of chickenpox. But with these overcome, the health of the children improved dramatically. Two of them had arrived marked 'probably mentally deficient'; in fact they were only severely undernourished, and were soon perfectly normal. Kindly middle-class ladies who visited the nurseries looked amazed at the babies in their prams saying, 'But these could be *anybody's* children!' There were plenty of problems, but somehow they were all overcome, and at the end of the war Jane was awarded the OBE and Miss Pudduck the BEM, which she always modestly concealed.

During the war Jane was still able to spend some time in London and carry on organizing with the help of an efficient secretary. For school holidays she rented local cottages where the family could be together. Jack occasionally visited the nurseries, and joined the family when he could. As well as writing, broadcasting and fire-watching, he became much more politically active, though he never officially joined any party.

Jack's were the politics of compassion, the liberal socialism that he had inherited from his father. In his youth he had seen the cruelties of the lower end of capitalism; on his *English Journey* he had seen them again, and had been distressed and outraged. The war revealed the possibilities of a life in which men and women could work together, often sacrificially, for the common good. 'The English', he wrote, 'are a good people. They have qualities that would make it possible for the new society which will not be Communism or Fascism or a capitalist democracy, to make a beginning here.' Jack had never been remotely attracted by any form of Fascism, though Oswald Mosley, Mussolini, and even Hitler, had their English admirers. He was critical of Marxism, believing it to be based on a 'false materialism', 'another extremely bigoted fundamentalism'. But he acknowledged, as one surely must, that 'from each according to his ability, to each according to his need' was a noble ideal.

Jack described himself as a 'critical left-winger': 'We should behave towards our country as women behave towards the men they love. A loving wife will do anything for her husband except to stop criticizing and trying to improve him.' So Jack went on criticizing the England that he truly loved. He deplored the English class system, the parade of the social season, and the House of Lords, which 'humbugged' us with its 'medieval masquerade'. He deplored the sale – in however subtle a manner – of honours and titles. 'From the moment it was known that honours could be bought, they should have been laughed out of existence . . . this foolish, snobbish tradition runs through our national life, and is one of the greatest recruiting forces for an intolerant and ungenerous Toryism.' It also sustained the special English vices of snobbery, complacency, and hypocrisy, and prevented the creation of a true democracy. We were 'a plutocracy pretending to be a democracy'.

While not opposed to inequalities of wealth – these could add to the interest and variety of life – he believed that there ought to be a minimum standard of living below which no one should be allowed to fall. He believed in the constitutional value of a reformed second chamber, and he gave an approving nod in the direction of proportional representation. He was critical of the Labour Party, and deplored its tie-up with the trade unions as undemocratic and representing too much of a sectional interest: 'If we ever do build Jerusalem in England's green and pleasant land it will certainly not be done with Trades Union rules.' Nor did he fall for the sentimentality of the Left, imagining all true virtue to reside only in 'the workers'. Unashamedly, Jack extolled what are called, sometimes perjoratively, 'middle-class values'. Of course, for Jack, a new society had to be one that would sustain and nurture the arts: 'These, with religion and philosophy, are the roots and nourishment of our national life.' In his final postscript Jack spoke of 'the growing hope of decent folk everywhere for a reasonable liberty along with a reasonable security', and he asserted that 'democracy is not an experiment that was tried and that failed, but a great creative force that must now be released again'.

NINE

ACTIVE POLITICS, 1945 AND AFTER

It was Jack's postscript of 21 July 1940 that caught the attention of an idealistic and politically radical young Member of Parliament, Sir Richard Acland. Richard had inherited large family estates in Devon and Somerset, but had come to believe passionately in the common ownership of land as well as of the basic industries and natural resources. And here was Jack:

> My own personal view, for what it is worth, is that we must stop thinking in terms of property and power, and begin thinking in terms of community and creation. . . . Property is that old-fashioned way of thinking of a country as a thing, and a collection of things on that thing, all owned by certain people and constituting property; instead of thinking of a country as the home of a living society, and considering the welfare of that society, the community itself as the first test.

Richard, true and consistent in his beliefs, did not feel that he could continue working for common ownership while remaining a large landowner; he began the process of handing over his 'great possessions' to the National Trust. He felt at once that his and Jack's political thinking were running parallel, and that together they could gather a powerful team for political and social reform. Out of this emerged the 1941 Committee, with Jack as chairman.

The committee met at the home of Edward Hulton, publisher of the progressive magazine, *Picture Post*; they were financially supported by Alan Good, a wealthy industrial 'whizz-kid', and manager of a large Midlands engineering concern. Members came from a wide section of public life and included publishers, journalists, writers and novelists, artists, sociologists, and a number of academics, including the economist Thomas Balogh, whose economic ideas were influential on the committee, though he and Richard Acland never saw eye to eye. Names such as Kingsley Martin, Victor Gollancz,

Ritchie Calder, as well as Acland himself would appear again in CND. Raymond Gauntlett became secretary of the group. Jack saw his task as chairman as trying to hold these diverse personalities together. When, as often happened, he was unable to attend meetings, Raymond Gauntlett, in whom he had full confidence, could represent him.

Richard Acland and his wife Anne spent two nights in the country with the Priestleys. Jack and Anne discussed literature, and Jack had them in 'tears of laughter with imitations of different kinds of chairmen at his meetings whose common goal was to work to the point of being able to describe him as a "good companion", as if this was something no chairman had ever said before'. Poor Jack, how he was haunted by *The Good Companions!* This meeting was constructive and encouraging, as well as being pleasant.

At first all seemed to be going well. The committee produced a number of publications, pamphlets, short books, and, of course, numerous articles in the Press. Jack with his usual speed and facility wrote *Out of the People*, an expansion of his general political ideas. The book had a huge sale, and had to be quickly reprinted. Jack gave people a vision of a new society for which many were searching, something that Jack's intuition told him, and which his imaginative literary skills enabled him to express – 'Where there is no vision the people perish.'

Although among Jack's many correspondents there were a number who challenged him to spell out his beliefs in practical terms, this was something he had always refused to do. It would, he said, be starting the wrong way round: we must begin by clearing the ground, exposing old and fallacious suppositions, creating a new atmosphere, a demand for change that would prove irresistable. Both Left and Right had to begin to think differently.

The 1941 Committee did, of course, discuss a number of constructive proposals, and in *Out of the People* Jack, in a brief appendix, spelled out a few basic political suggestions, for which he acknowledged his debt to the discussions of the committee, though what he wrote was always what he, personally, believed.

Jack was first and foremost a democrat; he wanted the devolution of political power, not its over-centralization. Democracy required local activity and responsibility: agriculture and village life must be supported, as must all those associations such as trade unions, the Co-operative movement, cultural, professional and charitable organizations. These were the sinews of democracy – 'Parliament should not drain away all the political life of the country.' Jack favoured a mixed economy: 'All very large-scale and absolutely essential utilities and services should be taken over by the community. But the main bulk of production would not be a state affair . . . because private enterprise permits more experiment, flexibility and efficiency . . . a rigid planned state economy means dragooning the people.'

Many of the ideas that the 1941 Committee favoured, such as joint industrial councils of men and management, national insurance, family allowances, and the basic minimum standard of living, may today sound 'old hat', but appearing, as they did, well before the publication of the Beveridge Report, they were at the time new and exciting. Jack insisted that there were no quick and easy solutions – there was 'no magic formula': 'You do not get rid of false values by substituting state ownership for private enterprise'; 'We must not let envy convince us that redistribution of the swag will do the trick. We must change the game.' It was the basic values of society that Jack cared about and these had to be, in the widest sense, Christian; that is to say, spiritual. 'We are not here', he wrote, 'to multiply ourselves senselessly, but to increase knowledge, to create beauty, and to experience love. Whatever helps to do these things is right, and whatever stands in their way is wrong.'

It soon became evident that Jack and Richard Acland were too temperamentally different to be able to work together for long. The Aclands were good friends of John's and mine, and we knew Richard as an honourable, sweet-natured and lovable man; his lively, clever and practical wife, Anne, described her marriage to him as like holding on to the string of a gas-filled balloon, and trying to keep it tethered to the ground as it dragged her along; I knew what she meant! Jack too had his vision, but his feet remained very firmly planted on the ground. Richard wanted a new political party to contest elections; this emerged as Commonwealth, and had a considerable success. Jack and others of the committee, though in theory supporting the aims of Commonwealth, were anxious not to undermine the Labour Party, only to convert it. Numbers believed that change should begin now, and that this would raise the somewhat sagging British morale, would attack privilege and inefficiency and help the war effort. Others, Jack among them, did not envisage any fundamental change until the war had been decisively won. Jack pointed out to Richard that many people would be unwilling to accept common ownership and Richard could hardly use the methods of dictatorship to coerce them. He also had to face the fact that Britain was overcrowded and not self-supporting; it was hard to see how she could afford a clean break with international capitalism. Richard recognized that he himself was 'a politician and nothing else'. By contrast, Jack, as an author and playwright, did not want to spend all his time on politics. Richard put the difference between them, as he said, 'rather brutally . . . Priestley wanted to blunt the cutting-edge of policy so as to converse with relatively small numbers of eminent people; I wanted to win by-elections with thousands of people who had not attained nationwide reputations.' Richard wanted political power; Jack, always wary of power, wanted influence. 'Despite our agreement on many issues,' Richard continued, 'it would have needed a miracle to keep us together in a fighting organization.' The miracle, of course, never happened, and Jack inevitably resigned.

This was by no means the end of Jack's active politics. He continued writing, broadcasting and speaking, and in the 1945 election he stood as an independent candidate for Cambridge University. University graduates were, at that time, entitled to two votes, one for their university member, and another for their local constituency. Needless to say, the first Labour government would soon put an end to this little piece of political privilege. Without a constituency, Jack did not have to do much in the way of compaigning. He sent round a published election manifesto, broadly in line with Labour Party policy and the Beveridge Report. He included a special plea for the arts, demands for the building of good theatres, galleries and libraries, as well as a suggestion for an arts minister and an arts council. Meanwhile, he toured the country, speaking tirelessly on behalf of the Labour Party. The Cambridge University election result was a personal disappointment for Jack. The sitting member, Kenneth Pickthorn, was returned with 73,641 votes. He was a well-known Cambridge figure, a senior tutor and history lecturer, a Conservative who had been a junior minister. Next came Wilson Harris, an independent of liberal views with 6,536 votes, and finally and rather sadly Jack, with 5,745 votes. Although Jack would not have had to nurse a constituency nor be subject to a party whip, had he been returned, I do wonder for how long he would really have stayed the course. However, it is no exaggeration to say that Jack's broadcasting, speaking and writing did contribute significantly to the swing in public opinion that brought Labour to power in 1945.

Throughout the war, Jack had continued writing plays. Perhaps his most important was *An Inspector Calls*, written in one week during the winter of 1944/5. The text of this play might well be, 'We are members one of another'. It has been seen as an anti-capitalist play,

A still from the 1953 film version of *An Inspector Calls*, starring Alistair Sim

and, set in 1912, it certainly illustrates the power that unrestrained capitalism puts in the hands of the wealthy and privileged, enabling them to destroy, albeit unwittingly, the most vulnerable members of the community. Nevertheless, the main thrust of the action is a matter of personal morality, conditioned no doubt by affluence and privilege, but personal none the less, as the two younger members of the family are quick to realize. Not only are we personally responsible for our actions, we are personally responsible for one another as members of the community. We are in fact 'our brother's keeper'. There is also in the play a time change; through the ambiguous character of Inspector Goole, played first by Jack's friend Ralph Richardson, the characters mysteriously experience the future before it happens. In 1993 *An Inspector Calls* enjoyed a triumphant revival in a new and striking production at the National Theatre, and happily two more of Jack's theatrical friends, Richard Pascoe and Barbara Leigh-Hunt, played important parts. Judging by the great enthusiasm of the audience, the play is as relevant at the end of the twentieth century as it was in the middle of it.

As there was no London theatre immediately available, Jack sent the play to his Russian translator, and it was quickly performed throughout the Soviet Union, partly no doubt because of its anti-

Jack enjoying the view from his balcony during his trip to Moscow in autumn 1945

capitalist slant. A number of Jack's books had already been translated into Russian and were widely popular. The Russians were great readers, and English was their first foreign language. Towards the end of 1945 Jack was invited to visit Russia, and he and Jane decided to accept the invitation. Jane, with her linguistic ability and her usual thoroughness, went on a crash course of Russian. Jack insisted that the visit had nothing to do with politics; they were guests of Voks (the society for cultural relations with foreign countries). For six or seven weeks they toured the Soviet Union, travelling by plane, by car and by train. As every visitor to Russia finds, they were welcomed everywhere with warm and generous hospitality – rather too generous as far as food and drink were concerned. The atmosphere seems to have been far less repressive than it became later at the height of the Cold War. They were free to stroll about as they wished and talk to people, who seemed happy to meet with foreigners; and they had no sensation of being followed or spied upon. They saw a people proud – as well they might be – of their victory over the Germans, and now enthusiastically setting about rebuilding their devastated cities. Jack wrote a series of more or less sympathetic articles. The trouble was that already anyone prepared to speak favourably of *anything* in Russia was regarded as either a gullible fellow-traveller or a crypto-Communist. Jack, needless to say, was neither. He wrote of what he saw, while aware of much that he did not see, but he was much moved by the enormous suffering these people had endured, and made hopeful by their warmth and evident desire for friendship – a genuine desire, all too quickly frustrated by the savage and suspicious character of Joseph Stalin.

After 1945 Jack and Jane returned to Billingham Manor, but it was not the happy family home that it had been before the war. The Army, as was too often the case, had left a trail of destruction. Many things were missing altogether; the girls could not find their treasures, nor many of their clothes; the boiler and the heating system, along with other household necessities, were not working. The separate lives that Jack and Jane had led during the war years had only widened any rifts between them, while the children were growing up, moving away, following careers and then getting married. There were no longer the close family occasions with all their laughter and fun; only the younger two, Rachel and Tom, were still at school.

Jane's financial advisors suggested to her that it would be a good time to invest in farmland. Jack would have liked to buy his own theatre, or even to invest in pictures, about which he knew a good deal, but he was somewhat in awe of his capable wife, and so a number of local farms were purchased. 'The last thing I thought I would ever become was a farming type,' Jack wrote to his daughter Mary. One way and another it proved too expensive to try to restore Billingham Manor to anything like its former glory, so they sold the house and the land, and rented Brooke Hill, which was nearer to Jane's various farms.

Towards the end of the war Jack was smitten with a serious kidney infection, which necessitated an operation. For the last four years he had been immersed in the war, writing about it, making films about it, talking about it, never able to stand aside from events. Now he was forced to stop. He enjoyed a period of convalescence in the western Highlands. I say 'enjoyed' because convalescence can be a time of regeneration of more than just the poor, battered old body, and that is what it was for Jack. He read and thought a lot about Jung since he had been asked to prepare a programme for that wise old man's seventieth birthday, and his creative depths began to stir and beckon. He looked slowly down the long vistas of memory, and so was born one of his most interesting novels, *Bright Day*. For a long time this was Jack's favourite novel, and out of all of his novels that I have read, I think it is mine also.

In one sense *Bright Day* is an examination of magic, and the dissolution of a false magic. Although Jack stoutly denied anything autobiographical, there is a wonderful picture of a young man growing up in Bradford before the First World War – memories need not necessarily mean autobiography, and here Jack draws happily upon boyhood memories. The book was published in 1946 and was well reviewed and well received. When it came to its publication in the Everyman Library in 1966, Jack was asked to write a new foreword, and in this he admitted the biographical background. He realized, he wrote, 'that my choice of theme and my treatment of it in *Bright Day*, were evidence of a change in the depths of my psyche, well below the conscious level. I was swinging away at last from a dangerously over-extroverted position towards the opposite pole of introversion, unconsciously restoring a balance to what was becoming menacingly one-sided.' 'On a superficial level', he said, he 'could not be accused of direct descriptions of persons or events', but 'on a deeper level where creation precedes a novelist's invention *Bright Day* is crammed with profoundly autobiographical material.'

The story centres around a family that the young hero, Gregory Dawson, invests with magic. The older Dawson, with whom the book opens, is a successful film-script writer. He is tired, stale and somewhat disillusioned. Slowly he remembers and reconstructs his far-away youth, and, as the magic of the family group dissolves in death, murder and much unhappiness, Dawson slowly comes back to life, and sees the world with renewed hope and zest. One of Jack's most sympathetic critics disliked what he called the 'fanfare of hope' at the end. Although I too was uncertain about the ending, looking at it again, I think 'fanfare' is much overstated; the hope is quite modest, a very Priestley kind of hope. Here it is: 'There was in my mind a little brilliantly illuminated stage on which ideas paraded and excitedly capered; and all round the stage, where timeless eyes watched in the shadows, was an atmosphere of tenderness for life. I hadn't known that mood, that theatre of creation for years and years. Something good might come out of it.' In later life Jack agreed that perhaps in 1945 and '46 he was too hopeful, too optimistic about the brave new world we were going to build. 'But,' he wrote later, 'I cannot help feeling . . . that I was, so to speak, wrong on the right side. We still have to live — in Wordsworth's wise phrase — by "admiration, hope and love".'

Jack with his Ford motor car outside Brooke Hill in the late 1940s (Ford Motor Co.)

Once returned to health, Jack did not, of course, turn away from the world of politics and events, he still felt himself deeply involved in the future of England. He couldn't help thinking that perhaps the Labour Party might owe him something for all his campaigning work. What he would really have liked would have been to be chairman of the newly created Arts Council, something for which he would have seemed especially well equipped – that did not happen, but Jack accepted an invitation to become a British cultural delegate to the first conference of the newly formed UNESCO. He began to get letters from the civil servant appointed to act as his assistant; she signed herself J.J. Hawkes. Whenever Jack saw this signature he couldn't help feeling a strange, unreasoning excitement.

PART III
JACQUETTA

TEN

EARLY DAYS

'"Aesthetic"; "passionate"; "intellectual"; "sensational" – that is, a purely sensuous experience': these words are how Jessie Jacquetta Hopkins describes the four different incidents that are her earliest memories; they are words that describe Jacquetta. All experiences were part of her secure and happy life in the Cambridge home where she lived until she married Christopher Hawkes, and became the mysterious J.J. Hawkes.

Jacquetta's father, Sir Frederick Gowland Hopkins, OM, winner of a Nobel science prize, was one of Britain's most distinguished scientists, the discoverer of vitamins, and father of the science of biochemistry. His father, Frederick Hopkins, was a bookseller, a second cousin of the poet Gerard Manley Hopkins, and an amateur scientist. He had died young, and had bequeathed his microscope to the young Frederick, who wrote later: 'I felt in my bones that the power of the microscope thus revealed to me was something very *important* – the most important thing I had as yet come up against, so much more significant than anything I was being taught at school.' After her husband's death, Mrs Hopkins had taken her young son to live with her brother James Gowland at Enfield, where there was a whole colony of Gowlands. 'Great Uncle James', as he was known to Jacquetta, was a bullying and domineering character. He was religious in a dark and twisted fashion, but he never went to chapel since he had quarrelled with his minister. Sin still loomed large, and in his view science was wicked, the work of the devil, so when Frederick was seventeen he was sent to work in a local insurance office. It was a long time, and a long, hard slog, before he was able to realize his scientific gifts. Fortunately, he was rescued by a cousin of his father's who recognized the young man's gifts and said that Cambridge was the right place for him. It was the right place, but there was no money to send him there. Scientific research was Frederick's passion and his aim, but he had to study and earn. He trained first as an analyst, ending up working for the Home Office in a number of celebrated murder cases. In 1888, at the age of twenty-seven, and helped by a small inheritance, he entered the medical school at Guy's

Hospital. In the evenings he worked in a private research laboratory, and at the same time managed to acquire an external degree in science from London University. He qualified as a doctor at Guy's and won the gold medal for chemistry.

The year 1898 was a momentous one for Frederick Gowland Hopkins. He fell in love with an outstandingly beautiful young woman, Jessie Ann Stevens. She too had lost parents at an early age, and she too was interested in medicine; she was a probationer at the Royal Free Hospital. Young 'ladies' were allowed to train as nurses, but had to do so at their own expense. Frederick was thirty-seven; there was no point in waiting, so early in the year they were married, and, as their daughter Jacquetta wrote, 'were to love one another for half a century or more'. Their early married life was not easy, as they had, at first, to live with Uncle James, who treated them like dependent children, insisted that they be in by 10 p.m., and refused to let them have their own latchkeys. They managed to escape to a flat in Lincoln's Inn Fields, and settled there happily. Then, in September 1898, Sir Michael Foster wrote to invite Frederick to become a fellow and tutor in chemical physiology and anatomy at Emmanuel College, Cambridge. Soon a small house in the college grounds became vacant, and it was there some years later that Jessie Jacquetta was born. She was very much the youngest of the family, separated by eleven years from her elder sister, Barbara, and by eight from her brother, Frederick Edward, so that for a great part of her childhood she was, quite happily, alone at home.

In his personal life, Jacquetta's father was infinitely gentle, unassuming, unselfish and kindly. He could not bear to hurt or upset anyone; people called him a 'scientific saint'. The steely strength of his character lay in his vision, and in his inflexible determination, whatever the obstacles, to pursue his scientific ideas. He had all the marks of true genius – the imagination and intuitive insights – with which such exceptional men and women seem to arrive in the world. His biographer, Professor Ernest Baldwin, wrote: 'His power of stimulating the imagination was one of his greatest attributes, and his own creative imagination was of such power that it could not fail to influence the thought and activities of everyone who had the good fortune to work in his department.' Throughout her childhood, however, Jacquetta was surprisingly unable to relate to her distinguished father. To her child's mind his gentleness appeared as weakness. Obscurely she felt that he leaned too much on the strength of the mother whom she dearly loved. Perhaps, she has suggested, looking back, she needed a stronger masculine authority in her young life. Was that the reason why she found herself only able to fall in love with considerably older men? Perhaps, perhaps not. What we have here, I think, is a real and profound difference in temperament between father and daughter.

Jacquetta's mother, as well as being irresistably lovely to look at, was kind, practical and public-spirited. She ran her home comfortably and efficiently, and supported her husband in every way. As a hostess she was able to create a friendly, informal and democratic atmosphere, in which young students could mix happily with older and distinguished scientists. She proved to be a wonderful nurse. Jessie Hopkins was interested in things of the past. She was knowledgeable as well, and collected antique furniture and china with taste and discrimination. She took her children to all the local museums, something important and formative for her younger daughter. Jacquetta never felt a hint of any tension or discord between her parents, and describes her childhood as 'steeped in sweetness and light with no awareness of harsher ways'.

By 1910 the amount of teaching combined with his own research proved too much for Frederick Hopkins, and he had a breakdown. Even though the children were developing whooping cough, his wife coped calmly with it all, and help was at hand. Trinity College offered

Jacquetta's mother, Jessie Ann Stevens

him a fellowship and elected him to a praelectureship in biochemistry. There would be no more teaching, and he was at last free to devote himself entirely to his own research. There was more money too, so he and his wife decided to have a house built for them in Grange Road, which was then on the outskirts of Cambridge, but still within easy walking distance of his laboratory. In front they looked out on the playing fields of St John's College, and at the back the sizeable garden led into open country. The house was a fine and interesting building in a mildly modernized Georgian style. It had a hipped roof with tiles of slightly different colours that blended happily together. The pleasant coloured brick with built-in columns of a darker colour flanking the leaded paned windows gave the house an imposing and elegant appearance. Doors from the dining-room and the drawing-room led out into the garden. The entrance to the house was imposing, too: a gravelled drive curved round a semi-circular lawn, and stone pillars crowned with round stone balls stood at either side of the entrance. The lawn had similar balls spaced round it: these were a problem, as they were always getting stolen by local lads.

Jacquetta was about ten months old when the family were able to move into No. 71. The appointment to Trinity soon restored her father to health, and, owing to the improvement in the family finances, they were now able to afford a cook, a house parlourmaid and a nanny for Jacquetta. For grand dinner-parties they could have special dishes delivered from the excellent Trinity kitchens. Downstairs the house seemed full of light, and must have been especially pleasant for living. There was a small study, but such were Frederick's powers of concentration that he would sit in the midst of family and visitors with a pencil and notebook scribbling formulae, his greenish eyes fixed on unseen images. Jacquetta cannot have been much more than a year old, still in her pram and not yet able to articulate words, but her memory is vivid:

It is that through-the-door world of coolness and light. On my back, pinioned in wool, the big wheels known below me. The canopy above. Tarry smell from those dark boards, the shed. That mysterious breath of out-of-doors on my cheeks. The canopy ripples and stills, ripples again. It ripples against the blueness – the bluest blue. What wonder. Arms out. I cannot touch it. Then joy. Against the blue swing yellow flowers. Trails of flowers swing from that tree. What joy the yellow and the blueness. The canopy stills, the flower trails hang straight down.

Jacquetta when a baby, 'counting her fingers' in the delightful garden of the family home in Grange Road, Cambridge

The laburnum tree that inspired such an ecstasy of delight in this baby is still there in the garden, as are the same roses, the syringa, the little box hedges and the rockery. The wooden bicycle shed is there, no longer, of course, smelling of tar. Lady Hopkins lived in 71 Grange Road until her death in 1954, and the couple who bought it from her estate have hardly altered anything.

Jacquetta's second memory is not so happy. Just before her second birthday her own trusted 'Nannie' was on holiday, and her place was taken by a temporary nursemaid. They are out for a walk, Jacquetta now in a push-chair. They pass a big ditch full of greenery, and covered with the great white trumpets of the large convolvulus. They are so beautiful, Jacquetta wants to take them as a present to her mother, who loves flowers. 'White as clouds. Mummy would love them. Mummy must get them. Stop! Stop! *She* must get them. Frown-face must get them. She flaps an arm and wobbles on the edge.' Jacquetta is stamping her little feet with impatience, but the ditch is full of nettles, and unfortunate 'Frown-face', who has no wish to get badly stung, says she can't reach the flowers. Jacquetta bursts into tears of impotent, infantile rage. 'Nannie would get them. Nannie would reach them. Hateful no-good Frown-face. She is pushing again. Stop! Stop!' She does not stop: 'Ugly face.' Some two years later, Nannie took her along the same road to see the smouldering beams of a house fired by suffragettes. She found this confusing. Suffragettes must be BAD. But when they held a rally in Cambridge her mother pinned on a large rosette and went to join them. Jacquetta was terrified she might be taken away to prison. To her immense relief her mother returned in time to read her little daughter to sleep, 'the only right end to a day'.

Jacquetta's somewhat intellectual memory comes a little later. Her mother was a keen gardener; Jacquetta is sitting on a warm step, watching her fork over her cherished rockery. Suddenly she starts up with a mouse in her hand. Jacquetta pokes it nervously, expecting it to run away, but it is still, stiff and cold. 'It is dead,' says her mother in a funny voice, so they sit side by side and have a little discussion about death. Jacquetta's nanny has told her about gentle Jesus, and encouraged her after she gets into bed to think a little prayer thanking God for his care of them all. So perhaps there was a question about mice and heaven. 'My parents', Jacquetta remembers, 'made no attempt to provide any religious teaching – except that my simple mother told me that "one could be just as good without going to church".' Manifestly, Jacquetta's parents were good people, but, for her father to become a fellow, Trinity had had to alter the college statutes in order to accommodate his principled agnosticism. Intellectual integrity was an absolute in the Hopkins family.

An intense and glorious experience of sensuous joy is the final early memory that Jacquetta records: 'It is a summer evening . . . nearly bed time. How the sun glows behind our ash tree. A warm bath of light. I *must* run. Run in the sun bath. Bare feet on grass. Run faster, faster. What speed, might I fly? Face to the sun, back to the sun. What joy all through . . . what joy.' 'I shared the glory of archangels before flopping down on the grass – I can re-experience that divine glow,' she wrote later; and many years later, as a scholarly archaeologist and prehistorian she wrote *Man and the Sun*.

While there was no religious instruction in Jacquetta's home, there was moral instruction. Most important must have been the example of her parents, but the two cardinal sins that impressed themselves most deeply upon the child were lying and stealing, so that her one modest fall from grace was traumatic.

On Sundays undergraduates came to tea, and cakes were set out on a stand known as 'curate's joy'. There was a plateful of miniature Swiss rolls to which Jacquetta was especially addicted, and on her way

Jacquetta as a young girl

up to bed she managed to steal one. Her mother must have noticed, because she challenged her; 'No, I didn't take it, I didn't,' Jacquetta declared, and as the question was repeated so was her denial. 'That', said her mother, 'is a lie.' In memory Jacquetta writes: 'I sobbed and sobbed until I was exhausted. I was a liar. I had committed the unforgivable sin. I was wrapped in darkness, bereft for ever and ever of love and happiness.' All through her life Jacquetta has been a most determined truth-teller. She finds it hard even to descend to the little social 'white lies' that we all use to smooth the ways of human intercourse; whenever possible Jacquetta avoids them. But the moral maze of grown-up life is bewildering for children. An imaginative child with a feeling for magic and mystery, Jacquetta believed implicitly in Father Christmas, until one day a tiresome older boy scornfully disillusioned her: 'that rubbish, nursery stuff. What a baby you are.' Jacquetta refused to believe this horrid child, and rushed home weeping to her mother, begging her to say that Father Christmas was real. But of course her mother had to admit the painful truth. 'The pain came from the fact that my parents had lied to me – I am still puzzled why they left me with my innocent faith . . . their honesty to me was absolute. I can only suppose that they did not think I could truly and fully believe in that red and white figure of the flowing beard.' Other 'white lies' figured at Christmas time, and had to be carefully explained to Jacquetta. Even if you received presents you didn't want and didn't like, you had to pretend that you did like them, and say how pleased you were, especially if they were presents from Great Uncle James at Enfield, at whose home they always spent family Christmases. For Jacquetta these provoked a mixture of emotions. She was often overpowered by all those grown-ups and their endless boring talk — talk at home was more interesting. Jacquetta's paternal grandmother was there, almost unbelievably old, hardly alive, sitting in her shawls and lace cap with lilac ribbons. When she died, the only surprise for Jacquetta was to see her father wiping away his tears, something almost impossible — grown-ups didn't cry, and the Hopkins family was normally almost excessively undemonstrative. However, Christmas was Christmas, and Jacquetta was a healthy greedy child who enjoyed the mountains of good food. She also particularly enjoyed swinging on the large front gate, and she did like presents. Especially remembered was a fine, strong bow with arrows. Jacquetta was a tomboy; she detested dolls and contrived to lose or break any given to her. In a passion of hatred she deliberately smashed a large blue-eyed china doll on her mother's rockery. She believes that this must have been due to her lack of any maternal instinct, but I think it had more perhaps to do with lively and intelligent girls of that generation instinctively rebelling against being stereotyped as future dutiful and loving wives and mothers. When Jacquetta finally had a child, I don't think she was without maternal love, and when it came to grandchildren, she surprised herself by the strength of her grandmotherly feelings.

Since her sister Barbara was so much older, it was not until Jacquetta was grown up that they were able to become real friends. But before he was sent off to his public school, Jacquetta was devoted to her brother, and loved to be able to play with him. She determined to harden herself so that he would not be able to look down on her for any supposed girlish weakness. She made herself endure mild pain, and then set about mastering those irrational fears. Mice, bats, earwigs and spiders were not too difficult, but the hardest of all was fear of the dark. She resolved that night by night she would walk a little further down the garden. This took some time. 'One sticking point was a rusty pump with threatening trees overhanging it. When, in time, my courage took me past the pump and on as far as the rough bottom of the lawn where the swing hung, the powers of darkness were in full retreat. Beyond the fence where there was meadowland the skies were more open, while my familiar sandpit was nearby.' Jacquetta cannot, at

The Hopkins family, with Sir Frederick and Barbara (back row), Jacquetta and her brother Frederick, and Lady Hopkins (seated)

this time, have been more than five or six; her courage, of which in later years she showed plenty, was not inborn, it was won – and that is usually the best kind of courage.

The garden of 71 Grange Road held delights more mysterious and exciting than Jacquetta's swing and sandpit. The house had been built where a Roman road was overlapped by an Anglo-Saxon cemetery. In the archaeological museum, Jacquetta had seen a grave group, and a beautiful amber necklace which had been dug out from below one of the gate-posts at the entrance to her home. She was fascinated by exhibits of ancient pottery and jewellery, intricate brooches and necklaces, and was aware that in her own garden Roman pottery and coins had been found. She was excited to discover that 'things made by one people, or at a particular time, could always be distinguished from those made by other people or at a different time. With the contrast between the soft, hand-shaped pottery of the Anglo-Saxon burial urns and the harsh, striated Roman stuff, I was introducing myself at the very root of the simple archaeology then near the beginning of its rapid growth and flowering.' Jacquetta longed to find some of these ancient objects for herself, but, to her surprise, was refused permission to dig in the garden. She resolved to creep out and dig after dark; it was beneath the front lawn that these treasures were said to lie.

I took a torch and my garden trowel and laboured greatly in the middle of the lawn to remove about one square foot of turf in many fragments. It would be much easier lower down. But it wasn't. I drove the trowel downwards again; it came up with only a desertspoonful of dull earth. Every time a bicycle went by, usually with a bobbing and wobbling front light, I put out my torch, and squatted over the hole. My right palm was beginning to blister, and I seemed to have been at work for hours. I stood up to survey my excavation by torchlight. The sides sloped inward meeting at a point about eighteen inches below the surface. It was no good.

Jacquetta doesn't seem to have got into trouble over this escapade. Her mother dressed the blister solicitously, and was perhaps impressed by her daughter's enterprise. Jacquetta's mind was made up, and at the age of nine, while still at her dame school, she wrote an essay announcing her determination to become an archaeologist.

ELEVEN

GROWING UP

Just before Jacquetta's fourth birthday in August 1914 war was declared. She saw the soldiers march away and then, all too soon, the wounded begin to return. Jacquetta's mother was called upon to become matron of a war hospital in the quiet backwater of Wordsworth Grove, and this meant she had to be away from home for long hours. Jacquetta hated her absence, especially the fact that her mother was now seldom able to 'read her to sleep'. As with a number of women during the First World War, Jessie Hopkins proved to be more than just a superb and dedicated nurse. She revealed powers of organization and administration of which she herself was perhaps hardly aware. The result was that her public life continued into the post-war years; she pioneered and organized infant welfare and children's aid in Cambridge until the local authority took them over.

By the time of the First World War Jacquetta's father had become a distinguished public figure. He had published his crucial vitamin discoveries, and had become the first Professor of Biochemistry in

Jacquetta and her mother distributing mugs of hot cocoa to soldiers during the First World War

Cambridge, with his own laboratory. With the war, he had to spend much time on government business, serving on the Royal Society Food Committee, which advised on food rationing and wartime nutrition, and becoming involved in other scientific wartime activities. He would do nothing military, for he abhorred war.

These were the external pressures that influenced Jacquetta's growing up. She wrote of other more intimate memories, of which the 'most significant to me is of a visit to the pretty Cambridgeshire village of Abington made quite unusually with my parents together on their bicycles. I rode astride behind my father on a cushioned carrier.' Once arrived, they dismounted and she and her father walked together among the timbered and thatched cottages. Jacquetta was already interested in the different kinds of buildings, and must have said something of her pleasure. Her father looked down at her and said, 'Why Jacquetta, your eyes are really sparkling.' She remembered each word: 'Perhaps they struck home with more force because I was seldom alone with my father. Now I felt a wave of excitement. So my eyes sparkled, did they? Then somehow I was I, whole and visible, a separate being. This was quite truly my first experience of self-consciousness . . . it was enhanced a year or two later when Nannie, who had left for another job when I was five, came back to see us. . . . I was within earshot when my mother asked her if she liked her new charge. "Yes," Nannie replied, "But she is not so interesting as Miss Jacquetta."' This, comments Jacquetta, is 'no doubt why I have kept this memory.' Of course, she was an interesting and an exceptional child, being always something of a loner, and always determined to pursue her own individual way. The two pictures she chose to hang in her nursery were an illustration of Rudyard Kipling's *Just-So* story 'The Cat that Walked by Itself' and a Rackham painting of Puck from *A Midsummer Night's Dream* inscribed 'Lord what fools these mortals be.'

Soon there was school and Jacquetta was sent to 'Miss Sharpley's', where the intellectual élite of Cambridge usually sent their children. She was not a particularly outstanding pupil. Though not unhappy at school, she was not a natural schoolgirl, and preferred one or two close friends to a social group. Esther Vernon-Jones was her first close friend. The pleasures of life outside school were incomparably more important, chief among them birds-nesting and collecting wild flowers, usually accompanied by Esther. Birds-nesting involved tree-climbing and this was Jacquetta's passion. 'I was as a child so passionately fond of climbing trees as to be seriously convinced of my membership of some tree-dwelling race of humans. I spent the greater

As a child, Jacquetta had a passion for climbing, and she is seen here after her ascent of a pillar at the entrance to 71 Grange Road

part of my time out of school in the branches of a large ash tree. . . . I can still recall my wordless longing to be climbing.' Eggs were collected and blown by means of a pin at either end, except for an addled swan's egg that had to be blown with a bicycle pump, and how it stank! Flowers were collected and pressed, and what a happy profusion of them there was, whole meadows of golden cowslips, and woods with pale and rare oxlips – those, because of their scarcity, were not, Jacquetta's father told her, allowed to be picked. At other times there were expeditions to study the architecture and interiors of local churches, accompanied by primitive brass-rubbings with 'heel ball' and 'cobbler's wax'. Vicars came in three categories: 1) No; 2) Yes, but be careful; 3) Tea in the vicarage. So these carefree children were able to bicycle fearlessly and happily about the surrounding countryside.

With a certain amount of pride, Jacquetta remembers protesting to Miss Sharpley about having to learn by heart such 'inferior poetry' as:

> Why do you walk through the fields in gloves
> Oh! fat white woman whom nobody loves?

On one occasion she went to tea with another school friend, Kitty Turner. Mrs Turner was showing her miniatures to an artist friend, and asked Jacquetta which one she liked best. Jacquetta rejected all the pretty golden-haired young girls in their pastel-coloured dresses in favour of 'an old woman dressed in black, her white hair and lined face the only source of light'. 'She is quite right,' exclaimed the artist friend, and as Jacquetta and Kitty headed for the garden, they overheard the visitor expressing astonishment at such artistic understanding in one so young.

It was Kitty, who, full of excitement, one day in school, 'drew us heads-together and told us in loud whispers exactly what our mothers and fathers had to do to get babies'. Just as Jacquetta's parents gave her no religious information, so they ignored the subject of sex. Jacquetta found Kitty's information startling, almost unbelievable, and promptly buried it. Throughout her childhood and adolescence, she remained completely uninterested in sex, and even at the age of fourteen, when she was a bridesmaid at her sister's wedding – partly memorable as the first time she wore silk stockings – she remarked: 'I can't see how going into a church and putting on a ring makes you have children.' The resulting faintly amused and embarrassed hush brought Kitty Turner's information suddenly back into her mind, and she felt painfully foolish. Even then, the information aroused no personal interest. For many years Jacquetta remained a sleeping beauty so far as sex was concerned.

At school Jacquetta had no great ambitions to be an organizer or a leader, but with a small group she did organize the kidnapping of Evelyn Herbert, 'a pale fragile child of well-to-do parents, who was fetched to and from school in a basket chair'. One afternoon Jacquetta's group ran away with Evelyn in his chair, in order to give him an afternoon of healthy play and good food – they had no doubt they were rescuing him from tyrannical and mistaken parents. (Had they been reading about Colin in *The Secret Garden*?) Evelyn seemed quite happy with the escapade, but of course they were soon pursued and captured. Their good intentions seem to have been recognized as they were merely reprimanded.

From an early age Jacquetta was familiar with the great men of Cambridge science who were often at 71 Grange Road (her favourite was Lord Adrian). Soon her father would take her along to his laboratory. On one visit she managed to slip a couple of white mice into her pocket, and kept them at home in a rabbit hutch. These, as mice are apt to do, reproduced themselves rapidly and incestuously, and when they were sufficiently well-grown, Jacquetta took them and sold them back to the laboratory, acquiring thereby some extra pocket money. Stealing evidently was not in quite the same league of wickedness as lying, or perhaps she thought that she was only taking what belonged to her father anyway. One other memory remains of the laboratory, when her father told her about the splitting of the atom, and a possible chain reaction of such power that it might even destroy the planet. Jacquetta was much alarmed and couldn't sleep for thinking how dangerously close 71 Grange Road was to the Cavendish Laboratory.

When Jacquetta was eleven years old, it was time to move on. Her clever sister, Barbara, had been sent to Cheltenham, but owing to a stupid matron had had to be rushed back to Cambridge with a septic appendix, from which she might well have died, had it not been for her mother's skilful and determined post-operative nursing. Jacquetta's reaction to the family distress was to invoke the powers of magic. She made a kind of talisman from cardboard and golden foil wrapping and hung it on the end of Barbara's bed; she was convinced that it would help to ward off the spectre of death.

Jacquetta was sent by day to the Perse School for girls, where she again pursued her individual way. She refused to wear school uniform, or to take part in any organized games: nobody seems to have objected very strongly. Jacquetta was not a 'joiner' and very much disliked Girl Guides with their badges and uniforms and camp-fires. Work went along in a middle-of-the-road manner – bad at maths, bad at Latin, good at anything requiring imagination, a feeling for poetry, a love of reading, and becoming increasingly enthralled by nature and the past. She was not thought of as an intellectual; she was a late developer. Her one community activity was the founding of a 'Trespassers' Society', with marks awarded for the relative daring of illegal entry into 'gardens, college properties, farms with ferocious farmers, and estates with outstandingly fierce gamekeepers'.

Family holidays were, in the early days, usually spent on the east coast, but the sea itself never much pleased Jacquetta – perhaps a premonition of the miseries of sea-sickness from which she invariably suffered in later life. But she loved the rock pools and their underwater life, and at Hunstanton she was 'struck by the extraordinary geological formation of a part of the cliffs; half white chalk, half a rich red, suggesting two worlds of heat and cold, mysteriously brought together'. Jacquetta never loved the flat Cambridgeshire countryside, but later when the family holidays were taken further afield, she 'responded ecstatically' to the mountains, lakes and rocky streams of North Wales and the Lake District. This, she saw at once, was what country ought to be, a delight she had unknowingly longed for.

Birds-nesting developed into bird-watching and so to ornithology, though Jacquetta was more of an aesthetic and romantic watcher than a scientific ornithologist. In her early teens she became friendly with a much older and eminent ornithologist, Emma Turner, a pioneer in bird photography, who took Jacquetta to the Norfolk Broads to stay on her artificial island in the middle of a dense reedbed in the centre of Hinkley Broad. They slept in a little thatched hut on the island, and Emma's houseboat, the *Ark*, was moored alongside, as well as a kayak-like Canadian canoe. When the skipper, as Emma liked to be called, 'tapped out a message on the stern board of the *Ark*, eels normally invisible would come crowding in to be fed. This ritual, established over the year,' said Jacquetta, 'heightened the participation mystique that came to me with this life among the waters, reedbeds and all their native creatures.' This was a wonderful place for bird-watching, observing all the little marsh tits, sedge-warblers and such rarities as bearded tits, and the booming bitterns. Jacquetta had one adventure on her own:

Waking early one still clear morning, I decided to venture out in the Canadian canoe. I felt like a trespasser in the calm beauty of the natural scene. It was happiness just to glide along, dipping the double paddle left and right, left and right as softly as I could. I thought of nothing, but opened up my consciousness to the rising sun, the shimmer on the water, the calls of the coots, and yes, a bittern. Suddenly there is a violence in the air, the stillness is shattered as a great bird, wings folded, talons thrust out before it, strikes the surface, sending a splashing column of water high into the air, nearly twenty yards ahead of me. As the water falls back, the osprey rises, its wings labouring from the weight of the taloned fish, then beating more strongly as the bird heads away towards its tree.

Other expeditions with Emma Turner were to the Brecks, 'golden heathland, set with the dark, noble forms of Scottish pines'. Here were new birds, rarer than those to be found nearer home – wheatears and crossbills.

How happy I was when one of the deep red cock birds came near enough for me to focus my field glasses and watch him at work on a pine cone. I could detect the stout little beak, its sharp tips crossed, levering open the scales to pluck out the tiny seed behind each one – a monotonous way to gain a living but for me a delight to watch. . . . What could be more unlike this secretive haunter of the fir trees than the stone curlew, so wild, self-assertive, a creature of earth and air? We came upon some towards sunset on a stony expanse of heathland. They leapt up in their flight, abusing us, their disturbers, with harsh cries before dropping down at a distance. As we hoped, they responded to our stillness by edging towards us, until I could see them in all their strangeness. They seemed to me to have a rare mixture of qualities. Their legs are disproportionately long, yet with the swollen joints and, it appears, large bones, awkward and in some way archaic. Their faces (one must use that word) show a fierce or perhaps desperate stare, yet they also convey an intensely haughty superciliousness. They stalk along lacking the delicate grace of many long-legged birds, with a stiff fastidious elegance. . . . Inevitably one describes these rare and remote creatures in human terms.

Birds have always fascinated humans. They mastered the air so gracefully aeons before we got our heavy machines up into it, and they are so remote genetically and in time; yet they have a strange affinity with us. Away back to primitive times and still among some countryside dwellers birds have been the subject of myths and omens. They have many of the rudiments of the arts, with their song and decoration, their amazing nests and the brilliant plumage of the males. Many of their courting rituals resemble our more sophisticated ballet dancing; indeed, famous ballets have been choreographed around them. Were not the mythical sirens half-bird and half-woman?

Another particular attraction of the Brecks for Jacquetta was visiting the flint mines of Grimes Graves. These were now only shallow, covered-in grassy depressions, but here once Neolithic miners with picks made from stags' antlers had driven shafts into the chalk to discover the beds of huge flint nodules, had dragged them up to the surface, and had trimmed them down, with sparks flying, for trade and axe-making. Jacquetta's imagination and increasing knowledge could picture this ancient activity, and when, years later, she returned to find that the Forestry Commission had planted young conifers all over the pits, she dashed about in a rage uprooting the little trees and hurling them away.

It was when Jacquetta returned home after her first stay with Emma Turner that she received something of a shock.

I found my mother inclined to be critical of her, even to say unkind things. This puzzled me deeply and may have goaded me into more and more ecstatic accounts of life on the island, and my admiration for its creator. I cannot now either remember or imagine how realization came to me, but I know it was as sudden as a physical blow. My mother was jealous. That my mother, who was normally as calm as a summer's day, as reliable as the air itself, should be jealous was utterly appalling. I did not try to do anything to reassure her, as usual with me I thrust the pang into my internal safe. . . . It was, as I see now, just one of the shocks of growing up.

Along with her passion for nature, the fascination of the past was increasing its hold upon Jacquetta. In the Cambridge Museum of Archaeology and Anthropology she had been happiest among the clues to Fenland prehistory yielded up by the peat. 'There was the perfect round bronze shield that conjured up visions of Bronze Age chieftains, and better still there was the Grunty Fen armilla, the golden curls of which, I was told, had sprung up as though by magic through the covering peat. Knowledge of such local treasures was beginning to inform and inspire my archaeological consciousness.'

It was time to move on again. Jacquetta had never doubted that she would go to a university, but where could she find her chosen subject? Then came the exciting day when she met the prehistorian Miles Birkett, who told her that an archaeological tripos was about to be launched in Cambridge. 'Just in time for you,' he said. So now it was settled, no other university had as yet a full degree course, so she would go to her sister's college, Newnham, to read archaeology and anthropology, Jacquetta was determined, if possible, to live in college, even though Newnham was only just down the road from No. 71, but very unfortunately she developed influenza just before the entrance exam, and had to sit it at home. 'I was confined to our drawing-room with a blazing fire to support my fevered state. It appeared that all the fates were against me, for as I tackled the first question, the chimney caught fire, the flames leaping through the winter soot. My mother and the housemaid extinguished them, but not without agitation – and some lingering fumes.' In spite of these set-backs, Jacquetta did well enough to be given an interview, which was no mean achievement, since there was intense competition for Newnham – seventy applicants for each vacant place – whereas you only had to be good at games to walk into some of the men's colleges. The principal, Miss Strachey, a gifted and witty woman, was not unsympathetic, and probably perceptive enough to recognize Jacquetta's originality and potential gifts. After a short discussion she held out her hand and said: 'Well, Miss Hopkins, I think you had better be *tottering* home.' Jacquetta, who had made rather much of her 'flu and other problems, recognized and appreciated the humour of Miss Strachey's concluding remark.

Jacquetta gained her entrance – no scholarship, a borderline case – but no matter: she was accepted.

TWELVE

ARCHAEOLOGY AND MARRIAGE

Jacquetta's father was knighted in 1925 and awarded the Copley Medal of the Royal Society in 1926. In 1929 came the Nobel prize. As her elder sister and her brother were already married, it was Jacquetta who went with her parents to Stockholm for the award ceremony in the presence of the King of Sweden. One of the local papers had got hold of the information that this good-looking young girl intended to study archaeology. The crown prince was a keen archaeologist, and as soon as he heard this he gave orders that she was to have a specially conducted tour of the National Museum. So Jacquetta had a wonderful time. She was met by the director and a whole retinue, and given an extensive and fascinating tour; she might have been royalty herself. Years later, in 1951, when she was archaeological advisor to the Festival of Britain, she was able to return the compliment. The crown prince was now the king, and Jacquetta was delighted to be able to conduct him round the British archaeological pavilion.

After this grand interlude, Jacquetta returned to her first day at Newnham. This, with its babel of voices, was bewildering. Jacquetta had never liked large gatherings, had hated children's parties and teenage dances, and now she was thrust into this unfamiliar crowd.

> Feeling remote and far away in such a chatter of strangers, I began to push my way among them without any purpose, and failing to distinguish any one individual from another. While in this haze of consciousness, I was seized upon in the mêlée by a thin girl with lank black hair, a sadly shallow complexion and a long pinched nose. 'I'm Johnson', she said nasally. 'Are you Hopkins?' I nodded my head aghast at the form of address. . . . Escaping I found myself near a girl with fair hair and brown eyes – brown eyes lit by a humorous smile. I felt immediately drawn to her, even more so when I heard her slightly husky voice. I told her how much I had been startled by being addressed as

'Hopkins' by one who called herself 'Johnson'. 'Surely that's absurd, isn't it?' We agreed that it was and laughed together. So I met Peggy Lamert, the young woman with whom I was to share a lifelong friendship that is with us still.

One of the many gifts of friendship with Jack and Jacquetta has been for me that Peggy has become my friend too. 'If I were a man,' I once said to her, 'I would fall in love with you just because of the sound of your voice.'

'At Newnham', said Peggy, 'Jacquetta stood out like a star.' She was certainly beautiful, but seemed strangely unaware, and had a certain, sometimes even ruthless, masculine quality. Like many complex and sexually attractive people, Jacquetta is attractive to women as well as to men, and though vulnerable to male charm and admiration, she also has a lesbian quality. She was somewhat in love with Peggy Lamert, and when, after two years, she learned that Peggy was to have a year off to go round the world with her father, Jacquetta wept tears of bereavement.

There were only four men and two women taking this new tripos, but Jacquetta seems to have been fortunate in her tutors and lecturers. The tripos was in two sections: a) physical and cultural anthropology and archaeology, and b) Anglo-Saxon, Norse archaeology and Roman Britain. Students had to learn Old Norse as well as Anglo-Saxon. Jacquetta would have liked to learn Celtic, but there was no one to teach it. But she was not particularly interested in linguistics as such, and preferred the more scientific aspects of archaeology. She elected to do these first: 'Rather strong meat, Miss Hopkins', she was told by her tutor, 'rather strong meat.'

Jacquetta worked steadily in the mornings, with something of her father's powers of concentration, and sometimes she would work in the evenings as well. There seems to have been only one occasion when she was threatened with any kind of trouble. Late one night she and a friend climbed out of the college – quite a feat getting over tall and heavy locked gates. The girls' object was to listen to the nightingales now singing at their passionate best. They were caught and hauled up before authority. Their explanation must have been accepted by the fellow in question, who appeared relieved. 'I thought', she said, 'that it might have been an assignation.'

Just occasionally Jacquetta does something that seems completely out of character. One such occasion was when she organized a rugby football match against the girls of Girton. 'Word of it got about, and when it was learned that male undergraduates intended to be present, the authorities obliged us to play before breakfast. This rather spoilt the occasion, but we did play, kept roughly to the rules, suffered no casualties, and quite enjoyed ourselves. Yet it still amazes me, that I conceived and carried out such a senseless idea.' Of course, however much the authorities may have disliked it, there were young men around. Some of them had cars, and when they discovered Jacquetta's interest in birds, they immediately delcared their own. Jacquetta accepted this innocently, and was surprised when one of them, who really was seriously interested in ornithology, ended up by proposing marriage to her. There seem to have been other proposals, all, to Jacquetta, uninteresting.

At the end of her second year, however, there was a much more serious meeting. Jacquetta's tutor, Miles Birkett, who considered her one of his most promising pupils, arranged for her to go as a volunteer on her first serious excavation. This was at Camulodunum, the pre-Roman Celtic capital of Cunobelin, just outside the ancient Roman city of Colchester. The director of the excavation was Christopher Hawkes.

Some of Jacquetta's fellow students at Newnham knew of Christopher Hawkes; he was not only brilliantly clever, but a great social success, with a number of glamorous girlfriends. They assured her that she would have no chance of being noticed by him. Jacquetta very much disliked the vulgarity of this kind of girl-talk, with its implied idea of deliberately setting out to capture male attention. She would never have lent herself to such behaviour, and in her case it was certainly never necessary. However, on this occasion she could not help feeling an interest and a sense of challenge around this director.

First appearances were disappointing. She had been told that Christopher had a Spanish grandmother, so she had an image of a dark and dashingly handsome young man. He was certainly dark, but he was rather short, and since he was very short-sighted he had to wear glasses. Later Jacquetta realized that it was never just a man's appearance that determined his attraction for her, and the men she eventually came to love would have been described as 'more or less ugly'.

'I soon found', Jacquetta wrote, 'that I could have a choice of suitors, but Christopher Hawkes could not fail to eclipse the rest – he was lively, clever, immensely energetic, a master of my beloved subject – and the boss. I cannot remember just when or how he first declared his love for me, but I think it must have been before the end of that season's excavations. Certainly he continued to court me, and meeting him on his own ground in London impressed me with his social confidence and knowledge of the world – largely illusory, but considerable when set beside my own total lack of them.' Meanwhile, Christopher, always a dutiful and affectionate son, had been writing to his mother about 'the charming Jacquetta Hopkins, daughter of Professor Sir Frederick Gowland Hopkins, discoverer of vitamins, PRS [President of the Royal Society], and Trustee of the British Museum [where Christopher worked] . . . she is such a nice girl, taking archaeology for her Tripos.' This recital of Sir Frederick's distinctions was doubtless intended to impress Christopher's snobbish mother.

Without the distraction of Peggy Lamert, Jacquetta worked hard during her final year. Christopher gave her a proof copy of a survey of British archaeology written by himself and Tom Kendrick, and to her surprise and delight she gained first-class honours in the tripos. On the basis of this, she was awarded a travelling scholarship, and went off to Palestine to excavate caves on the lower slopes of Mount Carmel, where she was to supervise the unearthing of a Neanderthal skeleton. This exciting dig left a deep and lasting impression upon Jacquetta – an excitement perhaps more personal than archaeological, though there were interesting discoveries as well. Although she had travelled in Europe with her parents, Palestine was new, strange and fascinating.

The labour of digging and sifting was done by Arab men and girls from the neighbouring villages. Jacquetta wrote that

The morning procession of Arabs was impelled, and that path worn, by ideas grown in the inquisitive minds of Europe and America. These minds, belonging to individual men and women, were so caught up in the tide of curiosity about the physical universe that they pursued answers like a pack of hounds. They had seen everything from microbes to the Milky Way, and now were in full cry after the answer to the question about themselves: what was the history of their own self-consciousness, how did their terrible and wonderful organs of thought, feeling and imagination come to be on earth? How on earth?

Jacquetta was especially fascinated by the grace and beauty of the Arab girls with whom she worked; 'they would sit in rings, the blues, pinks and greens of their cotton dresses and trousers giving each circle of girls the appearance of a flower'. Her own special assistant was interested and intelligent, and found in the dust of ages what was clearly a human tooth. And so, towards mid-winter, they discovered an ancient skeleton with characteristics that belonged indubitably to a Neanderthal man. It was the first time that any such discovery had been unearthed outside Europe. Jacquetta was much moved by this creature, 'with its low vaulted cranium, so close to the simian stock from which we are all descended.'

> Human consciousness had not been highly tempered when it was housed in that poor cranium, but now in us it was returning to discover, study and reflect upon its ancient haunts. . . . I was conscious of this vanished being and myself as part of an unbroken stream of consciousness, as two atoms in the inexorable process to which we all belonged. . . . With an imaginative effort it is possible to see the eternal present in which all days, all the seasons of the plain stand in an enduring unity. . . . But there is also a terrible reality in that opposing vision of the linear passage of time, of the continuous leaving behind which fills us with a cruel awareness of the wastage of our brief lives. Perhaps, of all men, the archaeologist must be most aware of time passing . . . . So, while we uncovered the skeleton detail by detail, and then shrouded it in plaster of Paris, I often looked at it with sorrow.

Sorrow was certainly not, for Jacquetta, an abiding impression of this time on Mount Carmel; rather it was of an ecstatic and mystical experience:

> One night when the land was still fresh from the rain, I was wandering near our camp enjoying the moonlight, when an intense exaltation took possession of me. It was as though the white goddess of the moon had thrown some bewitching power with her rays . . . the whole night was dancing around me. . . . It appeared that the moonlight had ceased to be a physical thing and now represented a state of illumination in my own mind . . . it seemed that my thoughts and feelings had been given a quite extraordinary clarity and truth.

Jacquetta climbed up on to a high outcrop of rock on top of the wadi, and knelt down: 'The moonlight swam around and in my head, as I looked across the plain to the shining silver bar of the Mediterranean.' From this vantage point she watched the slow procession below of a caravan of about twenty camels.

> My memory of it is dreamlike, yet embodies one of the most intense sensuous and emotional experiences of my life. . . . I had

the heightened sensibility of one passionately in love, and with it the power to transmute all that the senses perceived into symbols of burning significance. This surely is one of the best rewards of humanity. To be filled with comprehension of the beauty and marvellous complexity of the physical world, and for this happy excitement of the senses to lead directly into an awareness of spiritual significance. The fact that such experience comes most surely with love, with possession by the creative Eros, suggests that it belongs near the root of our mystery . . . it grants man a state of mind in which, I believe, he must come more and more to live: a mood of intensely conscious individuality which serves only to strengthen an intense consciousness of unity with all being – this mind is one infinitesimal node in the mind present throughout all being, just as his body shares in the unity of matter. So, as the moon leapt and bounded in the sky, I took full possession of a love and confidence that have not yet forsaken me.

This profound experience lay deep in Jacquetta's consciousness. In the early 1940s it inspired a long and beautiful descriptive poem, 'Man in Time'; it is repeated in an account in her book *Man on Earth*, from which these extracts are taken. This was published in 1956 and dedicated to Jack. Maybe she would not, or could not, have written it as she did before, as a mature woman, she had fallen so deeply in love.

During her sojourn on Mount Carmel, Jacquetta kept a framed photograph of Christopher in her little cabin, and every evening she looked at it trying to decide whether or not she should marry him. As time went by she felt more and more inclined to say 'yes'. 'I was genuinely moved that Christopher wanted me so much, I admired and in most ways liked him; we shared an earnest involvement in our subject. Did I "love" him? How could I tell? I knew I had felt little pleasure in such kissing and embracing as we had practised – but might not bliss arrive with consummation?' So, on Jacquetta's return the following spring, she and Christopher became 'officially engaged', and preparations were begun for their autumn wedding. At twenty-two, Jacquetta was emotionally younger than her years, the product of a protected, somewhat puritanical home, in which an undemonstrative self-control was the order of the day.

Charles Francis Christopher Hawkes was a brilliant and gifted young man. As top classical scholar at Winchester, he had gained a classical scholarship to New College. Oxford, where he had finished with a double first in Classical Mods and Greats. He was musical, could draw well, was a good actor and enjoyed the theatre. 'There's nothing that child can't do,' said the head of his early school. Now twenty-seven, he was a Fellow of the Society of Antiquaries, and the leading authority on Celtic Britain. While he was at Winchester, and later at Oxford, Christopher had been through a sincerely religious period, and had become a practising Anglo-Catholic, going regularly to the Eucharist, and to Confession.

Christopher's father, Charles Pascoe Hawkes – always known as 'C.P.' – was a barrister practising in London. He had been through the usual educational mill of the English professional and upper middle classes, and had read history at Trinity College, Cambridge. He was a fluent writer, and a gifted draughtsman, who made a name for himself with his cartoons, full of impish humour. These were published regularly in a number of periodicals including *Punch*. He was a convivial and sociable man, happy to be part of the London social life of the period, and inclined, in company, to talk too much. In 1904 he had married Eleanora Davison. It was her mother, Victoria Duarte, who was the Spanish grandmother of whom Jacquetta had heard prior to meeting Christopher. She was the daughter of Don Demetrio Duarte, a Spanish businessman who had operated in the lucrative trade of exporting sherry to England. Eleanora's mother had died with the birth of her second daughter Victoria, and the two girls eventually inherited a considerable fortune.

Christopher seems to have been a high-spirited, affectionate and outgoing boy, and, as can be imagined, he was doted upon by his possessive and strong-willed mother. There were always going to be problems with anyone Christopher wanted to marry. In fact, he was susceptible to feminine charms, and had twice fallen in love before he met Jacquetta. The first seems to have been serious enough for the contemplation of marriage, but then the girl walked away. The second was more serious, and the two became engaged. Once again, the girl retreated on the brink of marriage. Both experiences were naturally unnerving for Christopher.

When he first introduced Jacquetta, there was immediate trouble. His mother was extremely conscious of the subtle gradation of the English class system – perhaps because she herself only half belonged to it anyway. For her the Hopkinses were some notches below the Hawkeses in this absurd middle-class hierarchy. It was no matter that Jacquetta's father was at the pinnacle of his profession and had just been given the world's highest scientific honour for work and discoveries that were and are of incalculable benefit to the human race. Nor did the award in two years' time of the highest British civic distinction, the Order of Merit, make a great deal of difference. Mrs Hawkes's values were the false and superficial ones of social class. Meanwhile here was Jacquetta, who appeared shy and unsophisticated, who had not 'done' the London season and 'come out' properly, did not dress fashionably and had no small talk. Mrs Hawkes seemed to have nothing but small talk. She soon sent a message to Christopher urging him to tell Jacquetta to use make-up. She is also reported as saying to Christopher: 'She will be no use to you, she doesn't wear gloves. . . .' Even Jacquetta's beauty and cleverness seem to have counted against her, as being too great a threat, only too likely to entrap the susceptible Christopher. But as his determination to marry Jacquetta could not be shaken, his mother accepted the inevitable, and tried, as far as she could, to influence the marriage arrangements.

Poor Jacquetta was swept into 'a tide of events' entirely alien to her. Christopher, still under the influence of his Anglo-Catholic convictions, was determined to be married in church. Jacquetta, who had never been baptized, felt this to be hypocritical and wrong. 'There was a day', she said, 'at Winchester College when he marched me weeping, round and round the cloisters, until I surrendered, and agreed to be married in my father's college chapel.' Then there was all the business of the bridal dress and all the letters of thanks for 'unwelcome wedding presents'. Jacquetta's mother, watching her daughter, asked her several times if she 'really wanted' to marry Christopher. Jacquetta herself was beginning to have serious doubts, but she knew of Christopher's past experiences and did not feel that she could inflict upon him a third humiliating disappointment.

Of the actual wedding, Jacquetta wrote:

> I recall a sense of bewildered incredulity as I went up the chapel on my father's arm, my long train supported by six bridesmaids in their elegant gowns designed by Motley. I saw through my veil that Christopher was wearing spats. The knot was tied and we processed out into the glorious pale sunshine in Trinity Great Court. The reception in the college hall was crowded and well supplied with champagne . . . I floated through it all, lost in unreality.

Jacquetta had little to do with the service itself. The music was chosen by Christopher, who sang lustily, accompanied by his best man Count

Jacquetta on honeymoon on Majorca, following her marriage to Christopher Hawkes

Sergei Orloff, a Russian friend from Winchester, who had one of those marvellous deep bass Russian voices. At the reception Jacquetta's father felt too shy and out of place to be able to make the customary speech, so this was taken on by C.P. Hawkes. He had had rather a lot of champagne, and inadvertently ended his speech by saying how fortunate the bride was to be marrying such a splendid man as his son – was it a case of *in vino veritas*?

'That this expensive and conventional wedding had only a slender chance of lasting success will', wrote Jacquetta later, 'be obvious.' She described the honeymoon in Majorca as 'neither a joy nor a disaster . . . While I came nowhere near to passion, it would not be just to say that I was frigid. I wanted to please my husband and even gained some small pleasure in the attempt.' But the sleeping beauty remained unawakened, because, as she soon recognized, she did not truly love and desire Christopher. 'As it was,' she concluded, 'we enjoyed the sun, the bathing and visiting antiquities – and were not unhappy. Similar words might be used to describe the following years of our marriage.'

Jacquetta and Christopher Hawkes share a joke during their honeymoon on Majorca

THIRTEEN

MARRIAGE, ARCHAEOLOGY AND LOVE

After their honeymoon Jacquetta and Christopher returned to a rented two-storey flat in Cleveland Gardens near Paddington station. Christopher was working at the British Museum, and with some domestic help in the house, Jacquetta was able to continue her own academic work, and they could do some modest entertaining. But as newly-weds they had to be entertained by numbers of the Hawkeses' wealthy society friends. This meant long evening dresses for Jacquetta and starched white waistcoats and ties for Christopher, which in turn meant large laundry bills. Although Jacquetta's parents made her an allowance of £250 a year, British Museum pay was poor, and the couple were not well off.

Jacquetta always got on well with her father-in-law, C.P., for whom she developed a real affection, but her relationship with Christopher's mother, and with his sister Penelope, who lived at home, was always strained, with an underlying hostility. Christopher staunchly and sometimes angrily defended his wife against any criticism from his family. Even before their marriage he was complaining that his sister had been 'worse than icy' to Jacquetta. Eleanora ('Ellie') Hawkes evidently decided that she must do the best she could with her new daughter-in-law; she must, at least, be presented at court. Jacquetta knew that trouble with her mother-in-law meant trouble for Christopher, and since she would be able to wear her wedding dress, she could not even make the excuse of the unnecessary expense of a new court dress; so most reluctantly she agreed, though she thought the whole business unnecessary and absurd. However, luck, for once, was with Jacquetta. There was a limit to the number of young ladies that any one lady was allowed to present at court, and Ellie Hawkes, who clearly much enjoyed these excursions, had reached her limit. So, to Jacquetta's relief and not exactly charitable pleasure, the project lapsed.

Life assumed a pleasant enough pattern, with work in London during the week, and often weekends in Cambridge with Jacquetta's parents. Christopher got on very well with his distinguished father-in-law, and much enjoyed talking with him; Jacquetta too had grown to appreciate and to love her father. Of course, in such a calm and civilized home Christopher's mother-in-law was always pleasant and kindly, but with her feminine insight and knowledge of her daughter she had some reservations about Christopher.

Summers combined archaeology, meetings with local archaeologists, visits to museums and holidays. In 1934 Christopher and Jacquetta went together to assist in an excavation in France, near Clermont-Ferrand. The dig was at Gergovia, a rather bleak hill-fort, the stronghold from which a renowned leader of the Gauls, Vercingetorix, a kind of male Boudicca, had heroically repulsed the Roman invaders. The archaeologist Olwen Brogan was in charge, with her husband Denis, Professor of Modern History at Cambridge. Jacquetta and Christopher lived very simply. The company was congenial and interesting, the weather was kind, and the surrounding views over mountain and plain were magnificent. After two weeks of not very arduous work, they went on an extended holiday through the wonderfully unspoiled and beautiful countryside and the ancient cities of southern France.

At some point in their excursions in the next few years, Jacquetta and Christopher visited the Lascaux caves with their world famous palaeolithic wall-paintings. They were accompanied by the two proud French schoolboys who had discovered the caves when their dogs disappeared down a large hole in the hillside and the boys had climbed down to rescue them. Their schoolmaster, M. Laval, to whom they reported their adventure, had at once recognized the enormous importance of this find. Naturally Jacquetta and Christopher met and talked with M. Laval. They also met that most distinguished expert on palaeolithic art, the Abbé Breuil. They, with the rest of the British archaeological community, remained in contact with him, and during the German wartime occupation the Abbé continued to communicate with his British friends. His innocent archaeological missives contained coded information as to the location and movements of German troops.

Even the most archaeologically ignorant could not fail to be moved by the marvellously living wild creatures represented on the limestone walls in the dark and haunting subterranean depths of Lascaux. Jacquetta, as a professional, had a scrupulously scientific approach to her work, but she also brought to it her own poetic imagination. She was, of course, familiar with what was known of the Cro-Magnon tribes who roamed the area between fifty and fifteen thousand years ago, but these cave paintings were still a revelation; 'by some twenty thousand years the earliest art in the world':

> It has always appeared to me to be the most astonishing and improbable event in the whole of human history. Imagine these hunters! Behind them a vast span of animal forebears and a million years of dark, persistent savagery; round them the grim tundra and grassland of a sub-arctic continent.
>
> Suddenly out of this wildness and the brain and being of man there sprang a noble art. . . . These early Europeans in a world where, quite simply, there had never been art, took manganese and haematite and ochre, bone and stone, antler and ivory, devised brushes and chisels and painted, carved, engraved and modelled superb portraits of the wild beasts among which they found themselves. This is an originality unequalled and almost beyond understanding.

One might also add that these paintings high and low on the cave walls and ceilings were carried out by the dim and wavering light of animal fats burning in shallow stone saucers. The sheer physical skill involved in it all is nearly as amazing as the artistry.

When she wrote *Man on Earth* Jacquetta recollected her first and subsequent visits to Lascaux, as well as to the other cave paintings of the area, though Lascaux always remained supreme. She observed of those earliest artists:

> there was no bungling or hesitancy in them. Before long they were manifesting every subtlety of shading and foreshortening in a brilliant impressionism. They caught the force and malice of the bison and the fragility of the deer, the ferocity of boars, the sturdy ordinariness of wild ponies, and the mammoth's slight absurdity. . . . the swellings and hollows of the limestone fold one in their cloudy, dreamlike world. On every hand and overhead the forms of horned cattle, horses, deer and gigantic bulls run, leap, or stand waiting. They have been there so long in the darkness guarding the movement and life, the poetic intensity with which the Stone Age artists embued them. Now they live again. Some of the species portrayed have become extinct, their world vanished with the melting ice, yet art did what it was

always to do afterwards, it cheated time a little, allowing us to re-experience something of a strange and ancient emotion.

There was, and, I believe, still is, disagreement among the experts as to the purpose of these paintings, some even going so far as to suggest that the artists made their studies from the dead bodies of the animals they had killed. This Jacquetta rejected with scorn as being due to 'a total ignorance, only possible to men of the Machine Age, of the modes of artistic creation'.

For Jacquetta, the emotions that produced this living art went deeper even than the attempt to effect a successful killing through some kind of sympathetic magic. She observed how 'Many hunting peoples apologize to the animals they kill, asking their forgiveness, propitiating them.' Yet these people were entirely dependent on the animals for their food, their clothes, and for many of the tools and weapons that enabled them to survive in that harsh climate. At the same time, through their dawning self-consciousness and mental life, they were aware of their difference, their separation from the beasts to which they were so close. So 'they dressed themselves in their skins, horns and antlers, they ate ritual feasts, probably they imagined common spirit ancestors that made them one flesh with a totemic animal. They went into caves, sometimes far into the rock, and there made images of the animals, their work being, as all art was to be afterwards, another attempt at communion, at the recovery of unity with all existence. . . . It may be that the closed-in cave, cutting the artists off from the familiar world of action, helped them to visualize their images; certainly it well symbolizes the inner life of man that was then beginning.'

On her later visits to other caves in the area, Jacquetta noted, 'a few carvings of women, always wide-hipped, big bellied, and with full breasts. In one cave the woman, a dignified utterly impersonal figure sits holding a horn, in another there are three female bodies, carved among those of bison, horses and ibex, the inessential heads and feet missing, but the sexual organs emphasized'. 'Perhaps', she reflected 'they were images in some cult of fertility, which probably included both men and beasts. It is a truly astonishing thing to find the first of the world's artists already portraying the goddess of the feminine principle, who was to be worshipped under so many names by their still distant successors. . . . Here is the oldest symbol of all those we have created.'

Christopher was a fanatical worker – what we now, in that rather unattractive phrase, call a 'workaholic'. Along with his duties at the

British Museum, he was busy with his own work, a book on prehistoric Europe. Much of this had to be written at night. Jacquetta would take him a cup of tea around 11 p.m., and Christopher would go on working; that meant late breakfasts, and late arrival at the museum. Jacquetta, too, was starting work on her first book, *The Archaeology of Jersey*, but Christopher's exhausting regime was not helpful to the friendly and companionable life with which their marriage had begun. At one point Christopher was in serious trouble with the museum, even in danger of losing his position; he suffered something of a breakdown, due, his doctor said, entirely to overwork. A thorough rest and holiday restored Christopher, and he returned to the museum, which could not really afford to lose such a brilliant young man. In 1938 he was promoted to the position of first-class keeper, with an increased salary.

Nineteen thirty-six was the summer of Scandinavia. Christopher and Jacquetta were both invited to attend and to read papers at an International Archaeological Congress in Oslo. Christopher, always the dutiful son, wrote long letters home to his parents. He described his and Jacquetta's delight in Copenhagen, 'a really charming, human, civilized, easy-to-enjoy, happy, carefree sort of city. The museum is marvellous, and its staff most friendly.' At the congress he reported: 'Jacquetta's paper was extremely good – clear, controlled and assured. Mine was less good in that I had rather too much to say and exceeded my time!' Christopher was like his father – apt to use too many words.

After the conference, they were taken up the coast by steamer, visiting many of the Norwegian fjords, and being entertained on a lavish scale. They had excellent weather, and Christopher's only complaint was about the cost of everything, 'e.g. laundry 1/6d for a shirt'. There was more sight-seeing, swimming in the fjords, and a spectacular journey across the mountains, before their eventual arrival, rather exhausted, but still ready for more museums and sight-seeing, in Stockholm. Then came the real holiday at Visby, a fine old Hanseatic city on the strange, long island of Gotland, that lies in the Baltic Sea slightly nearer to Sweden than to its neighbour, the USSR. This proved to be the perfect holiday place. They did find the Baltic rather icy, but they were young and healthy and they enjoyed the long sandy beach, the continuing sunshine, and even, such as it was, the night-life of Visby. Towards the end they felt sufficiently energetic to contemplate walking round the whole 75 miles of the island, though they finally resorted to hired bicycles. Even this was rather hard work, since they chose the wrong north-south direction and seemed always to have the wind in their faces.

Later that autumn Jacquetta became intentionally pregnant. Rational and scientific as she was, she wrote, almost with astonishment, of her familiar physical self, 'now the slave of some great and marvellous and absolutely tyrannical purpose of which neither she nor he who launched the sperm has been vouchsafed any understanding'. Those were the days of domestic help, so Jacquetta was able to continue working. On the strength of a grant, she had been able to spend time in Jersey for the necessary research for her book. Here she was well entertained by the society of both Jersey and Guernsey, one of whose hostesses was heard to say of her: 'She wears her weight of learning like a flower'. *The Archaeology of Jersey* was eventually published in 1939, not exactly the best moment for publication, but since this was a particularly well-written work of scholarship destined for the archaeological community, it was able to find its permanent place.

During the last weeks of Jacquetta's pregnancy, her mother came to stay. 'She has been so nice with us these tedious, hot weeks,' Christopher wrote to his parents. The birth was not entirely easy, but all went well, and Charles Nicolas Hawkes, weighing 8½lb, arrived on 9 August 1937. Jacquetta thought him rather plain, but Christopher wrote that he 'looks a thoroughly agreeable and friendly sort of baby, and has nice little hands and feet'. Jacquetta soon recovered, and the family, complete with baby and monthly nurse, went for a holiday in Winchester.

In the summer of 1938 there was another joint excavation in Hampshire, this time with Nicolas and his nursery maid. Back in London, and with an expanding family, Christopher and Jacquetta decided that they must move. Had it not been for the outbreak of war they had intended to have another child as a companion for Nicolas. For a rent of 50s a week they moved to 39 Fitzroy Road, close to Primrose Hill and London Zoo. Jacquetta did some of the distempering, and, with a new sewing-machine that her mother-in-law had rather pointedly given her, she made some of the curtains, as well as a new dressing-gown for Christopher. The rest of the new furnishings had to be bought.

It might have been expected that the birth of a grandson – the only grandchild – might have made Ellie Hawkes more sympathetic towards her daughter-in-law, but the reverse seems to have happened. She became even more jealous and critical. When she complained about Jacquetta being over-extravagant and too slow in making the home comfortable Christopher wrote to her angrily:

Sir Frederick Gowland Hopkins in the Cambridge laboratory that was built for him with his grandson, Nicolas Hawkes

It is really time I stepped in and begged you to be more careful of your language – I mean this – your fatal passion for controlling others will lead to serious and irreparable harm if you do not check it where we are concerned. Your being 'horrified', and saying and writing these disagreeable things is extremely painful. . . . More than that, coming as it does on the top of a great deal of previous exhibitions of the same kind, and accompanied with language to Jacquetta on the telephone and whenever you have come here by yourself to see things has upset her more than I can say. . . .

Jacquetta happily is not easy to rouse, and we are both resolved to be as easy and sympathetic as we can for the sake of everyone concerned. But I warn you that your behaviour since Nicolas was born has been making me very uneasy. . . . I do not expect you ever to be fond of Jacquetta – that hope you killed a long while ago – but I do expect you to keep a proper hold on yourself and treat both of us with the good manners and consideration which Daddy and you yourself set before me as a rule of life when I was young . . . you are gradually antagonizing me from you by your ill-nature against my wife. . . you know we are both devoted to Daddy, and he is to you. Serious trouble between us would tear him in two. And as for Nicolas, it might well mean that he might never come to know his grandparents . . . we simply mustn't let it come to our facing that. But it is I who would have to decide, and a man's wife and family come inevitably first.

This was strong stuff, and does credit to Christopher, but curiously he did not show the letter to Jacquetta, perhaps from the (in my view, mistaken) idea then prevalent that it was a man's duty to protect women from unpleasantness.

In the summer of 1939 Jacquetta went alone to Ireland for the first excavation in which she was in sole charge. She was to explore a large Megalithic tomb in County Waterford, but first she had to get permission from the archaeologist at the head of all Irish archaeology, Adolf Mahr, a German. There was no trouble about the permission, and she found Mahr and his wife busily packing all their books up into crates. 'There is certain to be a war,' she wrote to Christopher, 'because the Mahrs are packing up everything, and are obviously leaving in a hurry.' (Later they learned that Mahr had also been head of Nazi intelligence-gathering in Ireland.) Jacquetta's living conditions were not pleasant. The food and the hotel were bad, and the hotel was full of Roman Catholic teaching priests, who disapproved of the study of prehistory and probably disapproved of women; she found the evenings very lonely. The tomb, however, proved interesting, even if her assistants were not particularly helpful – the labour she had been given was part of an unemployment scheme, and was completely unskilled, requiring more than normal supervision. The tomb had a large central corridor with a number of smaller ones branching off it. Jacquetta found an interesting little stone axe, a fine Bronze Age funeral urn, and a number of smaller urns designed to hold the bones of the dead. The evening after these finds she was late at the dig, and all her workmen had gone home; she carefully covered the urns, and secured the tomb. But as she bicycled back to the dreary hotel she was met to her surprise by a long procession of people making their way to the tomb. This she discovered was because rumour had spread that a magical hare, the guardian of the tomb, had been disturbed, and that a crock had been discovered which, on the stroke of midnight, would prove to be full of golden coins – the mythical 'Crock of Gold'. Jacquetta's rather more prosaic account of the excavation was published in an Irish archaeological journal. The following year, on the strength of her record of work, her writings and the publication of her book, Jacquetta was elected a Fellow of the Society of Antiquaries.

Back in London, Christopher and his colleague Tom Kendrick were fully occupied in packing up as many as possible of the British Museum treasures, so that they could be transported to some place of reasonable safety for the duration of the anticipated war. Jacquetta helped with the packing and once it was over she, Christopher and Nicolas went for a brief holiday at Chideock near the Dorset coast. In spite of Jacquetta's pleasure in her small son, and the rewards of her work, she was becoming increasingly restless and unhappy. Although she could still share archaeology with Christopher, his almost neurotic overworking made companionship less easy. Nevertheless this was a marriage that seemed to have so much in its favour. Much later Jacquetta recalled:

In all things social and intellectual it was admirably balanced and free. Yet it was also, I suppose, becoming every year more lifeless and stultifying. I will not say the lack was in our sexual life, that would be far too simple, but it was certainly in our union as man and woman. If we had ever known real passion together, everything else might have been well – but why had we not attained it? I now understand that all delight and intensity of love-making depend upon the mind and the imagination. That is true, but it only moves the explanation of our failure to another point. For the imagination to be kindled some profound psychological polarity between the individual man and the individual woman is evidently necessary. I could say that Christopher's instinctive life had been damaged by his dominating and possessive mother and by Winchester, while I went from becoming a late developer to becoming a case of arrested emotional development. Yet essentially the trouble lay in the absence of that polarity: it is a mystery and I hope will be allowed to remain so.

It is indeed a mystery, but a mystery with many faces. There is no single pattern of what is called 'successful marriage'; each individual, each couple must find their own way. Certainly passion and love are inseparable, but in the end it is perhaps love that proves the more durable. The surprising thing to my mind is not that so many fail, but that so many more succeed and do in fact live at least more or less happily ever after.

In Jacquetta's case, I think that at this stage in her life something more was involved in her own slow growth to maturity. There was a wildness inside Jacquetta, occasional desires to break the rules, something that belied her calm and formal exterior, something the restrained and conventionally educated Christopher could never reach. Now there was also a growing and unresolved tension between her rational scientific self and an imaginative and creative gift that was beginning more and more to seek an outlet. She may have appeared a highbrow intellectual, but, at heart, she was entirely romantic.

With a dreadful inevitability, war was declared on 3 September, and then nothing happened in Europe, only the tragic rape of Poland, during which the western allies, Britain and France, were able only to stand and watch helplessly. By the summer of 1940 everything changed, and it seemed at least prudent for Jacquetta to take Nicolas out of London. They went to friends whom they had made on their Dorset holiday, the Pinney family, who lived nearby in a fine old manor-house, and who were happy to welcome Jacquetta and Nicolas as their temporary evacuees. It was here that something of Jacquetta's suppressed emotional life burst out; she was overwhelmed by a violent passion for the lady of the house, Betty Pinney: it was a sudden undamming of feelings of an intensity that she did not know that she possessed. Betty Pinney seems to have been a strange, rather cruel character. She alternately encouraged and then repulsed Jacquetta, whose love was entirely romantic and ideal, an obsessive devotion and a desire only to love and serve her lady, like some young knight of old. Nor in Jacquetta's case was it particularly physical, and on the only occasion that Betty attempted to lure her into bed Jacquetta at once retreated. Eventually, aware of the absurdity of her situation, Jacquetta knew she had to extricate herself. She decided to take Nicolas and his Irish nanny to stay for the duration of the war with her parents in Cambridge. Meanwhile, in London, Christopher had been seconded to the Ministry of Aircraft Production, and bombs were falling. Jacquetta felt that, in spite of the danger, she must return to provide some measure of care and companionship for her husband. So she went back to Christopher, and had, as she said, 'for the only time in my life to experience and resist extreme physical fear'. As in her far-away childhood, Jacquetta's resistance to the inevitable fear remained resolute.

FOURTEEN

LOVE AND THE CIVIL SERVANT

Jacquetta quickly found work for herself. She became a civil servant, as an assistant principal in the Ministry of Post-War Reconstruction, and then in the Ministry of Education, where she rapidly progressed to becoming a principal, and finally an 'established' principal. Had she so wished she could have had a career for life, with a fine pension for her old age.

Christopher, of course, did his work as Secretary to the Air Supply Board admirably, but his heart remained with archaeology. Jacquetta felt that with his exceptional abilities, which she greatly respected, Christopher could have risen higher and found more interesting and responsible posts, but that was never what he wanted. He was busy with a book on *The Prehistoric Foundations of Europe*, which was published in 1940.

The affair with Betty Pinney had shaken Jacquetta; she half-wondered whether she would ever be able to find a full and happy heterosexual relationship. One or two experiments in that direction did nothing to reassure her; they may sometimes have been physically satisfying, but Jacquetta needed so much more. Meanwhile, life was full and often exhausting. There were regular weekends in Cambridge with Nicolas who seemed to be flourishing happily with his grandparents and a nanny. He still remembers his grandmother's 'lovely eyes' and 'lovely hands', and the way she could always help and soothe him if he hurt himself or felt ill. After the brief weekend peace of Cambridge, Jacquetta would return to London, often having to avoid broken glass and the debris of bombed houses as she found her way back to Primrose Hill. Christopher still wrote late into the night, and Jacquetta began more and more to make her own social life. Her closest Newnham friend, Peggy Lamert, now a reader for the publishing firm of Chatto & Windus, lived in a flat in Kensington, where Jacquetta arrived one evening for a small drinks party. Peggy introduced her to W.J. Turner and his wife Delphine. Walter Turner was a well-known poet, and a music, drama and literary critic. Peggy

W.J. Turner, the Australian poet and critic with whom Jacquetta enjoyed an 'electric' affair

remembers the immediate effect that he and Jacquetta had upon one another; she described the atmosphere between them as 'electric'.

Walter Turner was born in Australia, where he had lived until he was twenty-three. After the deaths in quick succession of his brother, his father and his grandparents he had come to London to be with his mother. He was a man of around sixty when he met Jacquetta, while she was still a young and beautiful woman lost in some kind of sexual and emotional limbo. Although Turner never left his wife, and, in his own entirely unconventional way, remained genuinely attached to her, he had many affairs. He was a remarkable, original and immensely gifted man; Jacquetta would unhesitatingly give him the accolade of 'genius'. It would be hard to imagine anyone more unlike a conventional English gentleman: he had a robust contempt for English politeness and restraint, despising purely social values, approved morals, and codes of behaviour; he was passionate and unrestrained, a wild man from the Antipodes who went his own way.

Turner had had a strict religious upbringing, coupled with a wide education, particularly a musical education. His father had been organist at the local Anglican church, where the young Walter had sung in the choir, often with a delight amounting to ecstasy. 'Like as the hart desireth the water brook, So longeth my soul after thee O God' was a psalm that he had taken for his own. Though soon

146

forsaking the forms and dogmas of religion, he was to be haunted for ever by a deeply spiritual quest. 'My heart', he wrote, 'goes searching over the sea, desiring that something that is more beautiful than the sun and wiser and deeper than the love of woman, that something which men call God.' He read widely in the philosophy of religion, and in the writings of the great religious mystics, and wanted himself 'to write a great religious philosophical book.' It was never written, but was always somewhere in the back of his mind.

Great art became Turner's religion, he defined it as 'pouring the infinite into the finite'. It was for him a revelation of the spiritual reality and the spiritual ecstasy that he sought, and that he found, pre-eminently in music – Beethoven to him was almost God-like. So for Turner the only valid morals were aesthetic, whether in life or in art – it was aesthetic and spiritual integrity that imposed the highest demands. Such a lofty view of the nature and function of art made Turner a demanding critic, fiercely dismissive of anything he regarded as mediocre or aesthetically false. His own views had, for him, an almost religious sanction, which resulted in an arrogance that frequently landed him in controversy and made him enemies. He admitted that he liked to shock and to provoke, even 'to baffle and mystify', but because he wrote with such originality and brilliance, his work was always fresh, independent and immensely readable. Among other things he was literary editor of the *Spectator*, and for more than twenty years, music critic of the *New Statesman*, until Kingsley Martin sacked him amid much ill-feeling.

It is interesting to find that although Turner tended to take the usual 'highbrow' view of Jack's work as 'popular and entertaining', that is to say somewhat lightweight, he wrote admiringly of *Johnson Over Jordan*, and attacked the hostile reviewers as 'typical of the sterile negative nature of so-called intellectuals'. It was 'the imaginative value' of drama that mattered more than the action; 'serious dramatists', he wrote, should 'set men not against men, but against fate or some intangible, indefinable background', should see them as 'symbols or vessels carrying a meaning that cannot be expressed in direct speech'. That, of course, is what Jack so often aimed to do, and what in *Johnson Over Jordan* he successfully achieved. Jacquetta and Christopher had bought tickets for this play, which, although slammed by many of the critics, was in fact being much talked about; but before they were able to see it, war had been declared and all theatres temporarily closed.

It was not long, however, before W.J. Turner and J.B. Priestley were plunged into a literary row in the pages of the *New Statesman*, of which Jack had recently become a director. While Jack's articles were highly praised, his novels and plays often suffered from the usual 'highbrow' criticism, about which he wrote what he described as 'letter after letter of passionate protest', all of which the editor refused to publish. 'Now,' said Jack, 'I was foolish enough to write something faintly derogatory about a series W.J. Turner (that fine poet) was editing. At once the enraged Walter Turner slammed in a letter telling the world that for years I had been notorious for my conceit, arrogance, refusal to take any criticism – a V2 of a letter.' 'Abominable I agree,' said the editor, 'and, of course, we wouldn't have published it if you hadn't been a director.' Ironically, not only was Jacquetta so soon to be passionately in love with Walter Turner, but she was a contributor to that same series, 'Britain in Pictures' that Walter Turner was editing. Her topic was *Early Britain*.

Although Turner made enemies, some of whom found it hard to forgive him, he also made many friends. In his diary he wrote of himself: 'I want love and affection; sympathy and tears – the cruel unkindness and disregard of friends, the hardness and selfishness of those around weigh upon me heavily. I am pierced to the heart when those I love are sad or distressed, and my inability to relieve them pains me.' But he also had to admit: 'My attitude to the world is so radically different from that of most other people that I can never judge what others feel or think.' And yet again, almost in contradiction – and who among us can claim to be free of contradictions – he could write to his wife Delphine:

As we grow older, unless we have kept ourselves continually in touch with the emotions of others, we lose the habit, the gift of communication, of intimacy; we become dry and withered from lack of life, like a parched orange skin . . . that sensitiveness to beauty and emotion which is the source of our greatest happiness is gone. The only way we can retain it is by feeling with others, by a wide and profound sympathy which can respond to the hopes and fears, the passions, griefs and joys of our fellows.

Turner fascinated his friends by his talk, by his outpourings of wit, of knowledge, and above all by a torrent of ideas – sometimes it was hard for anyone else to get a word in, let alone a contrary opinion. It is not surprising that such a man should also have fascinated many women.

Although Turner wrote numerous articles and books that included two or three novels and fourteen plays, few of which were performed, it is as a poet that he was pre-eminent, and it was his poetry that was most important to him. A few of his poems crop up in anthologies, but that is not enough for such an original and interesting talent. He was much admired by W.B. Yeats, and a critic, G.D. Zimmerman, wrote of his 'mixture of emotional energy and metaphysical intuition'. Turner fits no category. Although at first associated with the Georgians group, he was not a Georgian poet, and although he was modern, he was not altogether modern. Versatile and innovative, capable of many musically beautiful and moving poems, he was both metaphysical and romantic; he was himself.

At first Walter and Jacquetta met on an intellectual level. He was immensely well-read, well informed about all the arts, interested in anthropology and prehistory, in the discoveries of modern physics, and in the time theories of J.W. Dunne, which he had tried to use in one or two of his not very successful plays. Jacquetta's mind, stretched and expanded by all these stimuli, was well able to match Walter's own. It was not long before they became lovers. Though not in the full vigour of youth he was still an experienced and skilful lover. Jacquetta described their relationship as 'sharply divided between purely intellectual friendship and a shameless eroticism. We did not meet very often, but I became wholly infatuated.' As proof, if such were needed, Jacquetta recalls an occasion when, unexpectedly meeting Walter at an exhibition, she promptly – though briefly – fainted. Their relationship she said, 'produced a strange purity of its own, and brought me visions akin to those of godhead. I poured out verse, much of it bad, but containing some poetry and a few really good lines.'

None of this is altogether surprising: so much was stirring in Jacquetta, so much emotion, so much creative energy, so much that had to find an outlet. There was never any question or possibility of a life with Walter Turner, and through all these turbulent years, and those that were to follow, it was not until conditions changed radically that Jacquetta ever contemplated leaving Christopher. Nor was it surprising that Walter Turner, and many other men for that matter, should have fallen in love with Jacquetta. As Jack, the Jungian, was to write to her, 'There can be no doubt you are one of the Anima girls – hence the trouble you cause in literary and scholarly circles, where the boys are busy projecting Animas.' It was not simply that Jacquetta was a beautiful woman, nor even that she had what Blake so rightly saw we all require in the opposite sex, 'the lineaments of gratified desire', though, of course, she had that too, her nature being neither cold nor passionless. But Jacquetta managed to be fascinating and mysterious, and not all beautiful women are necessarily fascinating. With her sudden lovely but ambiguous smiles, and her cool exterior, she presented men with a challenge, an urge to discover what really lay within, and there was a great deal within to be discovered. I have written of her as a classical figure, something of the goddess, a mixture of Athena and Aphrodite; yet to return to Jack's words, 'I like to think I see you as a woman, and an exceptionally fine woman, a marvellous mixture of a rare, gifted creative, all very grand, and a honey of a girl – an entrancing combination.'

In November 1946 Walter Turner died suddenly from a brain haemorrhage; he was only sixty-three. Before she heard the news, Jacquetta experienced a frightening feeling of dark and deep foreboding. When she finally learnt of Walter's death she was prostrated with 'grief that was full of tears and an all-consuming sense of loss'. Nicolas remembers his nine-year-old self sitting on an arm of her chair and murmuring, 'Poor Mummy,' as he saw the tears in her eyes.

Walter Turner's last volume of poems *Fossils of a Future Time?* was published posthumously. He explained the title by a comparison with material fossils of the past:

> I see these fossils of past physical activity paralleled in intellectual activity by similar records. Our masterpieces of painting, of music, and of literature are just such relics of a vanished mental and spiritual life. If there is life in these poems, then they in their turn will become similar witnesses of a creative energy which flourished at a certain time in a definite place. . . . The reader will not fail to perceive the note of interrogation in the title; nor will he imagine – from my silence on the point – that I believe there is no connexion between one age and another.

So Jacquetta, who in her professional life studied the fossils of the earth and its strange past lives, now studied these different 'fossils', wondering, with anguish, which of the many love poems were addressed to her. And reading through them I believe that many were for Jacquetta. Walter Turner wrote in a number of different forms – classical blank verse, sonnet form, poems with rhyme and poems without. I will content myself with a 'song', one that speaks unmistakably of Jacquetta:

Her eyes are neither grey nor blue
Her hair is neither brown nor fair
Her level brows are dark in hue
He who has courage let him dare

Confront her gaze as deep as night,
Warmer than equatorial noon
When strikes through veils of heavy light
Heart of the tropic's blind typhoon.

Heart! Yes, it is her heart, the Sun
O'er earth goes staggering weak and pale,
It's fire that in her veins has run
Burns up the vessel mast and sail;

Naked and white I am as dawn,
Defenceless but that earth's white frost
Burns heaven as it is burning drawn
Into tumultuous daylight tossed.

Ah! that we two in one long night
Our dark blood in one black orb bent,
A moon of pure eternal light
Hung singly in the firmament.

Perhaps one might also add a few lines from the poem 'Comparison':

O call her not 'beyond compare'
Whom Agamemnon sought in Troy
Nor rave how she of midnight hair
Earth's triple pillar did destroy:
I know of one who need but move
To fill all heaven and earth with love.

And is she dark or is she fair?
Oh, she is darker than the Sun!
Her heart it is more light than air
So deep, it has been plumbed by none.
Who lies in love against her side
Has the volcanic earth to bride.

There are many beautiful 'fossils' in the collection; I hope that one day they may be rediscovered by some other poetic searchers to whom they will give the delight that many of them have given to me.

With the help of a friend, Jacquetta sorted through her own poems, and a small selection was published in 1949 entitled *Symbols and Speculations*. She dedicated it to her father, but sadly he must have died before it finally reached the public. Here is Jack's initial reaction to the poems: 'It is genuine original poetry, beaten out of life, and not out of other poetry. It is very like you, ranging from something awkward, bony, to something flashing and crying with beauty.' His complaint was that he found some of them obscure, 'an obscurity in the transitions of thought'. As one might expect, in the poems there are birds, flowers and butterflies, all expressive of Jacquetta's intent observation and sense of deep participation in the natural world and its marvellous manifestations. There are echoes of archaeology and much personal experience. 'Apples' records a happy moment sitting with Nicolas beneath an apple tree and watching a sudden flight of linnets:

> Housed beneath the apple tree
> Side by side my son and I
> Sit content to feel that we
> Share one green and private world.

Then comes the sudden flight of the birds:

> And their spangled passage flings,
> A miracle, an unknown sigh,
> On shade of leaves a shade of wings
> Bringing tears into my eyes
>
> I look wondering at the child
> He in wonder looks at me;
> Surely Adam would have smiled
> With us, beneath our apple tree.

Of course, there are also the love poems written for Walter Turner:

> I thought how I had only known you old,
> Strip't and planed by the years, ash tree made mast,
> A hard master in love, a destroyer
> Of treasured rubbish, lashing my last leaves

And, inevitably, there are poems of grief:

> I have felt sobs so deep
> I thought the earth must shake
> And bid her old rocks weep
> For my anguish sake.
>
> I have so plied my cup
> With joy, that on a hill
> I prayed heaven snatch me up
> Drunk with rapture still.
>
> The earth revolves unmoved
> And rocks are tearless yet
> My madness when I loved
> I live to forget.

After *Symbols and Speculations* Jacquetta wrote no more poetry, deserted beyond all conscious control by that so inconstant muse who comes and goes only at her own sweet and capricious will.

Under the entry for W.J. Turner in the *Dictionary of National Biography* the writer, after a brief biographical sketch, speaks of his 'Knowledge of the world, even a kind of ruthlessness, which was yet in perfect harmony with the innocence of a true artist. . . . His poetry was as idiosyncratic as was his nature. Although by experimenting with free metrical forms and colloquial idiom he made concessions to the spirit of the times, his poetry was too rich in imagery and sound, too lyrical and sensuous and unintellectual to belong to the fashionable trends of the inter-war period. . . . A few lyrics may justly be called perfect . . . and the poetic gift never left him.' The writer of this entry is Jacquetta Hawkes.

Fortunately for Jacquetta, she was interested and absorbed in her work as a civil servant. The Post-War Reconstruction Secretariat was housed in a small office with a few administrative grade staff. They were able to share in the work of their minister's private office, and Jacquetta learned about the subtle art of preparing answers to parliamentary questions. An old friend whom Jacquetta much admired was Henry Morris, Director of Education for Cambridgeshire, and pioneer of 'village colleges'. Jacquetta got him on to the Post-War Reconstruction Council, hoping to be able to introduce these colleges more widely. For this, the minister thought they would be better placed in the Ministry of Education, so Jacquetta was transferred there as principal, first under R.A. Butler and subsequently, following the 1945 election, under Ellen Wilkinson.

Instead of village colleges, however, Jacquetta was immediately put in charge of visual education. This involved film-making; an educational film featuring the history of Britain was projected. In this ministry Jacquetta made two of her best and longest lasting friendships. The first was with Helen de Mouilpied, who was nominally second-in-command, but who was really director of the film department of the Ministry of Information. Helen was already making films, and she and Jacquetta worked happily together, though, as principal and editor-in-chief Jacquetta had the final decision. If she approved a project, the money would be forthcoming. Jacquetta took responsibility for the earliest of the history films produced by the ministry, *The Beginnings of History*. For this she made an interesting and enjoyable visit to the Orkneys, those remote islands so rich in ancient monuments and remains. The Admiralty thought this educational filming mad, but was persuaded to give its permission.

The ministry was soon joined by a lively and attractive young man, Denis Forman, whose job was to assist Helen de Mouilpied with filming; she was to be his boss. Helen was a beautiful and clever young woman, with a first-class history degree from Oxford. She was tall, slim and dark-haired, 'always elegant', Denis said of her later. Helen had her own mysterious fascination, and her own special and unusual smile, and Denis immediately began to besiege her with ardour and determination. But Helen was entangled with another lover, another young man in the ministry. Her friends thought him a wet, not nearly good enough for the clever and beautiful Helen, whereas this new pursuer was clearly marked out as a high-flier, with an unquestionably exciting future before him. Helen wavered, pulled to and fro, frequently in tears, unable to leave Bill, unable to reject Denis.

Meanwhile, preparations had begun for the great six-week inaugural UNESCO meeting in Mexico. Sir John Maud, head of the department, and known as one of the founding fathers of UNESCO, was to assemble the British delegation, of which Jacquetta was to be the secretary. When she learned that Sir John had selected J.B. Priestley to represent literature, drama, and the arts generally, she went to protest. Priestley was not enough of an intellectual, altogether too lightweight, not a worthy representative. Jacquetta was still much under the influence of Walter Turner and her other highbrow friends who thought little of Priestley's work. But Sir John wisely disagreed.

Priestley had an exceptionally wide knowledge of the arts; he had practised many different varieties of literature and drama; and he was internationally known and respected as a dramatist and as a famous wartime broadcaster. So Jacquetta had to retire, and to begin dictating all those letters signed J.J. Hawkes.

The UNESCO delegation gathered for a briefing session and reception at an office in Belgrave Square. There was Jack, and there was Jacquetta. Some compulsion made her approach Jack, offering him a rather horrible looking pink sweet confection. So they looked at each other and smiled together, sharing a small private joke. They both remembered that significant moment. Then there was a splendid jamboree in July 1947 when the delegation with secretaries and appendages went to a UNESCO meeting in Paris. Jack, as a senior delegate, had been allocated two assistants, Jacquetta and Helen – lucky Jack! But Helen was still in an emotional turmoil, still uncertain, still inclined to weep. Jack, with his accustomed sympathetic insight, noticed her distress and took her out to dinner – perhaps to offer her some avuncular comfort? Naturally they discussed the delegation, including Helen's friend, Jacquetta. 'What a woman!' said Jack. 'Ice without and fire within.'

Paris had done well out of its wartime capitulation. It had been neither bombed nor shelled, and nor had it been fought over. The many senior German officers who had been quartered there had looked after themselves very well, so that the best French cuisine and the best French wines were in plentiful supply, in contrast to poor old war-weary England, where stringent rationing was to continue for several years. The delegation stayed in the best hotel, which was named the King George V – a compliment to the British perhaps. They all had a thoroughly good time, eating and drinking and visiting the famous French nightclubs.

As well as attempting to comfort Helen, Jack took Jacquetta out to dinner. The talk and the evening were pleasant enough, but they were both wary. Jacquetta was still in the shadow of Walter Turner's sudden death, and Jack, although he had discovered J.J. Hawkes, had troubles, worries and unhappiness at home; he was not seeking, and did not want a deep and demanding emotional commitment. In fact, family troubles had nearly prevented him from going away at all. His daughter, Mary, whom he regarded as exceptionally gifted and intelligent, had been showing signs of instability. Mary was a talented violinist, and, while studying in Geneva, had fallen in love with a penniless Danish music student. When she wanted to marry him her parents, not unreasonably, insisted that the young couple should separate for six months and think things over. The stress of this affair may perhaps have pushed Mary too far, for she suffered a severe breakdown. Jack, who had kept up a regular and loving correspondence with Mary, was distraught by this development, and felt that he ought not to go abroad while his daughter was so ill. He wrote to J.J. Hawkes cancelling his attendance at the Mexico conference. Mary was then taken into treatment at St Andrew's Hospital, Northampton, and family visits were prohibited. There was really nothing that Jack could do, so he was persuaded that it would be more sensible to go to Maxico after all, and he withdrew his cancellation, insisting on paying all his own expenses.

So, at last, towards the end of 1947, the British UNESCO delegation gathered at Southampton and boarded the Queen Mary en route for New York, from where they would proceed by train to Mexico City.

PART IV
JACK AND
JACQUETTA

FIFTEEN

THE COURSE OF TRUE LOVE

Jacquetta never enjoyed sea voyages, and this was no exception; all too soon she succumbed to sea-sickness and was confined below decks in a cramped and not particularly comfortable cabin. When Jack looked around for J.J. Hawkes he could not find her, and when she failed to appear at a meeting of the whole delegation which he was chairing, he was filled with a 'furious disappointment'.

Mexico City was not at first much better. The British contingent was installed in the Santa Christina Hotel, pleasant but relatively modest, relative that is to the larger and grander building that housed the Americans. Hardly had the British settled in than nearly everyone, including Jacquetta, was smitten with enteritis, and as the local plumbing left a great deal to be desired, the first few days were far from pleasant. Jack seems to have recovered quickly, and arrived in Jacquetta's room with brandy in a medicine bottle. 'That brandy,' she wrote, 'together with his irresistible voice, marked the beginning of a wonderful sense of being looked after.' As soon as Jacquetta was fully recovered, and could eat without fear of the consequences, Jack invited her to dinner at the best local restaurant. Driven by her compulsive honesty, and a recklessness induced by the high altitude and her first Martini cocktails, Jacquetta began by telling him that she 'did not much like his writings': not exactly a propitious opening, but Jacquetta always did put honesty before the desire to please. Jack, of course, was hurt and angry, especially as, like so many of those who criticized him, Jacquetta had read very little of his work. But the forces that drew them together were immeasurably deeper and more powerful than any surface misunderstandings, and walking back to the hotel 'along the noble and now quietening Pasa de la Reforma, there seemed to be just the two of them walking as one beneath the stars'. So Jack and Jacquetta crossed their private Rubicon together, and became forever lovers.

They had six marvellous weeks in Mexico City, trying to tell one another that this was just 'a rather special conference affair that must

Jack with Harold Macmillan during the UNESCO conference in Mexico City in 1947

be ended'. Though both marriages were falling apart, both were of longstanding, and the bonds of marriage, with children and other responsibilities, are strong, seldom broken without pain and the infliction of pain. They resolved that their respective obligations must not be broken.

Jack had to leave for New York before the conclusion of the conference, and even up to their parting they continued to tell each other that this would be the end. But Jack, at fifty-three, and deeply unhappy as he was at home, found that he could not bear to face such an end; he wrote from the train to Jacquetta:

I know I shouldn't be doing this – it's against everything I meant or even said – but I can't help it. I must write one letter to you – if only selfishly, to try and relieve myself of this terrible weight of sadness and loss. . . . You were right, of course, not to come to the station – it would have been a messy anti-climax . . . all went well until about six o'clock, when the whole landscape took on an unearthly beauty. I had opened my bottle of Scotch and was sipping and staring and brooding when you came flooding back to me in full and terrible force and then ever since it has been hell. Missing and missing and missing you. I'll get over the worst of it soon, I suppose, but just now I feel older and emptier and sadder than I ever remember feeling before. I seem to have walked straight into the emotional trap. Would I really have it different – remembering how miserable I was on my way to Mexico City? I don't know – honestly I don't know, my darling. In any case, I suppose, I've feasted – on beauty and strangeness and comradeship and fun – and now here comes the bill. Hell, that's my affair and at least I can thank you, which I do most humbly and tenderly, for all you gave and all you meant – all the enchantment that I thought had gone for ever. . . . I have known this last week, with every deepening moment, that we had gone further than we told ourselves we would. . . . How strange it has been – as strange as your curious changing beauty, which does not really belong to my world. (But I knew it deep down, from the first – recognized, before my heart was involved, the priestess of the archaic cult – said so in what I thought was fun. 'J.J. Hawkes' – My God!) Take this miserable letter, kiss it once, and then burn it.

Jack still clung to a hope, even to a deeper knowledge, that, just as he felt unable to break away from Jacquetta, she too would not finally be able to break from him. 'I'll get hold of you sometime,' he wrote, 'unless my family crisis develops. I sit here in the damned train, holding your lovely image in my arms – I can hardly see for tears. If it will make you happier to forget me, then do so – and God bless you!' Jacquetta's response was immediate, 'wandering joyfully through the streets of the old city hunting for a post office from which to send Jack the message that would put him out of his immediate misery'.

Back in New York at the end of November and after five wretched nights in the train, Jack penned an anxious note to Mary: 'You mustn't worry about money or practising just now, but simply try to get well first. We all love you very much. . . .' And as soon as he arrived home, he scribbled another brief letter: 'I have brought some pretty things to wear for everybody from Mexico City, which is full of them, though otherwise not a very pleasant city, being too high (7,500 feet) and upsetting for the tummy. . . . I will write again soon.'

And this he continued to do. But it was not a happy homecoming. Though it was the family who had urged him to go to Mexico City, Jane was now full of reproaches for his having left her alone to carry the burden of Mary's illness. The weather was dismal, and after

Christmas came one of the worst and coldest of winters, with power cuts and fuel rationing. Though heating was easier in the country than it was for people in the cities, Jack and Jane both succumbed to 'flu, and Jack wrote to Mary: 'I find these days in the dead heart of the winter period that I cannot work as well as I do when it is warmer and things are coming to life. I do not feel as creative or sufficiently alive myself.' Nevertheless it was during this dismal period that Jack was able to write *The Linden Tree*, one of his best plays, followed by another, *Home is Tomorrow*.

Life at home was emotionally easier for Jacquetta than it was for Jack. She and Christopher remained friendly and never quarrelled. Perhaps early training and a natural reticence, especially on Christopher's part, prevented anything in the way of scenes. Christopher was very much the English gentleman, his awareness of Jacquetta's infidelities only made him withdraw further into himself and cover up any pain that he might have felt. As a boy, Nicolas was never conscious of tension in the home, none of the raised voices, the banging of doors, the cold silences and general misery that disturbed the Priestley children.

Christopher had left the Ministry of Aircraft Production at the end of 1945, and returned briefly to his work at the British Museum, but in late July, he was elected Professor of European Archaeology at Oxford, with a fellowship at Keble College. He and Jacquetta contemplated moving to Oxford, but at that time it was impossible to find any kind of accommodation, and what was offered by the college was hopelessly unsuitable. So Christopher was given rooms in college, and took up his new post on 1 October 1946. Jacquetta continued with her civil service and UNESCO work, and there were long vacations when Christopher was able to work in London.

Jack and Jacquetta met when they could, and made love when and where they could. Jacquetta felt that she had been created anew, experiencing in her late thirties 'the pleasures and spiritual transformation of total love'. With Walter Turner, life had had to be lived on the heights, but Jack was a man for all seasons; tender, loving, sensual, humorous, always quickly intuitive and sympathetic, 'a good shoulder to cry on'. He was entertaining and stimulating, ready to talk on any subject with wide knowledge and personal insight; he was also – something especially fascinating to imaginative women like Jacquetta – a true artist. She loved him with her whole being, as he loved her. 'I must confess', she wrote, 'that I revelled in the wildness of those days, telling myself that to be such a mistress was a finer thing than to be a wife. . . .' They took time to come closer together; their backgrounds were very different, there was, as Jack wrote, 'a colossal gap to bridge, but I am absolutely certain that we need each other in a very special way – and only pride will prevent our admitting this . . . because, though we differ in so many things, each of us has a very personal vision of mankind as a whole, you through the long vista of prehistory, and I through drama and politics. We turn into poets, though of different kinds, more or less at the same moment.'

Jack was particularly anxious that their affair should not be discovered. He wanted Jacquetta to destroy his letters to her, which, of course, she could never bring herself to do, while he resolutely did destroy hers to him. She must have written something slightly critical, to which he replied:

> What you have to remember is that I have got you tied up in my mind, not as a person when I meet you, but when I read such a letter, with a type and generation whose attitudes I am tired of – its intolerance of work it does not happen to be interested in, work that may be immensely difficult to accomplish. (If it isn't, sit down and try it.) Hence the irritability which is not personal. . . .

On a more personal level, he protested that he did not read too many detective novels, his reading was as wide as any man's, he did not drink too much, very little in fact when he was at home working, and he did not write carelessly.

> I give an enormous amount of thought and preliminary attention to a really creative job of writing, which I never begin until after long preparation. . . . I am often able to write quickly now, just because I went through a long course of self-discipline in writing in my twenties. It is one of my grumbles that prose-writing is now so shockingly bad, chiefly because of the absence of this self-discipline, and lack of initial humility fostered by this conceit and intolerance, which in their turn have made contemporary criticism so poor. With much of this you would probably agree, but nevertheless I do feel you are much influenced by the attitudes of your particular generation and background. . . .

Whenever Jack and Jacquetta were able to meet, all such reservations melted away in their ever-deepening love for one another, but the meetings were too intermittent and too short. Jack, in particular, although he still felt he should try to make his marriage work better, was so harassed and stressed at home that he longed more and more for space and time with Jacquetta. They both had work to do – Jack's output during this difficult period was prodigious, including numerous plays, books and articles, as well as the libretto for an opera, *The Olympians*, with music by Sir Arthur Bliss. In addition he was leading an exceptionally active public life, and was chairman of numerous cultural organizations.

In 1947 *An Inspector Calls* at last reached the London stage, with Jack's old friend Ralph Richardson playing the part of Inspector Goole. Also, in August 1947, *The Linden Tree* arrived for a successful run at the Duchess Theatre, with Lewis Casson and Sybil Thorndike as Professor and Mrs Linden. This was a family play, 'technically', Jack wrote, 'a return to the method of *Eden End*, although rather more complex and subtle in its family relationship and making demands on much that I had learned since 1934. Let me say . . . that plays of this kind may call for no great mastery of language or imposing flights of imagination, but they have their own innumerable difficulties, not unlike the problems of tone faced by the old Dutch painters. . . .'

A scene from the 1947 production of *The Linden Tree* at the Duchess Theatre, starring Sybil Thorndike as Mrs Linden (photograph by Hailston Rogers)

The Linden Tree is not a Time Play, but in some ways, especially in its characters, it seems close to Time and the Conways, though, as Jack rightly says, the characters are more subtly drawn. The head of the Linden family tree is a man of sixty-five, a professor of history at a new university. Members of the university, his wife and at least two of his children feel he should retire, but the professor feels he must stay in order to keep his own values alive in the face of much of which he disapproves. The choice he finally makes is ambiguous: Jack doesn't take sides. As with so many of Jack's plays, music is a vital part, centred around the youngest daughter, Dinah, a cello player, and a Carol Conway kind of character. Jack's choice of music was not just to create a good or even a magical atmosphere; it was there for a meaning, just as his meticulous and detailed directions for staging were part of his conception of the play. In The Linden Tree it is Elgar's Cello Concerto that plays its part: 'A kind of long farewell – an elderly man remembers his world before the war of 1914 . . . a farewell to long lost summer afternoons.' In the same way, the music in Time and the Conways begins with Mrs Conway playing popular tunes of the period, all cheerful, superficial and trouble-free. By the third act, when we know of the troubles to come, she is singing Schumann's Der Nussbaum, about the lovely little nut tree with its whispering leaves, while the young girl (Carol Conway – doomed to die young?) is wondering what they mean. The play ends with the opening bars of Brahms's Cradle Song – goodnight and good morning – and leaves us with both.

Similar themes run through many of Jack's plays, representing a clash of opposites – the spiritual and the material, hope and despair, faith and cynicism, life and death, good and evil. Jack would perhaps not have used those big words (too grand, too explicit), but in spite of his feeling for the 'endless ambiguity of things' – his deep sense of cosmic irony – the big ideas are there. There is often as well in these later plays a comment in one form or another on the exploitative nature of national and international capitalism, contrasted with an emphasis upon the mutual responsibilities of life in a community. We find something of all these in Home is Tomorrow, a play about the work of a United Nations agency, and how right Jack is that it seems always to be 'good' men, not the villains, who meet the assassin's bullet. The themes are there again in the beguilingly romantic and symbolic fantasy of Summer Day's Dream. In both of these plays Jack's older and 'good' characters explain at some point that they believe in trying to live by 'faith, hope and love'. After his stern Baptist upbringing, Jack was familiar with the Bible.

Jacquetta too was writing. She wrote an interesting article for *Penguin New Writing* in 1949, called 'Art in the Crystalline Society'. Here she describes the older organic types of society as a tree with all the interrelated and diverse parts, whereas the crystal, with its identical particles, is an image of the new intellectual and increasingly atomized society. Of this she writes that 'with religion it has lost the motive of uniting itself with the universe, and with art one of the chief instruments for achieving that union'. The artist was once an integral part of the community, but now art is increasingly seen as 'no more than an unnecessary ornament tacked on to the edge of life.' 'It seems', she writes, 'that materialism must be modified . . . somehow the secularization of political theory must be reversed, and social institutions seen as expressions, no doubt happily imperfect, of a supreme spiritual reality. . . . Artists must forswear either enmity or humility towards science and accept their rightful position as its masters.' Though Jacquetta was never formally religious, neither was she ever a materialist. And she concludes with the quotation that artists must 'bring imagination to science, and science to imagination where they meet in the myth'. And that is precisely what Jacquetta herself proceeded to do.

She was already brooding on the book in which the two sides of her nature, the two strands perhaps of her Hopkins inheritance – her exact scholarly and scientific knowledge of geology and archaeology, and her creative and poetic imagination – were to be beautifully fused. She began work on her most successful book, *A Land*.

In the light of contemporary knowledge Jacquetta told the story of the creation of the land of Britain, and, in its later stages, its relation to the history of its peoples. As a counterpoint to this material and factual account she considered.

the growth of consciousness, its gradual concentration and intensification within the human skull. That consciousness has now reached a stage in its growth at which it is impelled to turn back, to recollect happenings in its own past which it has, as it were, forgotten. In the history of thought, this is the age of history. . . . Not that I would allow myself to repent the divine curiosity that has led to this knowledge. . . . I am committed utterly to *la volenté de la conscience et la volenté de la découverte*. To enjoy, to create (which is to love) and to try to understand is all that at the moment I can see of duty.

In her later writing, Jacquetta simplified this to 'to love, to create, and to try to understand'.

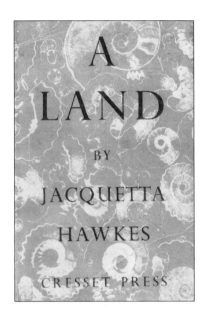

A *Land* received great critical acclaim upon its publication in 1951. H.J. Massingham commented in the *Spectator*: 'It is a germinal book and may well herald a change in cultural orientation that bitter experience has made tragically overdue.'

How these most vital of the qualities that make us human seem to fall into trinities! Jack's 'to increase knowledge, to create beauty, to experience love', Wordsworth's 'admiration, hope and love', and St Paul's 'faith, hope and love [charity]', and his fruits of the spirit as 'love, joy, peace'.

It is impossible in a short,space to do any kind of justice to such an original book as *A Land*. It is crammed with knowledge and information, yet is supremely the work of a poetic and vividly visual imagination. It could be so dull, and is instead so fascinatingly alive. Jacquetta constantly makes connections that bring the remotest past into our present experience. She makes us realize our unity not only with living creatures that we know, but with those ancient forms of life long since departed and fossilized. How extraordinary, for instance, to contemplate a time, aeons before the appearance of any form of life, when our world of rocks was without colour. Or to realize that it has taken three thousand million years to create the youthfulness of England in April, 'those fierce young buds and frail eggs, greenness that seems to cry aloud, those songs in the throats of birds, and hope in the heart of man. The resurrection of the spring god.' Then again, to consider our relationship to the earliest reptiles when

consciousness gained a new incentive and a tremendous new agency for its own perfection. For the first time, the male had to seek the female. . . . There is something here more than a sexual selection, immensely powerful as that has been in the evolution of life. The forces of attraction and repulsion, of mutuality in all their forms, have acted like some universal instinctive artistic genius, creating all that is most brilliantly coloured in the world; all that is furthest from the dead equality of chaos.

Until finally it is love, human love that 'refines and sharpens human personality, and provokes poetry and music'. Unbelievable as it may be, the truth is that 'those reptile couplings, all slime and scale', played a part in the creation of Héloïse and Abelard, and their tragic love affair, as well as of our own happier and more domestic loves and marriages.

Jacquetta's story of the creation of rocks and soil and the many different varieties of stone is enthralling, as is her account of the ways in which stone has been used by men for building and sculpture, as expressions of their apprehensions of the numinous, for the glorification of their gods and for their own homes. Jacquetta writes of how Henry Moore, 'our greatest sculptor', 'uses his understanding of the personality of stones in his sculpture, allowing their individual qualities to contribute to his conception'. She comments upon the way in which he uses the light and dark colours of Hornton stone: 'The sense of light and darkness seems to go the depths of man's mind, and whether it is applied to morality, to aesthetics, or to that more general conception – the light of intellectual processes in contrast with the darkness of the subconscious – its symbolism surely draws from our constant swing below the cone of night . . . Rodin pursued the idea of conscious, spiritual man emerging from the rock; Moore sees him rather as always a part of it.' 'It is hardly possible', she writes, 'to express in prose the extraordinary awareness of the unity of past and present, of mind and matter, of man's origin, which these thoughts bring to me. . . .' And I, a humble reader, can only feel equally if inarticulately amazed. . . .

The book is complemented by fascinating illustrations, photographs of curious fossils and stones, of buildings and of landscapes, and perhaps best of all Henry Moore's coloured drawings, including *Knights and Kirtled Ladies Waiting for Creation*. Although Jacquetta is unhappy about the onslaught of the machine age, and the dangers of over-population, she concludes with a 'Prospect of Britain' in which special areas of Britain with their different rocks, soils and building, and their inspiration for poets and painters, are all beautifully described. *A Land* was published in 1951, and was dedicated to the memory of W.J. Turner. It was not much approved of by pure archaeologists, but a great many people read and loved it. It well deserved the wide success that it achieved, and it established Jacquetta as a literary, as well as an archaeological, writer.

SIXTEEN

GROWING TOGETHER

These were difficult years, especially for Jack, with anxieties about Mary, and the fact that since the war it had become increasingly difficult for him and Jane to live together. Jane had been vaguely aware of Jack's infidelities over the years, but, apart from his temporary infatuation with Peggy Ashcroft, their marriage had never seemed seriously threatened; they could share a companionship of interests, as well, of course, as their sizeable family, and Jack had never wanted to leave her. Now, as the family had grown up and only Tom was still at school, there seemed little left between them. After a year or two, though she may not have known the particular person's identity, Jane began to realize that Jack was involved in a far more serious and finally threatening relationship.

For Jacquetta life with Christopher continued peacefully. Although she was increasingly turning to imaginative writing, she still wrote articles on archaeological subjects, and published her *Guide to Prehistoric and Roman Monuments in England and Wales* in 1951. When Christopher was at home, they entertained their friends. Denis Forman had married his beautiful Helen in 1948, and they were regular visitors. Mortimer Wheeler was also around, flirting outrageously with Jacquetta, and trying unsuccessfully to lure her into his bed. Christopher disliked and disapproved of Wheeler, but Jacquetta had a weakness for rather outrageous and flamboyant characters. Christopher, said Denis, was often the man in the kitchen, and seemed somewhat withdrawn and a little shy. He did not appear to be master in his own house and could be overruled and corrected by Jacquetta. But there was never any acrimony between them; there were always interesting people to talk to, and sometimes the parties became happily noisy and boisterous. Politically their circle was mildly socialist, though in the 1945 election Jacquetta, as a Cambridge MA, had agonized over whether or not she should vote for J.B. Priestley. She did in the end decide that she would.

Meanwhile Jack was in the background of Jacquetta's surface life, but very much in the foreground of her emotional self. His early letters to her reflect the swings of feeling, the surface misunderstandings of their steady growing together; they also reveal much of Jack's self-knowledge and his human understanding:

You have so much: a glorious honesty (which I deeply admire), passion, and a kind of frosty fire, like the Snow Queen on her birthday, a folded-in sort of handsomeness that turns into amazing beauty at the right moment . . . lovely intelligence, especially when you speak straight out of yourself and do not 'take a line', and somewhere – somewhere, I will swear – though I haven't reached it yet, and perhaps it isn't for me – an exquisite tenderness. It is odd how everything is reversed for us. I, the easy sensualist regard you most unsensually, except when immediately excited by you; whereas you find love for me in your body . . . but little or none, alas, in your mind. But this mind/body dichotomy won't work of course. It's really personality – and there I fancy, we meet on equal terms, with our own particular odd mixtures of masculine and feminine curiously balancing. But remember this whenever you find me lacking, that unlike you, I don't want to be in love. . . .

At other times, Jack would refer to 'the mysterious surges of antagonism coming up from the depths', or again:

There is no accounting for these queer ebbs and flows of feeling and pleasure and sense of rightness – the whole story seems to take place below the conscious level, which hasn't had much of a go with us, who rather tend to disapprove of one another on that level, and have to be prodded from below or is it above? But that seems to be the place to deal with – if one wants large and lasting satisfactions and all sorts of queer magics. . . . Probably on the conscious level we don't operate very much because it happens that both of us are more or less nicely fixed up on that level, got just the people we ought to have etc., etc. . . .

These were minor troubles, and could easily be accounted for by the fact that Jack and Jacquetta were so seldom able to spend any length of time together. 'What one misses most', Jack wrote, 'are not the two extremes of earnest talk and making love' [that had been Jacquetta's experience with Walter Turner], but all that lies in between – talk that is half making love and making love that is a kind of talk, for all of which one person is essential and no substitute can be found.' In fact, as Jack so often said, 'sex is a psychological act'.

Back at home, Jack was now often alone with Jane, but there were still family claims and occasions. Mary came out of hospital in 1948, and seemed fully recovered, so she married her Danish lover and went to live in Copenhagen. 'I knew it would be a disaster', said Jack gloomily, 'and it was.' Angela Wyndham-Lewis was already married, and it was not long before Barbara married a handsome young airman, Peter Wykeham. Sylvia followed: she married Michael Goaman, who shared her artistic skills and interests, and they worked together in a very successful designing enterprise, producing among other things designs for stamps for many different countries. Rachel too married young, announcing that she intended to have six children, which she eventually managed. She seemed a little on the periphery of the family, partly because of the ties of all those children, and partly because soon after her marriage to Dr Mark Littlewood, the family lived for several years in Saudi Arabia where foreign doctors were much in demand.

No amount of stress, trouble and unhappiness ever stopped Jack from writing. As in the wake of Pat's early and distressing death, Jack had settled down to write *The Good Companions*, his 'Holiday of the Spirit', so now, when his personal life appeared in such disarray, he set himself another challenge – another enormously long novel – 275,000 words of *Festival at Fairbridge*. 'I wanted', he said, 'to write a large-scale comic novel about post-war England . . . and stupidly as I now see, I chose the 1951 Festival of Britain, which I welcomed and never sneered at, as a peg on which to hang the tale.' He was disappointed by its reception, perhaps over-disappointed, because many people enjoyed it, and the idea didn't seem at all stupid and by no means all reviewers were hostile: 'It is all set down with the most tremendous gusto and above all with a sort of geniality that for the most part has entirely vanished from the contemporary novel. All the essential Priestley ingredients are there – the humour certainly'. The book included 'some of the funniest scenes I have ever imagined', Jack wrote, and so they are, and full of all varieties of English characters, some of whom, especially pompous males, come in for a good deal of knockabout fun. The *Times Literary Supplement* noted that 'his keen dramatic sense supplies unexpected climaxes, and illuminates backstage scenes – some of the best in the book'. And society, that other character in so many of Jack's novels, is there in all his gentle and affectionate satirizing of the English. And there are Jack's touches of poetry – the loveliness of the English countryside in summer, and, as so often with Jack, a sense of the underlying shadow and seriousness beneath all the fun and games, a feeling of the open-ended mystery of life, of something else just around the corner.

Around this time Peter Davison, the young son of Jack's old friends Edward and Natalie, came to stay, and became, on his own merits, not simply on those of his father, a lifelong friend. Peter is a poet and writer, and years later set down some interesting observations about Jack:

> There was an enormous distance between Priestley's image and his self, between his Persona and his Anima, as there was I discovered later with Robert Frost. Both men seemed simpler on the surface than they were within. Frost was witty while Priestly was comic. Priestley was unwary, ever reckless about showing anger. Like Frost he believed, and practised his belief, that language could be kept simple and translucent without betraying the depths beneath it, but he chose to scatter himself broadly, out of a prose writer's impatience. . . . Both Frost and Priestley have been much misunderstood, and both have given cause for misunderstanding. Once I brought them together, the only time the two men met. They misunderstood each other to the bone. Priestley said, 'What a sweet old man.' Frost said, 'I was glad to meet your friend the Socialist.'

Jack had trouble with his temper at this period, though, remembering his father, he tried hard to keep it under control. But he and Jane seemed continually to rub each other up the wrong way, and to bring out the worst in each other. Jack was gloomy, grumbling even more than usual, and generally ill-tempered; Jane was unreasonable, emotional, resentful, taking to her bed with psychosomatic illnesses. There were times when they simply could not speak to each other. Jack found help from his readings of Ouspensky, and particularly from Dr Maurice Nicholls's massive commentaries, with their emphasis upon 'self-remembering', that is pausing to remember your true and fundamental Self, and his advice not to identify yourself with those other false and undesirable selves, the self-pitying self, the misunderstood and unappreciated self, the vain self, and the angry self. Jack wrote to Jacquetta:

> Re-reading Ouspensky expounding Gurdjieff, some interesting stuff about personality (almost the persona) and essence; and it occurred to me right from the first, while our personalities were

almost antagonistic, our essences felt the rightness of one another. With Jane, I think, it was the opposite, as I think it probably is with you and Christopher. Your personalities fit in all right – similar background, interests, friends etc. – but your essences are all wrong. But perhaps this is all too easy. Some fascinating stuff, mixed with nonsense, in the Gurdjieff/Ouspensky theories. . . .

Analysis is one thing, but love is another; Jack concluded by describing Jacquetta as:

a fascinating creature who still looks (and always will, I believe) like a high priestess from some strange race, but is also the sweetest, kindest and most companionable being on earth – what an astonishing mixture! And what do you get – merely a fat man from Yorkshire – though, of course perhaps among members of that strange race there have always been wonderful legends about fat men from Yorkshire – and you have been sent on a mission to enthral one of them.

It was in this difficult period that Jack also produced his 'grumbler's apology' for his family, that enchanting little book, *Delight*, where all his little pleasures and happiness seemed so healingly far away from his present turmoil.

As well as reading Ouspensky and Maurice Nicholls, Jack wrote to Jacquetta that he found himself wanting to read and think about Jung again, this time with certain reservations:

This all-knowingly, highly selective Unconscious worries me. How can an Unconscious without an ego carefully appraise an elaborate situation, select the right symbols etc., etc.? This is God – or one of His lieutenants – and not the primordial rudimentary mind. It is the Jungians, in their analyses, rather than Jung himself, that worry me here. Last night I re-read that analysis of me based on *Rain Upon Godshill*. It seemed to me rather better than it seemed the first time, probably because I began last night by accepting its faults. You might probably agree with its conclusion that I am kind, generous, gifted etc. etc., but over-extroverted, demanding from the outside world something it can't give and so on, and probably with Shadow and Anima trouble. . . . 'Even', it says, 'on his Shadow side he remains honest and candid, and there were few people of whom so much could be said' and my Shadow 'is neither repulsive nor evil but not unlike one of those genies or spirits in the fairy tales which accompany the wanderers in secret'.

Not too bad, Jack concluded, and so would I, though I probably have more knowledge of Jack than I have of Jung.

Jung was certainly in Jack's mind when he conceived a new and doubly exciting idea. With the success of *A Land* he thought that he and Jacquetta might collaborate on an experimental play. While in New York in the autumn of 1951 he had seen a performance of Shaw's *Don Juan in Hell* produced by Charles Laughton. There were none of the normal dramatic aids to performance, no scenery, no stage lighting, no costumes, no make-up, and the actors – in evening dress – read their parts. Against all Jack's expectations it seemed to succeed; it was something fresh and original that captured the imagination of the audience. Jack immediately wanted Charles Laughton to produce something similar for him. Jacquetta had been lecturing in the United States, and when she came to join Jack in New York the idea for *Dragon's Mouth* was born.

The play was conceived as a dramatic quartet with four characters representing Jung's four functions of sensation and intellect (written by Jacquetta), and intuition and emotion (written by Jack). Two men and two women are cruising in the West Indies on a luxury yacht, belonging to Matthew (the bass voice), a successful, thrusting and ambitious businessman who is married, perhaps a little surprisingly, to Nina (the soprano), about whom all we know at first is that she is 'quite a figure in the world of wealth and fashion'. Harriet (the contralto) is employed as a personnel manager in one of Matthew's companies, and Stuart (the tenor) is an academic, a man of letters, and an old friend and admirer of Nina's. We don't actually hear any music in the play, but there are musical references. The yacht is anchored in a cove surrounded and sheltered by great rocks. 'They look', says Stuart, 'like a jaw full of ragged teeth with one sharp fang among them'; hence the name of the cove is 'Dragon's Mouth', suggesting no doubt 'the jaws of death' or, as Nina observes, 'the mouth of hell – and we are the souls awaiting judgement'. A deathly plague has hit the crew: one has died, and two more are sick. A port doctor from Port of Spain has been out in a motor launch to take off the sick, and to take blood samples from the four main characters. Now they await the results – infection means certain death.

Jack was responsible for the planning, the stage directions and the

Jack and Jacquetta with the cast of *Dragon's Mouth*, 1952, including their close friends Dulcie Gray (left) and Michael Denison (third from the right, behind Jacquetta), together with Rosamund John and Norman Wooland (Cheales Adams (Photographers) Ltd)

linking passages, and he and Jacquetta each wrote the parts for one man and one woman. By now they were so much together in their thinking that people at first found it quite hard to decide which of them wrote which two characters. Jack, with his novelist's ability to create characters, wrote the parts of Matthew and Harriet, and Jacquetta took those of Stuart and Nina, the two sides of herself, the academic, detached and scientific man, and the very feminine woman happily enjoying the pleasures and the beauties of the world. There are no props, only a length of white rope that could suggest part of the rail of a ship. The characters gather on deck, staring out at the sea. They discuss their situation and their prospects, they consider their lives, their views of themselves and their approach to life; and perhaps not surprisingly each thinks their approach the best, and so very cleverly, and in compelling and often beautiful prose, they argue with each other. When Stuart, the detached 'man is nothing but' kind of person maintains that he is the one who, with no illusions about God or life after death, enjoys and savours 'whatever it is possible for a man of taste to enjoy, while keeping his intelligence free and critical, giving no blank cheques to self-deception', Nina replies and then sums them all up:

I'm not sure you have much of a self to enjoy. It's chiefly your own cleverness you enjoy, and I suspect that becomes very dusty after a time. I believe that of the four of us, I'm the only one who who can really be happy. Harriet is too conscientious, emotional, self-sacrificing. Stuart is too intellectual and finicky, Matthew is too ambitious, too busy, always desperately arranging to arrive somewhere quite different, where life will really begin. And happiness is in the moment, the actual living present, nowhere else, and I know how to find it there – that's what always attracted you, isn't it, Matthew darling?

Matthew agrees: 'A man like me needs a woman like Nina to complete him . . . why, I've seen a few roses turn Nina into a lighthouse. And to me that's wonderful, that's magic.' He goes on to assert in the face of his friends' disbelief: 'Yes, I'm a kind of poet, and what I've always wanted is magic.' They continue with a good deal of man/woman repartee until their fascinating conversation is cut short by a booming, frightening sound. 'That', says Matthew, 'means that a message is coming through', and he goes below. There is a moment of darkness before the second part. The message is that one of the four is infected and a motorboat is coming to take away the one doomed to die, but before they can be told who it is, the radio breaks down.

The imminence of death, as Dr Johnson observed, 'concentrates the mind wonderfully'. The talk changes. 'The Moment of Truth,' says Stuart, 'that wounded bull the Ego sinks to the reddened sand, and self-knowledge, coming from God knows where, prepares to lean upon its thin bright blade.' Slowly the characters expose themselves, stripped of all pretence, all postures – Matthew, Stuart and Harriet declare in one way or another that they are the ones who should die. Nina, on the other hand, says only that she who lives so much through her senses, who has so joyfully accepted life, will now accept death: 'Perhaps because I have so much desire for shapeliness, for perfection of form, I want to cut short my life before it blurs – to die while I am still in possession of the rose. . . .' It is Nina who draws the characters together, sets them in context and in balance. She speaks for both Jung and Jacquetta. Her speech is profoundly autobiographical: 'I have grown fat on experience, my senses have gone out and in like bees bringing home nectar. I have joined myself with the whole world, sharing its darkness as well as its light. . . . Matthew said there must be conflict: I would go so far as to glory in the clash of opposites.' Here she is expressing the Jungian belief that it is only the acceptance and reconciliation of opposites that can produce the truly integrated self; and that is what Nina, I believe, represents. 'You know I am Nina,' Jacquetta said to Dulcie Gray when she undertook the part. 'Yes,' said Dulcie gently, 'but every actress has to be free to make her own interpretation'; Jacquetta naturally agreed.

The four characters recognize that their differences are contained in a unity: 'at the four points of the compass', says Harriet, 'we embrace the globe of human personality'. 'Each one of us can discover the other there in nucleus. It is a trust,' says Matthew. As they hear the sound of the returning motorboat getting louder and louder they decide to go to meet it together, and that is the end: we never know which is the one to die.

It proved impossible to find a theatre to stage the play in New York, and so Jack decided to produce the play himself in England. He turned to his old friends Michael Denison and Dulcie Gray. They were both excited by the play. Michael would play Stuart and Dulcie the perhaps more challenging part of Nina. Norman Wooland and Rosamund John were soon lined up for the other two parts. Rehearsals were not without incident. Michael Denison remembers rehearsing in the brown gloom of St Pancras Town Hall when the rehearsal was not going well. A frail old man suddenly appeared among them. 'Excuse me,' he said, 'but is this where you get death certificates?' Rosamund John redirected him, and Jack chuckled delightedly. 'You know,' he said, 'I invented him.'

Dragon's Mouth went on tour and then ran for seven weeks in London. Criticism, as might have been expected, was mixed, but some was appreciative and understanding and there was universal praise for Dulcie Gray's Nina. Even the unsympathetic Kenneth Tynan admitted that the play contained 'several flights of the best rhetorical prose' that he had ever heard on stage. I find the play both interesting and gripping; I would have thought that it would work excellently as a radio play.

Apart from the pleasure of creation, their collaboration provided Jack and Jacquetta with an excuse to meet openly. At one point, when Jane was away, Jacquetta went to stay for a night or two at Brooke Hill. Jane was often away now; it was better for her and Jack to be apart. After this happy interlude Jack wrote to Jacquetta: 'It gave you at least a glimpse of the kind of atmosphere in which I have to spend much time, but on the other hand the queer nervous strain did mean that I was always rather preoccupied, but I felt you understood that . . . this sharing of experience is very valuable, and it is a weakness of clandestine relationships that they have so little of it.' He concluded more happily: 'I know two people who have pretended to be tough characters. . . . He is a fat, conceited chump, bumptious and aggressive and tactless, though now and again he does something thoughtful and charming. I mean in relation to her. She is extraordinary, at once exquisite and delicate and yet earthy and fruity, a lovely ardent woman who is at the same time a rich character.'

Episodes like this could, however, be unsettling. 'I don't want any more domestic ties,' wrote Jack, 'but the fact remains that I miss you, just as you probably do me, and its damned silly we have to be away from each other when we might both be quietly working down here, and walking and talking our heads off as well.' And a little later he would write: 'Darling, soon I must bring you into my life more, or turn some of you out of my heart and mind. This present balance doesn't suit me, though God knows I couldn't offer myself with confidence as a house partner.'

SEVENTEEN

DIVORCE AND MARRIAGE

In 1951 Nicolas went to boarding-school. Jacquetta did not want him to be put through the conventional strait-jacket of Winchester. She and Christopher discussed their son's education at length; unlike his father, Nicolas would not be in college with the scholars, and this, for Christopher, made a difference. In the end, they selected the more relaxed, mildly progressive, but still academic atmosphere of Bryanston School. Nicolas arrived at the school, just as Tom Priestley, now aged eighteen, left it.

Tom was to go straight off to do his national service, and then on to Cambridge. Jane took him for a walk, and told him that she was now thinking seriously of divorcing Jack. But she still hesitated. It was hard to disentangle two lives that had been meshed together for twenty-five years. And while Jack may sometimes have been difficult, he was a natural life-enhancer, a man it was easy to love. It was 1952 before she took the decisive step, and finally asked Jack for a divorce; she wanted to marry David Bannerman, an old friend and admirer, and a distinguished ornithologist. Jane bought herself a house in Scotland and prepared to move. Through all the upheavals Miss Pudduck and Gertrude quietly and efficiently kept Brooke Hill going.

Just before the first performance of *Dragon's Mouth* Jack had invited the Denisons to Brooke for a weekend; he wanted them to see more of Jacquetta. Before they all left London he told them: 'I've just heard that my wife has left me for a bird man. I told Jane she could take any furniture that she wanted, but she won't have done it yet.' However, Jane had wasted no time, and when they arrived they walked into an apparently empty house. Jack immediately took over, and, as Michael said, 'never in our experience had his gifts of hospitality been more hilariously displayed . . . the high spot of the evening was Jack accompanying the pianola as a dancing cellist without a cello'.

Jack and Jacquetta had found their collaboration on *Dragon's Mouth* so successful and creative, that they embarked together on a new play, *The White Countess*. Jack had been asked to do a three-week lecture tour of Japan in the autumn of 1952. They decided they would go together, complete work on the *Countess*, and return via the United States to explore possibilities for an American production for both plays. Nothing came of this, and nobody ever liked *The White Countess*. Maybe this expedition was a little reckless, as they had not finally decided what to do with their joint lives, and Jacquetta had said nothing to Christopher about the possibility of a divorce.

Christopher was upset about this latest development, although, since his move to Oxford, he had become increasingly aware of the

Jack and Jacquetta at a rehearsal of *The White Countess* in 1953 (photograph by Erich Auerbach; *Illustrated*)

failure of his marriage, and was also aware of Jacquetta's relations with Jack. A legal end to the marriage must have seemed inevitable. Christopher's father was a senior lawyer, and a registrar for divorce and probate. He was a sympathetic advisor to his son over this difficult period. It was he who told Christopher that, as a precautionary measure, he should get a letter from Jack setting out the purpose of this trip to Japan, and the reasons for Jacquetta accompanying him. The divorce laws were still a miasma of absurdity and hypocrisy, and if it were to appear that Christopher had in any way condoned his wife's adultery then the divorce would not be allowed. Adultery had to be proved, but without 'collusion, connivance or condonation'. Since it was generally accepted that the woman's name must be protected, the man, innocent or not, was often expected to submit to a faked adultery – a night in a hotel in Brighton was a common solution. Of course, nine times out of ten there was collusion, connivance, etc., but to this the judges of the day appeared to turn a blind eye. So Christopher wrote to Jack to ask for a letter as to the purpose of the Japanese visit, in order, he said, 'to have something to show his family'. Jack was extremely reluctant to write any such letter, but he was put on the spot. If he refused to write, that might look like a confession of guilt, and since there was as yet no talk of a divorce between Jacquetta and Christopher, he could hardly announce that he was taking his mistress with him. Although it was possible to produce a professional reason for Jacquetta to accompany him – their collaboration in two plays, their work together in UNESCO – Jack was intensely reluctant and unhappy at the prospect of writing something that was essentially untrue, or at least, to a high degree, 'economical with the truth'. But Christopher was very insistent, and, though Jacquetta did not understand the reason for this insistence, in the end she said, 'Surely it can't do any harm, since they seem to want it so much.' So Jack reluctantly wrote something: not a lie, not a fabrication, but not the whole truth.

Jacquetta returned from Japan bringing, perhaps a little guiltily, some rather special Christmas presents for Christopher, a Persian rug and two Japanese prints by Hokusai. But with Jane about to divorce Jack, it seemed absurd to go on with their present unsatisfactory arrangements, and on Boxing Day she found herself, almost without premeditation, asking Christopher for a divorce so that she could marry Jack. Now that the moment had arrived, Christopher was very upset, but, as Jacquetta wrote to Edward Davison, 'He was very sweet about it, most of the agonies having been assimilated . . . when I went to Japan.' In the emotion of this final break she found that it was she who felt 'most horribly sad, and kept weeping'.

So now the dreary preparations for divorce began – lawyers, accountants, money, furniture, all the practical unhappiness and worries. 'I wonder you don't go abroad,' Jack's accountant said sympathetically. Since Jack was so well known he preferred to go abroad for a night of faked and collusive adultery, so he made arrangements with the Hotel Scribe in Paris. Jacquetta did not wish to put Christopher, always a faithful husband, through the usual absurd farce. She, an independent modern woman, was the 'guilty party'; she would accept the blame and would be the co-respondent. This was honest; the dishonesty and hypocrisy of the law turned it into what Jacquetta saw as 'a dangerous folly'. She reproached herself for the element of pride in her decision. Perhaps, too, there was the lure of a night in Paris with Jack.

Farce pursued them to the end. When lawyers went to the Scribe for evidence the manager refused to supply it, declaring that 'the English Monsieur must have his pleasure'. However, the lawyers managed to cook up something sufficiently convincing for a judge.

The divorce took place on 6 June 1953, and Jack's letter to Christopher was duly produced in court. There is no doubt that Christopher, at this period, was under a great deal of pressure from his parents, in particular from his mother, who had, of course, never liked Jacquetta. He was devoted to his father, and would certainly have wished to follow his advice. Whatever lay behind the final decision to produce the letter in court, Christopher would have been acting on legal advice. It was on the basis of this letter that the judge proceeded to attack Priestley as 'a writer of fiction', asserting that he had written the letter 'in a deliberate and cunning attempt to deceive Professor Hawkes as to his conduct'. 'I think Mr Priestley mean and contemptible,' he said. Judges are there to expound the law, not to pronounce ill-founded moral judgements, especially as the unfortunate recipient has no remedy; one can hardly sue a judge for slander. With such well-known figures, the judge's remarks were splashed all over the newspapers, and did Jack considerable personal harm. Divorce in those days was a stigma, whether you were the guilty or the innocent party. Christopher's lawyers had advised him to sue Jack for heavy damages, but Christopher refused to have anything to do with such a proposition. Jack was a rich man, and he had already made a generous financial arrangement with Jane. In fact, since David Bannerman had very little money, Jack supported both of them to the end of their days.

Immediately following the case, and while waiting on Paddington station for his train back to Oxford, Christopher wrote to Nicolas:

> All went smoothly and without fuss except that, at the end, the Judge made a little speech saying how 'mean and contemptible' (I just quote his words) he thought Jack's conduct had been. I do regret this, especially as it will be reported in the papers, and will give pain to Mummy. I hope you will be able to see this thing, now as before, in fair perspective. The Court has given justice, but the real Judge of human conduct is a higher authority than we can know.

Neither Christopher nor his father had realized the amount of damage Jack's letter to Christopher was to cause, and Christopher was deeply upset by the whole episode. He had had no intention of damaging either Jacquetta or Jack. His biographer, Diana Webster, writes:

> He destroyed the letter shortly after the divorce, feeling a mixture of anger and remorse. . . . His way of dealing with emotional problems was to dig the biggest hole he could, shovel in as much heavy material as he could lay his hands on, and build an impregnable fortress on the top of it. In some respects this was a product of his upbringing; but it was also his only defence against any assault on his surprisingly delicate, emotional nature. . . . I know that he was deeply ashamed of the hurt this action caused, but what was left of his pride refused to let him admit it.

Immediately following the divorce and its attendant publicity, Jacquetta's anxiety also was for Nicolas, away at school. She wrote to him immediately: 'I am afraid the case went as horribly as it could on Friday. I do hope you won't have been made to suffer for it in any way. The judge took it upon himself to say things about Jack which were absolutely unjust.' In a second letter she wrote again: 'I hope you have had no serious repercussions from the beastly divorce publicity. . . . Several legal people have written to Jack saying how scandalous the Judge's behaviour was, but of course, that doesn't help with the public — please let me know about this, because I've been much worried for you and have heard nothing.'

Nicolas, the innocent sixteen-year-old and an only child was more vulnerable than the Priestley children, and he did suffer, especially as a school fellow, with the cruelty that some children delight to inflict on each other, had drawn his attention to a newspaper report, and had made various unpleasant observations. Jacquetta wrote again:

> I am very sorry if you felt anything was kept from you, I had no intention of it . . . as far as what the judge said about Jack I can assure you it was absolutely unjust. It is too long and complicated a business to explain on paper, but I will if you like when we meet. I am glad to say we have neither of us had any critical letters, while Jack has had a good many sympathetic ones. Also another legal chap has written to a law journal to protest at the judge's action of blackguarding someone who could not make any defence. Still, it's no good going on like this I know; I only hope that you'll be tolerant. Wisdom is very hard to come by.

'Fair perspective', 'tolerance' and 'wisdom' seem rather a lot to expect or hope from a vulnerable sixteen-year-old.

Jack and Jacquetta were married in July, and Jane married her ornithologist. Jack happened to meet Jane's sister, who told him that

Jack and Jacquetta at their wedding in July 1953

Jane appeared 'happier than she had seemed since she was eighteen, and that old Bannerman orders her about and she apparently likes it'. Jack and Jacquetta returned to live at Brooke Hill, where Miss Pudduck and Gertrude were relieved to find that Jacquetta had no wish to make any changes and the household continued to run as smoothly and happily as ever. Miss Pudduck and Gertrude had great loyalty to both their employers, but Jane explained that her new establishment would be much smaller and more modest than Brooke Hill, and so they decided that they would stay and continue to look after Jack.

Marriage for Jacquetta was, I think, a true liberation, a commitment to love with the whole of her life and being. For Jack it must have been peace: not simply a release from argument, turmoil and trouble, but the lasting peace of heart and mind that is regenerative and creative. And contrary to a few dire warnings, Jacquetta says that she could not have found a companion sweeter and easier to live with than Jack, and he would have said the same about her.

Some six years later John and I were spending a weekend at Brooke Hill with the Priestleys when Jacquetta got a letter from Christopher announcing that he was about to marry Sonia Chadwick, a fellow archaeologist. I recall the depths of feeling with which Jacquetta said: 'Oh, I do *so* hope that he will be happy.' And so, for thirty-three years, he was. Just before his marriage Christopher had written to his bride-to-be:

the fact is, I really have no very marked emotions about the Priestleys, who seem to me people in another world, so that I seldom remember that they exist, and when I do I don't bother anyway. I think one can say quite objectively Jacquetta's would have been a hard case − and mine perhaps still harder − if she hadn't behaved as she did . . . and looking back − as I never do usually − on my grief when it all broke up, it seems to me just a matter of fate, and 'a case' more than a moral outrage, because she remained a charming and affectionate and natural mother to Nick all through, so that he is a perfect chap altogether, and we have all been entirely cheerful for so long now, that as I say, I never worry my head about it at all, we almost never meet, nor need to. Naturally, Nick's affection was a wonderful help and, naturally, the friends who helped by their affection included women as well as men. . . . I'm awfully grateful: and to archaeology I've been grateful ever since I took it up as a boy;

because it's such an endlessly gay and exciting subject, so many of my friends are in it, and it always seems to provide the stuff of life so happily. No, honestly, I've no grudge or grievances against life at all . . . and I don't carry any burden of inner woe. . . . I like gay things and amusing things and interesting things and strenuous things and beautiful things. . . .

So the cosmic dramatist unveiled his final act. To all four players in this small personal drama, he gave four truly happy endings.

EIGHTEEN

CREATIVE HAPPINESS

'Happiness', wrote Jack, 'cannot be adequately described, that is why we read so little about it, while the dark wastes that lie around it are strewn with millions of words.'

Jack is writing of first love, of his two young lovers, *They* who *Walk in the City* (1936), and he does so in a prose poem invoking the imagery of spring, the enchantments of art, the magic of Christmas . . . and he adds: 'You will not understand the happiness of these two unless you remember your own, and set it glowing behind the pages, turning the poor dim picture into a glorious transparency.'

It is the poets, the dramatists, the composers of music and opera who show us the heights and the depths of human love, the ecstasy and the agony, but rarely the sunlit plains of happiness in between. Fairy stories, and love stories that are not tragic, end with the hero and heroine living 'happily ever after'. And perhaps, since among other things, this is a love story, that is where I too should have ended. Yet I still want to celebrate our friends, and the years of our friendship. Jack and Jacquetta were generous with their happiness, they shared it around, theirs was no '*egoisme à deux*', and John and I were fortunate to share in their happiness, and so to enrich our own.

Jacquetta soon gave us a copy of her follow-up to *A Land*. *Man on Earth* had been published in 1954, and she had dedicated it to Jack. It is a mighty book, fascinating and erudite, and in it Jacquetta takes up her theme of the development of human consciousness. She stresses again her knowledge of the unity of all life, and of our own inescapable unity with those first tiny, struggling, unrecognizable creatures of mud and slime. Jacquetta's childhood sense of identification with nature, her 'participation mystique', may well have been an intuition of the truth that she was later to discover intellectually through her studies. Although she accepts that the development of life, with its abundance of species, has taken place as the biologists and geologists have discovered, she parts company with their conclusions. She cannot accept that we and our development are simply the result of random selection, a series of cosmic accidents. Jacquetta repeats her disagreement and her beliefs: 'That natural selection alone produced the mechanism for writing *Hamlet* and the last quartets [of Beethoven], I find myself unable to believe. . . . I simply cannot explain our beautiful, surpassingly various and supremely imaginative world by the orthodox tenets of evolution. . . . There is, I believe, an all-pervading and transcendent significance in human evolution, which we now know enough of the past to comprehend.'

It is the mechanism that we now comprehend, and though I fully share all Jacquetta says, I feel that there remains a question mark over those words produced by human consciousness, 'purpose', 'significance' and 'transcendence'. And if we say, as she does, that the purpose of evolution is the development of human consciousness, we are still left with the question, and with the mystery of ourselves and our species.

Jacquetta uses words carefully. For her 'transcendent' does not mean the religious conception of a creator outside and beyond our comprehension. We are not, and should not pretend to be, moving towards a kingdom of heaven on earth or beyond it. The kingdom of heaven is here within us, it is in all that Jacquetta understands by human consciousness, the heightening of which is the whole duty of man on earth.

With skill and artistry, Jacquetta traces the long, slow evolution of conscious man. She has fascinating things to say about the development and structure of the human brain, and the connection

In her writing, Jacquetta, here photographed by Mark Gerson in the 1970s, explores the 'distinctive flavour, colour and form' of different cultures

between the 'Old Brain', the thalamus, and the 'New Brain', the cerebrum, that slowly grew from it. The thalamus is the intermediary between the unconscious life of the body and the cerebrum 'the prime seat of consciousness'. Little known in the world, hidden out of sight below the enveloping folds of the cerebrum, the thalamus has yet been recognized as 'the power behind the throne of human nature'; it is the source of emotion, love and imagination. The thalamus is feminine in its nature, in contrast with the later and essentially masculine nature of the cerebrum, the head opposed to the heart. It is the interplay between these two areas of the human brain, 'one so much more ancient than humanity, the other in its full development as young as our species, that produces what is best in a rich, creative life'. Jacquetta continues: 'While one honours the intellectual achievement of our species, it is the works of imagination and feeling that give cultures their distinctive flavour, colour and form, their power to delight and inspire. It is through them that a people is mainly remembered and judged.'

Jacquetta the prehistorian observes that mankind's earliest religious symbols that we know of, first that of the Great Mother Goddess, and then that of her dying and resurrected son, to be followed much later by the Apollonian sky gods – the full light of consciousness – may well indicate that 'We have expressed in these worldwide religious symbols an image of living forms that the evolution of consciousness has built up in our brains.' Jacquetta points to another connection, when she explains that 'the world that man was to inherit, the life that was to be the matrix for his own, and the stuff of much of his religion and art were already present on earth seventy-five million years before man himself appeared to recognize and claim them. The properties of mind and imagination were being assembled, but as yet there was no consciousness to give them the reality of a name.' Since I believe that the creation myth of Genesis tells us not of a fall, but of the advent of human consciousness, this recalls to me that Adam's first task was the naming of all living creatures. The eating of the famous, or infamous, apple, that moment of true self-consciousness, brings about our endlessly painful knowledge of good and evil, and hence the experience of guilt. Adam and Eve recognized themselves, and 'knew that they were naked'.

Jacquetta is a humanist, so for her there is no absolute morality, because most of it is and should be transitory. 'Any ultimate morality must evidently relate only to the supreme values,' and these are to be found in our art, our mystical experience, and in all the fields of pure thought which she sometimes calls 'intellectual love'. 'These developments', she writes, 'are limited to a few among millions, but all true experience, all active beings have their value, and help too to nourish and support the creative power of the most gifted.'

After taking us through the rise and fall of civilizations, Jacquetta's final chapter of *Man on Earth* is 'A Myth for the Future'. With much that she deplores I am in agreement, and many of the destructive trends that she identifies seem to get worse:

> If we feel confident of anything in the modern world which has grown out of the Renaissance, it is that we have gone astray. . . . Even the artists have shown our loss of confidence by becoming unable to portray men in their full humanity. Afraid to claim the qualities of spirit, mind and heart which their predecessors showed in terms of Christian humility [man made in the image of God?] or humanist pride, they have escaped into non-committal abstract forms.

Jacquetta concludes:

> I am confident in the goodness of existence, and the need for it to go on. Our individual lives are of their very nature tragic, yet mind and senses together have grown up out of the darkness to equip us for delight. To be stretched between these two poles is the best exercise of the psyche. For the rest we can but look our ignorance in the face, for it is one of our few certainties. No religion, no philosophical or scientific system claiming any absolute and exclusive knowledge of truth is proper to our condition as inmates of one speck in a universe the vastness and wonder of which even our trifling minds are beginning faintly to apprehend.
>
> It is because I accept our inevitable ignorance and the room within it for every kind of experience that I have dared to attempt this book, setting down my vision of our lot, and affirming my faith in human life – and my love of it.

Since I am not writing biographies of Jack and Jacquetta, only a personal memoir, I am selective in their lives and in their writing; there are many more works I would have liked to discuss had space permitted. I have spent time on *Man on Earth* because it raises so much that interests and excites me, and because it so well illustrates Jacquetta's thinking and temperament.

By 1959 the Priestleys had moved to Kissing Tree House at Alveston, just outside Stratford-on-Avon. This fine eighteenth-century house, white and harmonious, is surrounded by green space, stretches of lawn and field, with belts of trees to shield it from the roads that run down the east side and along the southern boundary. It is a far cry from the wild and spectacular beauties of Brooke Hill. Here all is calm and restful; to the south of the lawn is a wide green field, sometimes full of grazing cattle, to the west more fields, one of which Jack lent to the village as its cricket ground, and beyond it the village church – an English idyll in what must be the centre and heart of England. John and I spent many happy and sunlit weekends at Kissing Tree House, and we did still manage to bring the 'Collins weather' with us.

Inside the house all is light and spacious; a long marble-floored and elegant passage runs the whole length of it from the front door to the south door that opens on to the garden. All the main rooms on one side or the other open off the passage. Jack's study is at the far end, with its large windows facing south and west; he got the best views, the sun and the sunset. Jacquetta said she didn't mind about views, and preferred a smaller more shut-in room in which to work. This was conveniently located upstairs off her bedroom. When you read numbers of books by these two, you can't help beginning to think in symbols: Jack, the large open-hearted extrovert in his sunlit study, and Jacquetta, the reserved introvert, hidden away in her little north-facing room. Perhaps, really, she just wanted Jack to have the best room and the best view; he was certainly a man who needed space.

The Priestleys were very happy at Kissing Tree House; Jack loved it. It had been Jacquetta's choice. 'If it suits you, it suits me', said Jack. So much of the arrangement and decoration reflected Jacquetta, but there was plenty of Jack around as well – his possessions, his huge library of books, his pictures, his piano, his billiard table; it was a happy blend of them both. They still came fairly regularly to London, particularly to Albany, and they travelled abroad for work and for pleasure. Otherwise, during the week at Kissing Tree House, work went steadily on, and the household, in the expert hands of Miss Pudduck and Gertrude, ran along as easily and comfortably as it had always done. Jack continued to produce novels and plays as well as personal essays for the *New Statesman* on all kinds of topics as his fancy took him. Jacquetta wrote articles and reviews for learned archaeological journals, as well as her own personal books.

Jack, never one to spare himself, was soon engaged on a gigantic enterprise, nothing less than a magisterial survey of the literature of western man from the fifteenth century to the present – 'western' interpreted not just geographically, but culturally to include Russia and America as well as England and Europe. 'A young man couldn't write it, because he wouldn't have the necessary reading; and an elderly man, who might have the reading, would have more sense than to attempt such a book.' So wrote Jack, now in his early sixties, and about to put sense aside. Just as he couldn't stop writing, so he couldn't stop thinking, continually exploring and reflecting upon the mysteries of human existence. 'What really tempted me, so that I fell,' he wrote, 'was my conviction that ours is an age of supreme crisis, when the most desperate decisions have to be made, and that some account of western man, in terms of the literature he has created and enjoyed, might help us to understand ourselves (and doing the work has certainly helped *me*), and to realise where we are and how we have arrived here.' So began another stage in Jack's lifelong search for wisdom and for truth.

Literature and Western Man is not primarily a work of scholarship, nor a literary history, it is a personal book, the result of nearly half a century of reading and thinking based upon Jack's own reading of ten thousand or so books, and written with a background of history,

Kissing Tree House, Alveston, which became the Priestley residence in 1959

philosophy and psychology as well as his own creative experience. It is the personal emphasis that makes this weighty book so consistently readable and alive, and with his knowledge and intuitive perceptions he has fresh and illuminating things to say about the seven hundred or so authors whom he selects – it has to be his own selection, because, as he says, 'I am the Western Man I know best.' Somehow he manages to maintain the impetus, the zest and the interest throughout; there is never any feeling of satiety, never a hint of dullness – one thing Jack could never be was dull.

A French writer has told us that if we can discover what a writer's favourite word is, the word he cannot help using over and over again, it will give us the essential clue to his personality. One word is hardly enough for such a prolific and varied writer, such a many-sided personality, as Jack, but there are words in his work that stand out and recur. First must come 'magic' and its handmaid 'enchantment'. Critically important too are 'breadth' and 'balance', and we might also add 'irony'. These are what Jack found in the authors he liked best, and these are what he sought to express in his own work.

Literature and Western Man is in five parts, each with its own poetic title. The first part is entitled 'The Golden Globe'. Here Jack looks briefly back to the Middle Ages, when there was 'a truly religious basis and framework for the life of Western Man'. Perhaps Jack is a bit over-romantic when he suggests that 'the Western mind, in both its conscious and unconscious aspects, found a home in it and was for a little time at peace with itself, related and integrated as it it has never been since. . . . For man has come down the eons a religious being, who must needs worship something, and the Gothic, its consciousness soaring with its towers and steeples, was for the West the last truly religious age.' True, in many ways true, yet is our restless species ever at peace? In this period, man failed miserably to come to terms with his sexuality, the body was evil, celibacy and virginity were the greater good: witness the tragic loves of Héloïse and Abelard Augustine, after his own years of pleasurable and extramarital indulgence, announced to the world that all sexual pleasure even within marriage was sinful; the sexual act was only to be performed for procreation, and as far as possible without pleasure. The feminine and the masculine were seriously out of balance.

The invention of printing leads us through the later fifteenth century, that age of transition, of unbalance and uncertainty, its literature divided between 'a sardonic realism and a romance that loses all contact with actuality, a split only closed by great art', but where

A shop-window display for *Literature and Western Man*, published in 1960 (John R. Freeman & Co.)

was there that great art? Then, with new inventions and new discoveries, the world was 'suddenly enlarged, was bright with the promise of new knowledge, new freedom, new opportunities. Men knew that they lived on a globe; and now, in the sunlight of this new age, it began to look like a golden globe.'

Jack turns first to the Renaissance in Italy, 'where genius drew strength from the community in which it was rooted, and the spirit of the community was leavened and raised by the genius it helped to nourish'. With his own feeling for community this was something Jack felt that he missed and needed. At first this was an age 'when an essentially Italian pagan spirit was still contained within the easy bonds of the Church, when a sense of beauty and natural piety still worked in harmony and the new humanism was modified without defying tradition'. Jack was well aware of the dark side of humanism, wild superstition, cruelty, murder and dubious morality. He spends time on an interesting discussion of Machiavelli's dissection of the dangerous politics of power.

In France the reader meets two of Jack's favourite authors. First Rabelais, 'a monk-scholar, physician, a humanist, at heart a sensible moderate who could tolerate anything except fanaticism, life-despisers, power-worship, a bogus spirituality based on narrowness

195

and pride; but he was also a humorist, in fact one of the greatest humorists of all time'. With his 'carnival display of giants, dwarfs, freaks, wild clowning and obscenity . . . [he] always returns, as all the greatest writers do, to a reasonable and balanced acceptance of continuing life; his enormous roars of laughter have only cleared the air and made it sweeter.' Jack did admit that Rabelais was 'a man's author, whose cheap cynicism about women is his weakest feature'. Quite different, but for Jack particularly attractive, was Montaigne, a fellow 'humanist under God', disliking 'pedants, intellectual bullies, bigots and fanatics . . . not irreligious but deeply sceptical about the claims of the theologians', the writer who 'created a literary form, the personal essay, that has been since used, more or less as he originally used it, by innumerable good authors not only in French but in other literatures, notably English'.

So to England, and its 'sudden dazzling height of poetic genius', and its Shakespeare:

> Words, magnificent words, wonderful words, words of power like those in some musician's incantation, were needed now to express all that must be expressed; and fortunately the language, suddenly arriving at maturity and an extraordinary richness of vocabulary (Shakespeare's is phenomenal), had such words; a man could get drunk on them, a society turn to poetry as it turned to food and drink. And this it did. Finally, perhaps because the rapid transformations of the time and the flood of energy stirred the depths of the unconscious, where all is magical, there seemed to be a strange magic pervading and illuminating the whole scene, miseries and cruelties and all, a magic that lingers to this day in an Elizabethan song, a speech by Hamlet or Cleopatra.

This is a marvellous chapter, and Jack rises to the height of his magnificent subject. He ends as Prospero and Shakespeare end: 'Be cheerful, sir, our revels now are ended.'

> That 'Be cheerful' coming before a speech that dissolves the very globe itself is wonderfully characteristic of Shakespeare. With him, though he takes us as far as human imagination can reach, we always come home: the balance is restored; life – ordinary sensible life, in which it is best to be cheerful – goes on. . . . Shakespeare was not a religious man . . . but in the broader sense – and this man needs breadth – we can justly call him religious.

This is not simply because he has the illimitable charity of the imagination, a tenderness for so much in man and Nature, an instant appreciation of whatever makes for love, affection, understanding, good-fellowship, sympathy and harmony, but because he recognises that life is a mystery, that man and Nature are symbolic representations, that we can feel if not think our way, through our sense of beauty and goodness, to a reality behind appearances. . . . This magnificent king of all our poets and dramatists might be not unjustly described as a gigantic ordinary man of goodwill, who desires, no matter how many adventures of the depths and heights his spirit undertakes, what sensible Western men, all down the years, have themselves desired. . . . Though he conjures up everything from lyrical young love and gossamer fairylands to darkest witchcraft and bloody murder, always he leads us home: 'Be cheerful, sir, our revels now are ended.'

Finally to Spain, where the reflection of the great golden globe shows us another much-loved genius, Cervantes, the creator of Don Quixote and Sancho Panza. 'The secret of Don Quixote's wide and timeless appeal is that it can be appreciated on many levels' and Jack proceeds to uncover for us layer after layer of irony.

This grave Spanish irony descends beneath the surface of boisterous humour and obvious satire like a mine-shaft, taking us to level after level, each more profound and universal than the last. We are involved in the regressive tragi-comedy of illusion and truth, appearance and reality. . . . [Cervantes] wrote the best novel in the world. . . . [He is] the magical ironist of the relativeness of reality, of truth at war with illusion. . . . Of all our great novelists he is the youngest, because he is the first, and the oldest, because his tale of the mad knight is an old man's tale. He is also the wisest.

In Part II of *Literature and Western Man* the reader is invited into 'The Order'd Garden', where Alexander Pope could write:

> Nature and Nature's laws lay hid in night.
> God said 'Let Newton be', and all was light.

This was the age when consciousness and the intellect were in the ascendant. God was still there, but says Jack, 'inspiring and directing scientific enquiry like the all-powerful head of some institute of research'. Jack was by temperament a romantic, but that does not mean that his criticism was one-sided; he was an all-round man of literature, appreciating and praising talent, skill and imagination wherever he found it. He writes of 'that mutilated giant, Jonathan Swift', and of his masterpiece, *Gulliver's Travels*. 'Swift is a master of irony. But Fate is a greater master . . . a savage satire, one of the most ferocious indictments of the human race in all literature . . . is transformed into a nursery favourite.' Of Molière, Jack writes that he has 'balance, that illimitable common sense of the born satirist and comic writer' and also 'an unusual warmth'. And it should not surprise us that of the novelists, Jack's favourite is Fielding, he of 'the generous heart and the unperverted sympathetic imagination'.

We move through the Enlightenment, with the towering figures of Voltaire and Rousseau, the latter seeing further than his contemporaries and into the Romantic movement proper. Jack explains this great upsurge of the unconscious: 'a one-sided attitude if persisted in, inevitably produces its opposite equally one-sided. Too much dependence on reason inevitably produces unreason.' Pope's ordered garden could no longer be recognized; it was beginning to produce strange weeds and flowers, and 'above it the moon was rising, to create fantastic shadows in which reason was lost to romance'. Here, in Part III, 'The Shadows of the Moon', the pace quickens, and the writers and philosophers multiply. The canvas widens, and by the time we reach Part IV, 'The Broken Web', literature is all over the place. The great Russians make their appearance, to be followed by the Americans and the Scandinavians. There are too many of them all for me to begin to select. It is because of Jack's theme, the interplay between the conscious and the unconscious of western man and his loss of the symbols of religion, that Jack is able to maintain the unity and the coherence of his work. He continues to organize the immense amount of material that is increasingly at his disposal, while at the same time remaining a lucid, perceptive and illuminating critic of the authors and poets whom he selects.

It is in 'The Broken Web', that we meet Marx and Engels who, says Jack, 'succeeded where other and perhaps sounder critics failed, chiefly because they created a new myth, when a new myth was urgently needed . . . they managed, without being aware of what they were doing, to produce a substitute religious basis and framework. . . . They created the Frankenstein monster that went stumping away . . . and History, so ingenious at devising ironies, never did better than this. . . . in

Jack in the study at Kissing Tree House in the 1960s

their dream of freeing the industrial workers of Western Europe, they helped to establish a grim autocracy stretching from Warsaw to the China Sea. . . . Whatever else they intended their doctrines to accomplish, Marx and Engels have done literature more harm than good.'

The fifth part of the book has no poetic title; it is called simply 'The Moderns'. It is us; though Jack makes no reference to any writer still living. Now, in the background we meet the depth psychologists, Freud, Adler and Jung. Out of these three, Jack writes:

> Jung's thought is at once bolder and more subtle; his theory of the collective unconscious and its archetypes; his account of the four functions, thinking, feeling, sensation, intuition, and the Types that result from them; his equation of the integrating principle transforming the ego, still at the mercy of unconscious drives, into the freed Self – with religious experience: these not only bring him much closer to and in deeper sympathy with art and literature, but also turn him into one of the few great liberating thinkers of the century.

Jack also quotes from a historian of psychology who observes that each of these three great analysts was finally led 'to an experience of the spiritual core of man's being . . . each gave it a different name . . . [but] each of them referred ultimately to a contact with a larger realm of reality in which man's psychological nature transcends itself.' And so, says Jack, 'ignoring all our reports of progress', we are brought to 'the great blank face of death, and . . . the hunger of "the man of flesh and bone" for immortal life'.

Man, industrialized and urbanized, is uprooted. 'Patterns of living that have existed for thousands of years are destroyed within a generation,' and without any religious framework the helpless individual 'is at the mercy of his unconscious drives and, at the same time, is beginning to lose individuality because he is in the power of huge political and social collectives'. Literature too has become one-sided, over-introverted, 'a literature largely for specialists . . . and people in general, for whom it is really intended, find it either too "difficult" or too "neurotic" and "unhealthy".' There appears to be nothing left but sex (the only green thing in a grey world), and 'we are now piling on to sex the whole gigantic load of our increasing dissatisfactions, our despair, a burden far greater than it can safely take. . . . Religion alone can carry the load, defend us against the dehumanising collectives, restore true personality. And it is doubtful if our society can last much longer without religion'. But Jack sees no possibility of going back:

> . . . no church existing today has the power . . . to undo what has been done. . . . the symbols [of religion] no longer work, and they cannot be made to work by effort on a conscious level. The stammering helplessness of the Churches during this age of war and more war and now, the final horror, of a nuclear arms race is proof that, whatever they may do for this man or that woman, they are now among the institutions contained by our society, compelled to follow every lunatic course it takes. No matter what is willed by consciousness, that which belongs to the depths can only be restored in the depths: the *numinous* lies outside the power of the collectives. . . .

We ask what must we do to be saved? 'We must wait,' says Jack:

> We can stop disinheriting ourselves. We can avoid both the *hubris* and the secret desperation of our scientific 'wizards' . . . We can challenge the whole de-humanising, de-personalising process, under whatever name it may operate, that is . . . gradually inducing the anaesthesia that demands violence, crudely horrible effects, to feel anything at all. . . . We may need much more to establish order, justice, real community, in the outer world, and may not ourselves find the right healing symbols for the inner world, but, just as a first step, we can at least believe that Man lives, under God, in a great mystery, which is what we found the original masters of our literature, Shakespeare and Rabelais, Cervantes and Montaigne, proclaiming at the very start of this journey of Western Man. And if we openly declare what is wrong with us, what is our deepest need, then perhaps the despair and death will by degrees disappear from our modern arts. Literature, where the whole man should find himself totally and touchingly reflected, might then look both outward and inward, as it should: and so bring with it a rich new life, a life sometimes tragic, at other times careless and gay: as different and as satisfying as Shakespeare's midnight heaths, where good and evil battle in thunder-and-lightning, and his Forest of Arden, where, the West meeting the Ancient East for a moment, the young voices pipe up in an eternal spring. . . .

Literature and Western Man is, in itself, a work of art. We do not have to agree with all Jack's conclusions to see that it is also in the broadest sense a deeply religious book, full of wisdom for our bewildered and tormented age. In it we find Jack with one of his favourite quotations from Wordsworth, for the book is full of admiration, of love, and finally of hope. And as the mark of a true and creative critic, he makes us eager to read the authors he writes about, and to re-read those we already know.

I once offered *Literature and Western Man* to a widely read and intellectual friend. 'I've never felt I *had* to read Priestley,' she said, 'Well,' I replied, 'try this.' And, of course, she was enthralled, and came back glowing with praise, having revised all her second-hand opinions. Indeed, one of our sons found the book enormously helpful in passing his university entrance examination; it seems that his interviewers, too, had perhaps imagined that they 'didn't need to read Priestley'.

Jack wrote this huge book in eighteen months, and by the end he was really knocked out, physically and mentally. But being Jack, his well-spring of ideas soon began to bubble up again, and before long he was back at work. What a man! And what a truly great book! The dedication is suitably short and simple – 'For Jacquetta'.

NINETEEN

SUNLIGHT OVER ALVESTON

Weekends at Kissing Tree House assumed a pattern. John and I would arrive from London on a Friday evening. The front door opened to the friendly face of Gertrude or Miss Pudduck, and there at the far end would be the bulky figure of Jack emerging from his study, followed by Jacquetta coming downstairs. It was a warm welcome.

After unpacking, cleaning up and changing we would assemble in Jack's study for drinks. There was his grand piano, though he played it less and less, his gramophone, the television and his desk with typewriter and a large bowl full of pipes. The walls from the floor to the high ceiling were lined with books, and a secret door – secret because it too appeared to be lined with books – would open into a sizeable cupboard which housed a sink, a refrigerator, and shelves for glasses and bottles, and for Jack's large collection of records. It was beautifully convenient for the production of his exhilarating dry Martinis.

After a candle-lit dinner, and Miss Pudduck's excellent cooking, there would be coffee next door in the green and gold drawing-room. Books and books again on either side of the fireplace, and on the walls Jack's fine collection of early English watercolours. We had afternoon tea in this elegant drawing-room, but somehow it was Jack's study that seemed the focus of the house. It was there that we gravitated at the end of the evening for nightcaps, or earlier when John and I were on our own, for music or television or just talk. Usually the Priestleys entertained at the weekends with friends to stay, or with people who lived locally, writers and theatre people and others, always interesting and lively – all of them – there was plenty of good talk and amusement. Sometimes we were there with members of Jack's and Jacquetta's families.

As well as lawns and trees and a wonderful springtime display of daffodils and narcissi, there were two large walled gardens to the east and north of the house, one for fruit and vegetables, and the other with herbaceous borders round a hard tennis-court. Jacquetta looked

The entrance to Kissing Tree House (photograph by Rosalind Pulvertaft)

after the house, the garden and the rest of the property, but she wasn't interested in tennis, so she thought that Jack might do his bit by seeing that the court was kept in order, but of course he never did, and it fell into sad disrepair. My guess is that Jack was always spoiled by his women.

With two large greenhouses in addition there was an ample supply of fruit and vegetables, as well as scented and sometimes exotic flowers for the house. Jack's gardener, Hales, from the Isle of Wight, had uprooted his family, and come to take over the garden, and to live in the small lodge-house at the entrance. Yes, it was certainly 'gracious living', in a style to which, in post-war Britain, neither John nor I, nor most of our friends, were accustomed, but, of course, we loved it, as did all the Priestleys' friends, left-wing or otherwise. And that was because of the relaxed informality of it, where all was peace and harmony, an atmosphere of comfort and pleasure which was the perfect background for the steady creative work that never slackened.

Of course, the life of a professional writer is not just writing books. There are constant requests for articles, reviews, interviews for press, radio or television, invitations to speak or lecture to this or that society, or on this or that occasion, not to mention correspondence, all of which means time and work.

Jacquetta, photographed at Kissing
Tree House by J.S. Lewinski

Perhaps we should look at an interesting article, 'The Proper Study of
Mankind', that Jacquetta wrote for *Antiquity*, in which she expressed her
views on the state of archaeology. Jacquetta often likes to lead into her
subject by way of art or nature; here she starts from a Pinter film *The
Servant*, in which 'the rich and dashing master is undermined, then
diminished and finally destroyed by his servant'. She fears that owing to
the rapid increase in technology, mankind in general, and her beloved
subject archaeology in particular, may be heading in the same direction,
'the scientific servant may be usurping the throne of history'. She writes
of the understandable desire of archaeologists 'to participate in the
prestige of the natural sciences', but she points to the important
'difference between the values of archaeological and other types of
scientific fact – accepting as a premise that archaeology exists for the
service of history . . . the facts of biology, chemistry, physics are virtually
universal and unchanging . . . once they have been checked by the
experimental method they become part of an unchanging body of
knowledge that can be used again and again'. Archaeological facts
cannot be experimentally checked in the same sense; they are open to
subjective interpretation, 'relevant only to one particular fragment of
history'. 'The natural sciences', she continues, 'have triumphed through
analysis, through breaking down larger into smaller parts. Scientific

archaeologists try to emulate them. . . For those of us who believe that history is an art and therefore concerned not with breaking down but with creating larger meanings these methods need constant checking and to be kept firmly in place.'

This was Jacquetta's eloquent and repeated plea for the preservation of human values. Of course, she was not opposed to the new technical aids for dating, location, and the like; how could she be? Partly a scientist herself, she was well able to understand and use modern technology. What she deplored was 'the relative neglect of the higher human achievements . . . Art and religion receive very little of the serious attention that is available in our world of archaeology.' Jacquetta was delighted by the reaction to this article: 'It is a long time since anything I wrote was greeted with such enthusiasm. I had letters of support from all kinds of people and from many parts of the world.' Jacquetta kept well abreast of her subject. Apart from her own reading, study and reviewing, she was now the archaeological correspondent for the *Sunday Times*, which helpfully sent her off to report on important and interesting excavations. Her independent career, she felt, was a source of enrichment in her marriage and her companionship with Jack.

His output continued at its usual pace. I must proudly mention *Saturn Over the Water* (1961) because that was the novel that he dedicated to John and me. 'A sheer piece of self-indulgence', Jack called it: 'I decided to write the kind of story I love to read but that nobody writes for me. I sat down every day determined to enjoy myself. . . . I enjoyed the sheer narrative power of it, I enjoyed the parable, and enjoyed making use, however briefly, of a number of out of the way places I happen to have visited.'

Saturn Over the Water is indeed an immensely enjoyable thriller. And, of course, it is much more – a threat and a warning; in all Jack's books, as in Jack himself, there is more than meets the eye. In many ways this is a more complex and updated version of *The Doomsday Men*, for now we have nuclear weapons and the cold war. Again we have the alliance of money, science and fanaticism, this time linked to a lust for power. The threatened destruction is more subtle, too, as the 'villains' are cleverly hotting up the cold war with a view to the nuclear destruction of the northern hemisphere, after which they plan to retreat to the uncontaminated south, and build a new world order of which they will be the absolute masters. The conspiracy is foiled by the engaging hero Tim, an innocent painter, assisted by the feminine fifth column, the attractive Rosalia. It isn't quite a 'they lived happily ever after' ending, because the threat still lingers. According to *Saturn Over the Water*, mankind is moving into the age of Aquarius, whose ruling signs are Saturn and Uranus, while water represents the influential unconscious. Saturn, as power and destruction, is busily stirring the unconscious to a nuclear holocaust of hate, to prevent which Uranus, the sympathetic imagination, the artistic and feminine principle, must become the ascendant sign, and this is the task not for Tim and Rosalia alone. You have been warned!

Jacquetta was soon involved in community affairs. She became an active member of the Warwickshire branch of the Council for the Protection of Rural England, of which she later became president. She also joined the Stratford Society for the preservation and protection of the town, and of this too she was eventually elected president. In 1963 Stephen Pratt arrived to be headmaster of the King Edward VI Grammar School (Shakespeare's school). He and his wife Amy soon became friends of the Priestleys, and when a vacancy occurred on the board of governors Stephen proposed Jacquetta. There was some opposition, because of her connection with that dangerous revolutionary movement, CND! Jacquetta was nevertheless elected and proved, said Stephen, to be an invaluable and outstanding governor. In fact, Jacquetta's views on education are traditional and conservative. She was much opposed to the rush to comprehensive education, and fought hard for the preservation of K.E.G. as a grammar school. She and Jack both helped to raise money in case it were forced to become independent and self-supporting. This was in fact prevented when the Conservatives returned to office in 1979, and K.E.G. remained as a voluntary aided grammar school. The local girls' grammar school of which Jacquetta soon became a governor, also survived in the same manner. After a year or two Stephen invited Jacquetta to be the guest of honour and main speaker at the K.E.G. speech day – the first woman ever to be asked. It was a great success, and everyone was much impressed when Jacquetta quoted from a translation of an ancient Egyptian document advocating selective education.

As a little postscript to discussion of Jacquetta's public spirit I might mention something that I discovered when we were staying with them one cold winter weekend. Jack said to me: 'Jacquetta buys coal for old people in the village.' Jack and Jacquetta were also generous supporters of John's and my various causes, and when Jacquetta became a founder member of the Homosexual Law Reform Campaign, she easily persuaded John to join the committee, not exactly a help to his ecclesiastical career, but happily he never thought about that.

I have to pass by two of Jacquetta's delightful and lighthearted publications. Her book of *Fables*, which she dedicated to Nicolas, and *Providence Island*, in which a group of archaeological and anthropological academics set sail to investigate rumours of an island where an untouched race still lived as if in the Stone Age. Jacquetta writes about this island, its trees, its flowers, its coasts, rivers and mountains, and its beautiful people, as if she had left it only yesterday. It is an exciting story, too, for a group of Americans arrive determined to use this remote place for testing nuclear bombs. But these strange islanders have developed remarkable psychic powers which they use to repel these threatening invaders. There was talk of making this Garden of Eden story into a musical, but it never happened. One of our lost pleasures, alas.

It was in the early sixties that Jacquetta finished *Man and the Sun*, the book that completed her imaginative scientific and anthropological trilogy. Her first chapter is a strictly scientific account of the birth of the sun, but Jacquetta, the poet and ornithologist, does preface it with the dawn chorus and the sunrise. All people and all civilizations have worshipped the sun in one form or another, and Jacquetta takes us through their mythologies and their rituals. 'Sun Father and Earth Mother', 'Sun of Justice', 'Sun Royal', 'Sun of Life', 'Sun of Death' (the Aztecs), 'Sol Invictus', 'Sun of Salvation', 'Sun of Intellect' – the chapter headings tell the story. There have been noble sun religions, and there have been fearsome corruptions. 'The Aztecs perpetrated the most dreadful deeds ever celebrated in religion's name. Speaking from their conscious minds, the priests still proclaimed the virtue of loving-kindness, the glorious duty of maintaining the light of the world, but the dark side of the psyche that is in us all had grown, had corrupted and had taken possession. . . . They enjoyed what they did.' With reference to the present day Jacquetta comments:, 'Prometheus stole fire from the gods, the fire that has so often been kindled as a symbol of the Sun. We have stolen the secret formula of the Sun itself . . . Man's first artificial sun rose above the Pacific, but it was not a star of peace.' Jacquetta concludes with the familiar Priestley theme:

We cannot live without religious meaning, although we may well do without religious institutions. (The time may come when even those few who still follow them turn against priests who, in

Jacquetta and Sadie Wykeham, Jack's eldest grandchild, at Hidcote Manor Gardens, Gloucestershire

gem-encrusted copes and mitres, serve Him who taught poverty and humility, and love of one's enemy, by raising no murmur against a nuclear holocaust of hate.) If we cannot find God in the world, we lose him in ourselves and become contemptible in our own eyes. . . . Science is uniting man with the Sun in a totality of energy and matter. That is communion in the lowest level of being. But we have always been right to seek the highest.

Jacquetta wants a new religion with a new morality 'that cannot be of the prohibitive life-denying kind . . . but a less strenuous positive morality directed towards creative love in all its manifestations'. I am not defending institutional religion when I say that Jacquetta is by nature a religious pagan; very different from the religious atheism of our mutual friend Marghanita Laski, who incidentally shares the dedication of *Man and the Sun* with her publisher husband John Howard.

One of Jack's sadnesses was his inability to return to the theatre after the war. Although his plays continued to be successfully revived, and although he wrote a number of new ones, he made no real headway with them. However, there was one brilliant success: his collaboration with Iris Murdoch in the dramatization of her novel *A Severed Head*.

Jack had at once spotted the emergence of a major new talent with the publication of Iris's early novels, and they soon became friends. Iris went to spend a weekend with Jack and Jacquetta at Brooke Hill. She was wondering whether she would marry John Bayley, and how good it was that she did! There were many walks from the house, one along by the sea where Iris sat on the beach gazing out over the water, and Jack sat up on the cliff behind her, and painted the scene. In the evening they took the 'east walk', up through the pine woods to a piece of open ground where nightjars could be seen, turning and twisting on their long soft-feathered wings as they chased the flying insects. These birds produced a whole crop of country legends: to some they were the 'goat-suckers', able with their long, wide beaks to milk any wandering goat, while the cottagers hearing those strange churring calls of an evening gave them names from the sounds of their own daily lives – 'Spinner', 'Wheelbird' and 'Churn Owl' – and then there was Thomas Hardy to give them a poet's name:

If it be in the dusk when, like an eyelid's sudden blink
The dew-fall hawk comes crossing the shades to alight
Upon the wind-warped upland thorn, a gazer may think
To him it must have been a familiar sight.

I don't know what these three gazers thought, but Iris was so impressed that she asked the Priestleys if they would mind if she brought the nightjars into a novel. They thought this the height of literary integrity.

Iris had written a dramatization of *A Severed Head* but was not happy with it, so she took it to Jack. He read it and said: 'This won't do, Duckie!' ('Duckie' was one of his favourite endearments.) He proceeded to make a number of changes, one or two very slight – a significant pause, a significant word – but which made all the difference. There were other larger alterations in structure and dialogue on which they worked together, and Iris felt that she learned a very great deal. It was nearly a year before they found a cast and a theatre, and then the play ran with enormous success for two-and-a-half years. It was dramatic, funny and moving, and the dialogue sparkled with wit.

In the early 1960s Jack tackled that major theme that had continued to haunt him, and in 1964 a huge effort, *Man and Time*, was published. The book opens with a historical survey of what philosophers, theologians, novelists, playwrights and scientists have

Jack with Iris Murdoch, May 1963, during their collaboration on *A Severed Head* (Horst Tappe)

thought and discovered about time. A section entitled 'Examples and Speculations' follows. In a television interview Jack had invited viewers to send him their own experiences of strange coincidences, presentiments and precognitive dreams. He received a flood of answers. 'After a thousand', he said, 'I stopped counting.' He subjected these to truly scientific rigour, rejecting any that seemed in the least suspect, and was left with a considerable number of dreams and experiences that could not be explained away. The final chapter is called 'One Man and Time', that man of course being Jack. Drawing on his correspondence and on the theories of Jung, Dunne and Ouspensky, Jack states his own personal belief, 'that our lives are not contained within passing Time – we may not be immortal beings – I do not think we are – but we are better than creatures carried on that single-line track to the slaughter-house'. Jack argues that we survive into what he calls Time Two, where we become more essentially ourselves: we 'transform the one-sided ego into the broadly based and integrated Self' – in Ouspensky's terminology we discover our 'Essence'. (Could this be a little like the Roman Catholic doctrine of purgatory?) There follows Time Three, when, according to Jack, we finally dissolve into a selfless consciousness. He concludes:

> There is, of course, a purpose in all this. I am not an atheist, but I cannot agree with men who talk about God as if He had once attended a speech day at their theological college. (Far too many clerics, I fear; I have voiced similar complaints.) Whatever else this Universe might be, it is obviously very large and extremely complicated. It must therefore contain innumerable levels of being about which we know no more than a beetle does about the proceedings of the British Academy.

And our task on earth? We should know this by now: 'to bring consciousness to the life of earth, or, to quote Jung, 'to kindle a light in the darkness of mere being'.

Immediately following this huge task, Jack produced one of his finest novels, *Lost Empires*. The narrator is Richard Horncastle, a skilled watercolour painter, who mostly paints Jack's much-loved Yorkshire Dales. Before he becomes this successful painter, young Richard has spent several years on the variety stage as assistant to his uncle Nick, an expert illusionist (a deliberate allusion). With Richard and the group of artists we travel around the pre–1914 music-halls. It is a little like *The Good Companions*, but with a wonderful variety of strange, sometimes grotesque characters and much more light and shade – there are some dark shadows here, but it is a marvellous story. After many misunderstandings our hero finally gets his girl and settles down to paint and to live happily ever after. Jack was one of few serious modern authors who was not afraid of happy endings; he liked them, and was able to create them with conviction and without sentimentality.

One of the criticisms made of Jack was that he failed to create evil. Not that he wasn't painfully aware of evil, not after the First World

Jack and Jacquetta pictured in Moscow during a visit to Russia in the early 1960s

War and our increasingly horrible, cruel and violent world. He inveighed against all that produced such horrors – dictatorships, totalitarianism, megalomania, fanaticisms of all kinds, block thinking, hypocrisy, plain stupidity and the tyranny of fear. It was when it came to human beings that he had difficulties. Perhaps he had an exceptionally large amount of what he has called 'the illimitable charity of the imagination'; perhaps one of the reasons that he loved Chekhov was that he shared his 'immense brooding tenderness' – a tenderness that could only view with compassion the suffering, the tragedy, the struggles, the pathos, and the absurdity of human beings. Jack's 'bad' characters are usually absurd, often humorous caricatures. Jack's own humour was never black; he maintained that the best writing should come out of affection: 'Affection not only brings warmth into humour, but also insight into character, so creating more humour.' That was Jack.

Of course, we all met quite frequently in London. We would lunch or dine in Albany and Jack and Jacquetta would have dinner with us in No. 2, Amen Court. Although we couldn't quite manage their style of gracious living, the surroundings in our, or rather the cathedral's, beautiful Wren House were quite up to Kissing Tree House. When John and I eventually bought a modest little house on the Essex-Suffolk border, Jack and Jacquetta came to stay several times. They would arrive with some of Miss Pudduck's delicacies, and we couldn't have had nicer or more appreciative guests, and that, for all his reputation, included Jack. He didn't even grumble (perhaps he did afterwards) when I nearly poisoned him with smoked eels – normally one of his favourites – which had been kept too long. We had local friends to meals. One of the funniest lunch parties I have ever given was when Angus Wilson and Tony Garrod came, and Angus regaled us with his experience of chairing the Booker Prize judges. Denis and Helen Forman lived locally as well, and that was a bonus for us as well as for Jack and Jacquetta. Sometimes Jack brought his painting gear with him, and I have two fine gouaches of our lovely view over the Stour Valley. Although there was an attractive little summerhouse in the Kissing Tree garden, Jack seldom painted there, keeping the pastime instead for his holidays and travels; he really loved his painting. 'What happiness', he wrote, 'came from the con-centration, the deep absorption, and the result if I felt I had caught something essential and (to me) memorable in the landscape . . . there was an instant magic in handling brushes and paints, matching or contrasting colours, bringing character into design, attempting an all-

Jack became a keen painter, and he is seen here in the summerhouse at Alveston, summer 1967 (*Leisure Painter*)

over tone. No wonder, at least in my experience, painters are happier than writers.'

Jacquetta wrote a number of books drawing on her 'weight of learning'. In *Dawn of the Gods* and *The First Great Civilization*, her fine prose brings the ancient peoples to life for us. As a prehistorian she was also asked to contribute a chapter to the UNESCO *History of Mankind*. Jacquetta, with many others, was fascinated by the Pharaoh Akhenaton, his stimulus to a new realistic form of art, and his monotheistic and visionary religion of the sun. She had devoted a whole chapter of *Man and the Sun* to Akhenaton and his beautiful wife Nefertiti, and she wrote a novel around his life called *Man of Two Worlds*. The first part of the novel, drawing on existing material that Jacquetta knew, is beautifully done; the second, the sad and mysterious ending to his career and his parting with Nefertiti, is I think less successful. Present-day archaeology thinks poorly of Akhenaton, and Jacquetta herself is uncertain about this book.

In 1971 Jacquetta was asked to deliver the prestigious John Danz Lecture at the University of Washington. She was always modest about her credentials and expressed her genuine surprise at the invitation:

Jacquetta at Kissing Tree House
(photograph by Bern Schwartz)

Long ago I gave up a safe specialization in prehistory to become the kind of generalist most widely deplored. I have never held office in the academic world and therefore am not on the network. Since I became a generalist most of my published works have occupied a no-man's-land between scientific and imaginative ends. I have advocated subjectivism in the writing of archaeological works; I have attacked statistics. I have denied that Stonehenge and other monuments are computers. . . .

The lecture, 'Nothing But or Something More', developed from Jacquetta's article in *Antiquity* and her trilogy of books in the 'no-man's-land'. She also derived a great deal from *Beyond Reductionism*, a book comprising papers and discussions from a remarkable symposium held at Alpbach in the Austrian Tyrol, which had been attended by highly distinguished biologists, geneticists, neurologists, psychiatrists and students of linguistics from all over Europe. The symposium arose from a general feeling of the inadequacy of simple natural selection in accounting for the development of that remarkable species Homo Sapiens. Jacquetta had found immense encouragement for her ideas from this eminent gathering, and the realization that these distinguished academics were moving away from the reductionist views that had held sway for so long. She advances her own thesis:

It is probably right to see these genetically inherited mental forms as an accumulation from the past, but I want at the moment to disturb you by making a contrary proposition. It might be called sending up an intellectual balloon, or jumping in at the deep end. The proposition is that these things are given to us not by past aeons but as a process that is unrolling into the future. In other words, that our world, and heaven knows how many others, are involved in a development that can be likened by one of those dangerous analogies, to an egg developing into a man, an acorn into an oak, and so on. . . . I was delighted to discover that much of the interdisciplinary discussions at Alpbach were leading to this idea. . . . Provided we can prevent ourselves from destroying both ourselves and the world in which we live this could hold out wonderful possibilities for the human race. . . . Essentially all that I have tried to say to you is that we still inhabit a mystery, and that the best of scientific wisdom recognizes that this is so. Those scientists who live as whole and imaginative men do not believe that anyone has proved that their minds, their individual psyches are nothing but chance responses to chemical and molecular games played on the skin of the earth. The degraded masochism of this 'nothing but' does not represent a rational view of the universe. Let us have the courage to accept the inner experience that tells us that we are something more – and that we may be part of a process that is something much greater still.

Jack, meanwhile, with undiminished energy, went on trying his hand at different forms. There was a continuing stream of essays; there were thrillers and detective novels and children's stories; and then, at the age of sixty-eight, came a huge burst of exuberant humour and enjoyment in his longest ever novel, 300,000 words of *The Image Men*. This is a wonderful send-up of all the absurdities and paraphernalia of the professional publicists – the image makers, who swarm like parasites over our public life. Politicians, for instance often seem to worry more about their images than about the policies that they inflict upon us. *The Image Men* became Jack's favourite novel. In fact, he found himself sadly reluctant to say goodbye to his two heroes, Professor Saltana and Dr Tuby. He admits that perhaps his affection for them is partly because he put so much of himself into them:

To a limited degree there is an authoritative side to my character, and there is also – perhaps to a lesser degree, perhaps not – a persuasive and rather seductive side. So I took these two traits, enlarged and decorated them, and created the commanding Professor Saltana and the artful and pleasing Dr Tuby. . . . With all their impudent adventures – among, academics, media types, businessmen, senior politicians – I had given myself a well-earned holiday.

He was pleased with his leading ladies as well, complete characters of their own and the 'sex' (of which there is quite a lot) 'seems to me', he wrote, 'about right. You know what's happening in the bedrooms without having to undress everybody.' There is a proper distinction between 'serious relationships and rather casual impudent adventures'. Dr Tuby goes in for the latter rather successfully until he gets properly entangled with one woman, Lois. And finally Jack gives these, his favourite characters, 'a tremendous unabashed happy ending'. I certainly recognize the seductive Dr Tuby!

The Image Men got splendid reviews: 'The rigour and fluency of this latest offering puts most novelists half his age to shame.' . . . 'I can't resist a creativity so exuberant that it seems not a surrogate for life, but a kind of para-experience on the same level of immediacy.' . . . 'Huge and irresistable enjoyment' . . . 'All his admirable energy, humour and steam-engine narrative power . . . brilliant professional skill.' And perhaps the one that gave him most pleasure was the comment from his old friend Iris Murdoch, no easy critic: 'A very clever and funny book with real people in it'.

TWENTY

THE SUNSET YEARS

In the sixties and seventies Jack was offered various honours. He was not, I imagine, displeased by the offers, but he had no intention of accepting anything from any politician: he had attacked political honours in writing, and that was that. No, he didn't want to be Sir Jack. Then there was the peerage: Harold Wilson wanted him as a spokesman for the Labour Party in the House of Lords. Jack would never be a spokesman for anything or anyone but himself, and neither he nor Jacquetta was attracted by the prospect of becoming 'Lord' or 'Lady'. Once, when Jacquetta returned from one of her archaeological expeditions, Jack hired a car and went to meet her at the airport. 'I've just refused the CH,' he announced. It was the only occasion in their married life when they came anywhere near a quarrel. Jacquetta did feel that she might have been consulted, the Companion of Honour did not involve any change of name, and was less obviously political than earlier offers.

Meanwhile, Jack continued to write – novels, books of history, essays and reminiscences. 'I've written too much', he used to say. He felt that if he had concentrated his work, instead of hopping about from one literary form to another, chasing after every new idea, he might have been taken more seriously and appreciatively by the literary pundits; those who supervise university departments of English might more easily have found a pigeonhole for him. With a huge output, the work was bound to be uneven, and it is, but everything that Jack wrote is readable and worth reading. As a young writer he had taken enormous trouble over his style, trying to simplify it, so that, however complex, however difficult the ideas, the argument would be clear, readable and reasonably easy to understand, and he was undoubtedly successful in conveying difficult and complicated ideas. But 'simple' does not mean plain or unadorned; happily Jack never wholly disgarded his talent for fine writing. As I once said of him.

He created unerringly those marvellous rhythms and cadences of English prose at its best. Metaphors leap out at you one after

219

Jack is honoured with the freedom of the city of Bradford on 8 September 1973

another; he moves you to laughter – plenty of that – to tenderness, even to tears; his writing is alive with poetry in the widest sense; ripples and bubbles of humour are never far away, however serious he is, and he can be very serious, he never loses his lightness of touch, his humour, nor his power to entertain. He is always stimulating, and never, never dull.

And the result of all that early painstaking work is, to my not entirely unliterary mind, some of the best English prose of the twentieth century.

Over the years Jack kept up a steady correspondence with his daughter, Mary, who wrote to him almost once a week. Mary had divorced her Danish husband, and had come to live in England. She still suffered from periodic breakdowns, but used her musical talent to pioneer music therapy for disturbed mental patients in hospital. She became an acknowledged expert in this field, wrote books and articles, and did some broadcasting. She relied a great deal on her father, and his letters to her are full of wise fatherly advice and encouragement, as well as interesting comments on his own writing.

Soon after completing *Literature and Western Man* he wrote to Mary:

> The more I study the work and lives of the really great writers,
> the masters, the more I discover that they were able to bring rich
> natures, full of contradictions and opposites, to a sort of balance,
> unlike lesser geniuses who are intense and often compelling from
> sheer one-sidedness. I am myself not much of an artist,
> everything I have done will be forgotten in fifty years – some of
> it is almost forgotten now. But in a very, very, very humble way I
> belong in temperament and outlook somewhere far at the back
> of the procession of really great ones whom I at least understand.
> I have never put cleverness before wisdom.

This was a somewhat over-modest assessment, I think. Jack said that he
wrote 'out of a heightened ordinariness', and that he attempted to
balance his conscious and his unconscious perceptions and intuitions,
though the balancing was in itself unconscious and not a matter of will.

Jack's special personal relationship with the *Zeitgeist* came in a
children's story. Several years before *E.T.* arrived on our screens, to
draw huge crowds into the cinemas, and send them out in tears, Jack
wrote *Snoggle*, 'a story for anybody between 9 and 90'. The book tells
the story of what happens after a spaceship arrives from some remote
galaxy, and lands two strange little extra-terrestrials. They are found
by three children, who name them Snoggle and Snagger, and who
protect and rescue them from authority which arrives with police and
army, who are convinced, in the light of current space fiction, that
these must be dangerous invaders, bent on the conquest and
exploitation of our little blue planet. These creatures must be shot; it
was not conceivable that alien creatures could be friendly. The
children manage to outwit authority, and the friendly and endearing
Snoggle and Snagger return safely home in their spaceship to their far
more advanced planet. My grandchildren loved *Snoggle*.

In one of his occasional pieces, 'They Come from Inner Space',
Jack reflected on various forms of science fiction, and reports of flying
saucers. They 'seem to me important', he wrote, 'because they show
us what is happening in men's minds . . . they are the myths and
characteristic dreams of our age, and are psychologically far more
important than our more rational accounts of ourselves. They take the
lid off. They allow us a glimpse of what is boiling down below.' Of
our own efforts at space travel, Jack wrote that 'the rocket ships no
longer represent man's triumphant progress. They merely show him

hurrying at ever-increasing speeds away from his true life as a spiritual being. He is trying to escape from himself. . . . So uncertain is he now, so deeply suspicious, that a ring of friendly faces may be suddenly transformed into dreadful invaders from space.' So perhaps Jack's unconscious was telling him that he must make his own small effort towards restoring this dangerous imbalance.

Jack experienced success and failure in his work, and since writing is so deeply personal, the disappointments were correspondingly painful. But he wrote of them philosophically in a letter to Mary:

> I have lived long enough to know that life is like a road on which you turn one corner to find everything dismal, ugly and wretched, but then just as you may be beginning to give up hope, you turn another corner and the sun is shining on the bright fields again. All my working life has been spent in these alternatives of dark and light, success and failure. I don't consider myself a particularly brave, resolute character. Indeed I know I'm not – but I do try to keep going along that road, believing as I go that life is a mystery, and that far more is happening than we can know or understand.

Weekends at Kissing Tree House were always a pleasure, but a few seem to stand out in my memory. In summer we went for picnics into the Cotswolds. Priestley picnics were no ordinary affairs of sandwiches and cheese – they were feasts. Jack would sit and paint, while the three of us walked or visited the famously beautiful gardens of Hidcote Manor. There was one magical evening when we went to the theatre to see the Royal Shakespeare Company's production of *The Cherry Orchard* with Peggy Ashcroft playing Madame Ranesky – Jack's favourite play, and Jack's favourite actress.

There was a weekend with Paul and Marigold Johnson, when Paul put John and me to shame by getting up early to go to church, and when he exercised another of his talents in a skilful sketch of Kissing Tree House as a present for his host and hostess; Jacquetta had it framed and it still hangs on one of her walls. During a weekend with Jack and Catherine Lambert we had long discussions about the work of Francis Bacon. We agreed that whatever his remarkable painting skills, there was something deeply unhealthy about those hideously distorted figures. Then there were John and Marghanita Howard. There was always plenty to talk about with Marghanita (née Laski), with her determinedly ideological atheism and reductionist observations. 'Love is

Jack and Jacquetta enjoy a relaxing Sunday morning at Kissing Tree House
(photograph by Tom Priestley)

just a mating device', 'Poetry is just an arrangement of words and
sounds', etc. Jack was fond of Marghanita, as indeed, were we all, and
he maintained that her natural instincts were completely in opposition
to her advertised views. 'Atheists', it has been said, 'are people obsessed
by God', and that was certainly true of Marghanita, who liked nothing
better than attendance at Anglican church services, and theological
argument, for which she was well equipped. She had high moral

223

standards, and was one of the kindest of people, and a good and true friend – Jacquetta and I both miss her greatly.

When he was in the mood, Jack could turn himself into a real clown, as Bob Robinson remembers. Their friendship began when Jack, always on the look-out for good writing, wrote to Bob to congratulate him on an article in the *Sunday Times*: 'Just a note to say how much I liked your piece on Sinatra, such a lot of print arrives here on Sundays, and so little real writing. Keep it up.' Jack also, not surprisingly, took a fancy to Bob's attractive wife, Jo. The couple were invited for a weekend to Kissing Tree House, and told to bring tennis things. Bob brought his cine camera, and remembers Jack on the tennis-court putting out his tongue at it. Later, as Jack was strolling with Jacquetta and Jo in the garden and walking past the camera, he announced: 'Captain Priestley and his two trained sea-lions'! When Jack was on form he could be hilarious.

There is one weekend that stands out in my memory above all others. As we were all busy people with full diaries weekends had to be arranged well in advance. We arrived as usual on Friday evening pleased to hear that John and Iris Bayley were coming to dinner. 'Come down in good time,' Jacquetta had said, 'we are going to have champagne.' I had thought no more about that – it was probably some special celebration for John and Iris. But when we were all assembled in Jack's study, I did begin to feel that something unusual was afoot. 'We must just wait for Miss Pudduck,' said Jacquetta. Miss Pudduck arrived and so did the iced champagne. Our glasses were filled and Jacquetta stood up in front of the fireplace to announce: 'I want to share with you our dearest friends and with Miss Pudduck the news that beloved Jack has been given the OM.' That was truly a moment of emotional delight; we knew that the Order of Merit was the only honour that Jack had said that he would ever accept, as it was not political, being in the sole gift of the Queen and given only for genuine merit and special service to the country.

Jack enjoyed Buckingham Palace and subsequent lunches with his fellow OMs. Jacquetta, with her feeling for ancient history and mythology, had always believed in royalty. Jack, the egalitarian democrat, thought their existence added to the social silliness of the English, until that is, he watched a television documentary and realized that the royals were hard-working professionals, entitled to respect and understanding from another hard-working professional.

Over the years, Jack produced three volumes of occasional essays. I have already quoted from a number of these. They are full of penetrating social criticism, and, of course, are revealingly full of Jack himself. *Thoughts in the Wilderness* came first. He introduces it by recounting how a poet told a friend, who of course repeated it, that Priestley had 'a second-rate mind'. Jack announces cheerfully that, yes, he has a second-rate mind, and has never pretended to have anything else, but he has some advantages: 'some sort of intuitive insight into what the English people in general are thinking and feeling, a glimpse of the national mood of the moment . . . and the other small advantage . . . my mind is my own, nobody has hired it, no hidden campaign guides it, and what it chiefly desires, even more than applause, is that English people should have a good life.' The 'wilderness' in which Jack finds himself is political, though he firmly defends himself against any idea that he has moved from Left to Right. He is critical of the Labour Party that he once helped to elect, and finds it lacking in vision, and trotting out stale political dogmas. And now that the parties are moving closer together, politics has become something of 'a yawning parade of opinion'. Jack deplores what he calls 'block thinking'. In addition to the Communist block – not just Marx and Lenin but a complete outfit, anti-this and pro-that and no questions asked – he identifies a Pacifist Block, a Catholic Block, a Rationalist Block; 'and the vanity of severely rational people is astounding'. All have complete systems of ideas and entrenched positions, and if, like old J.B.P., you have no such outfit, you just shiver in the wilderness.

Jack's views on 'Censorship and the Stage' might seem surprising in that he was in favour of some form of censorship. Once a play had a licence it could be performed anywhere, and was not at the mercy of puritanical and reactionary local councils and Mrs Grundys. He pointed to the difference between what is *read* in private, and what is *seen* in public. Take sex: 'I don't like hot revealing sex on the stage, not because I'm a prude but because sex needs to be described from the inside as a poet or novelist can do, and when it is shown from the outside, with solid bodies on the stage, we are turned into "voyeurs".'

Jack also disliked explicit violence on stage or screen. One article for the *New Statesman* was called 'Don't Feed Ghoul': 'In our inner world there live all kinds of creatures . . . if we feed them they grow bigger and stronger, perhaps so powerful they try to take us over.' One of these he called Ghoul, 'for whom we are now creating a heyday'. 'Ghoul delights in blood and violence, cruelty and broken bones and limbs. . . . Some West End cinemas [we should now include the suppliers of 'video nasties'] are laying on lunch, tea,

Jack and Jacquetta at the time of their silver wedding anniversary, 1978

dinner and supper for Ghoul.' We are told that all this is cathartic, purging us of our hidden lusts and violence, but, says Jack: 'If catharsis worked, then there ought to have been less and less violence in real life, whereas there has been more and more.'

Jack examined the State of England in the light of its heraldic emblem . . . in an article entitled 'The Lion and the Unicorn'. He observed that the people of England were doing their best to keep the poor old lion going because that was how the populace and the politicians imagined that they impressed the world. But the world was less and less impressed; Jack argued that English people needed to turn to the other side of their national character, to that magical creature the unicorn, symbol of all that is imaginative, creative, boldly inventive and original: 'It is the Britain of the poets, the artists and scientific discoverers and passionate reformers, bold inventors, visionaries and madmen that still dazzles the world . . . the Britain of the Unicorn.'

I once asked Jack what in his life had been most important to him. 'The Moments,' he replied. And here they are:

All my life, I now realize, I have been nourished and secretly sustained by certain moments that have always seemed to me to be magical . . . it is neither conscience nor energy that has kept me going, but the memory and the hope of that magic. It has visited me before, it will come again. Sooner or later I would taste the honey-dew once more. . . . [These moments are] out of the prison of cause and effect . . . in a flash they add another dimension to life . . . they are not earned or deserved . . . they belong to the fairy-tale world . . . they arrive when they choose. . . . In my life I have suddenly known the greatest happiness *when there was no apparent reason for it* – when out of nowhere came floating up the great blue bubble.

For someone who disliked the process of travel, and was increasingly reluctant to leave home, Jack, with Jacquetta, did a great deal of travelling. Jack's daughter Barbara's dashing young airman had become by the 1960s Air Marshal Sir Peter Wykeham, KCB, OBE, DFC and bar, AFC, and he was Air Commander of the Far East based in Singapore. Jack was very fond of Barbara, and so was Jacquetta; all four had spent happy holidays in France. So off went Jack and Jacquetta for an extended holiday to Singapore and the Far East. Then in August 1967 Jack uprooted the household, rented a house in Daytona Beach, and arrived with Gertrude and Miss Pudduck for a month with the London Symphony Orchestra under André Previn, for the first Florida International Music Festival. The music was fine, and Jacquetta went bird-watching in the Everglades, but the house was something of a disaster. The literary result was *Trumpets Over the Sea.*

A holiday in Poland where Jack had royalties to spend, was not successful. A grey pall of dull, dreary Communism seemed to have settled over the lively country Jack had once so much enjoyed. He hardly stopped grumbling, and when they got home announced that he was never going any further away than Tiddington (the nearest village). None the less it was not long before Jack, now approaching eighty, decided that he would like to go to New Zealand, on the recommendation of Ralph Richardson, who had told him that it had the most beautiful scenery in the world. The visit was a real success. They were pleasantly entertained; Jack painted happily and Jacquetta was enchanted by the countryside and all the strange new trees, flowers and bird and animal life. The resulting book was published as a limited edition entitled *A Visit to New Zealand* and was illustrated with Jack's paintings.

It was 1977 when John and I began to go on holiday with the Priestleys. We only once went abroad, to Amalfi in February. After that Jack didn't want to travel too far. John and I had never been to Yorkshire, and Jack wanted to introduce us to his favourite part of

227

England, the Yorkshire Dales. They were, for Jack, 'the finest countryside in Britain, with their magnificent, clear and austere outlines of hill and moor, their charming villages and remote whitewashed farms, their astonishing variety of aspect and appeal, from the high gaunt rocks down to the twinkling rivers'.

Jack loved to paint in the Dales. He wrote about 'their ever-changing panorama and pageant of light and colour', 'a scene, forever shifting, that entrances any sensitive eye and drives any landscape painter mad. . . . At one moment the slopes of the fells will be smothered in grey cloud, and a few moments afterwards they will be there in the sunlight looking like magic carpets.'

We stayed in a pleasant hotel in Arncliffe, and visited various pubs for lunch. It was rather like a royal progress. Jack was the local hero, and wherever we went people came up, wanting to shake him by the hand and tell him how much they admired him, and how much they had enjoyed his books. This was the kind of situation that Jack hated. He felt deeply embarrassed, and his reactions were anything but gracious; his many admirers must have been sadly disappointed. There was only one pub where John got more attention than Jack, and that was run by a pair of ex-Roman Catholic priests. And there was one extra-special picnic at Jack's favourite place, unspoiled little Hubberholme: 'one of the smallest and pleasantest places in the world,' Jack wrote, 'an old church, a pub, a bridge set in a dale among high moors. In summer, long after the snows have melted, there is rarely much water in the river, so that it glitters and winks; and a man who has been walking for an hour or two can loiter on that bridge for quite a time waiting for the pub to open, and staring at the river.'

John and I never saw the grumbling Jack in full spate, just a few semi-humorous rumbles here and there. As far as any criticism of him went, Jack always got there first:

I grumble if I don't get letters; I grumble if I do. . . . I am the worst present-receiver in the county of Warwickshire, for I can hardly manage a smile or a few pleasant words of thanks, and am obviously going to point out what is wrong with the present as soon as the giver is out of the room. . . . Few men have ever done more grumbling than I have. For writing I have a certain talent, but for grumbling I have indefatigable genius. True, I expect the worst, but when it is worse still, as it nearly always is, I am the loudest complainer.

Jack thought optimists were, on the whole, shallow, silly, unrealistic fellows. He himself might justly be called 'a life-enhancing pessimist'. He did add that he knew he was always his own worst enemy. Jack could and did write delightful and charming letters of thanks; it was just having to say it that he found so impossibly difficult.

Jack's publisher, Charles Pick, remembers a classic occasion when Jack had agreed to speak at the official opening of Heinemann's new warehouse. He was to come up from the country, and be collected by car from Albany. He arrived grumbling – there had been no heating and no coffee on the train. They started late, and Jack went on grumbling: he couldn't speak in the open air; he didn't want to meet a lot of city types; when was he going to get his lunch? Hoping to soothe him, Charles produced an inscribed gold watch as a present from the firm. Jack took one look at it and said: 'I can't wear a watch.' Of course, in the end, Jack rose to the occasion with a fine Priestley speech.

Charles was very fond of Jack: he found him always easy to work with, and generally appreciative. He wouldn't take any advance or sign a contract until a book was published. They never argued; and Charles appreciated Jack's loyalty. There was a time when Heinemann was in financial and other difficulties, and there was a meeting of its top authors in Albany. It was suggested that the main authors might wish to transfer to the Bodley Head. Jack was outraged; with Richard Church he walked out saying: 'Heinemann's made me, and I'm not going to desert them now.'

Over the years Charles Pick organized on behalf of Heinemann a number of dinners at the Savoy for Jack. The first was in 1962 to celebrate forty years with the firm. Then came the birthdays – the seventieth, the seventy-fifth and the eightieth. In memory these occasions tend to merge into one another. I think Ralph Richardson was at the first one, and his was more of a performance than a speech – a real Richardson delight. The seventieth birthday stands out, because it might so easily have been a disaster. Sir Charles Snow was the chairman and the main speaker, supported by Angus Wilson, who made a witty and clever speech. But when Sir Charles rose there was no mistaking that he was dreadfully drunk. His wife Pamela Hansford-Johnson was ill; had she been there she could have controlled things. Poor old Charles bumbled away, saying all the wrong things. Jack was 'no intellectual', he was always such 'a good companion'. Charles got muddled over the plays and waffled on about *Journey's End*. There was one phrase that he fancied and kept on repeating, that Jack was 'the whisper of the conscience of England' –

one doesn't normally think of Jack as a whisperer! Charles couldn't be persuaded to sit down. One or two neighbours nearly succeeded, but up he popped again with his 'whisper' until he finally collapsed. We all sat in the most excruciating and miserably uncomfortable embarrassment. Jack rose to speak, and I don't think I have ever admired him more; humorously, delightfully, he pulled it all together, he laughed at himself, made us laugh with him. 'If you will accompany me down to the river, I will walk across the water' – it was the way he said that, with his true dramatic instinct; he made us all relax and feel happy again. Charles Snow and Jack were good friends: Jack never bore him any grudge, and never let the occasion make any difference to their friendship.

I know that Jack's old friend, Richard Church, spoke charmingly and delightfully at one of the birthday dinners, and there were brilliant speeches from Robert Robinson and Iris Murdoch at the seventy-fifth. Iris had no script, but Bob let me see his. Here is an extract:

What I've been trying to single out is the quality that I honour in Priestley above all – the sense he gives me of inviolable identity – we do *ourselves* a favour if we celebrate a man who never peddled anything to anyone in his life. . . . I once went to dine in a restaurant with Priestley, and the waiter asked him if he had a reservation. I remember thinking that no, he has no reservation, but in the roll call of time he will turn out to have been among the founders of the feast.

For the eightieth birthday again I have hazy memories of the speakers. One was an old friend from America, Evie Ames, who spoke beautifully and movingly. Another was the head of Harpers and Row, Jack's American publishers, who arrived by plane literally at the very last minute. For one of these birthdays another old and dear friend, Susan Cooper, came over from America. She, with Jack and Jacquetta, watched a celebratory television programme on our rather poor black-and-white set up in the nursery of 2 Amen Court. Towards the end came a condensed version of *Johnson Over Jordan* with Ralph Richardson playing his original part. In spite of the unpropitious surroundings, Susan wrote later: 'The magic that one had been hoping for all along suddenly came filtering through this T.V. programme. Time had made one of those curious spiralling turns, for Richardson had grown older to meet the play he played it without a

Jack welcoming John and me to his seventy-fifth birthday party held by Heinemann at the Savoy Hotel, London, on 13 September 1960 (Tomas Jaski)

false note or a marred inflection.' When it ended, Susan looked at Jack. Rather gruff and low, he said: 'I shed tears not for what I have seen, but for what I have been remembering.' 'But,' wrote Susan, 'Priestley wasn't really remembering, not really looking back; he was looking outward, into the level of Time where there is no forward or backward, no youth or age, no beginning or end. Like all the great enchanters, he has always seen it plainer than the rest of us.'

Pictured at the dinner table with Jack and Jacquetta on the occasion of the seventy-
fifth bithday party are Iris Murdoch and Sir Kenneth Clark (Tomas Jaski)

We met Jack's family on some of our visits to Kissing Tree House,
and, of course, they were at the birthday parties. Nicolas Hawkes we
knew quite well, partly because he had been a keen CND
campaigner. But there was one Priestley occasion we were sorry to
have to miss. A picture gallery in Wimbledon put on a Priestley
exhibition, to which each member of this talented family was able to
make a contribution. It included a number of Jack's pictures, of
course, and several from Barbara, who is an accomplished artist. Sylvia
and Michael are both artists, and their daughter Vicky was becoming
well known as an illustrator and flower painter. Mary had made pen-
and-ink drawings of conductors, Rachel contributed a piece of
sculpture, and Tom produced drawings and paintings. Jacquetta, too,
contributed a picture. Think of all this talent, scattered down
succeeding generations, in art, literature and music (Mary was not
alone in being musically gifted, as Sylvia was a talented flautist).
Sometime these gifts may all come together again in other exceptional
individuals; one way or another I do not believe they will be lost.

Jacquetta was rather more anxious for holidays than Jack. After
Gertrude surprised everyone by saying that she wanted to retire much
earlier than anyone had expected, Jacquetta had all the problems of

Jack's biographer, Susan Cooper, joins him for coffee in the garden at Kissing Tree House

trying to find replacements. And soon Hales the gardener died, so she had that responsibility as well. Miss Pudduck remained, a rock of support throughout, and somehow managed to maintain her exactingly high standards.

So we continued to go away with the Priestleys. Jacquetta and I were usually the sightseers, Jacquetta more of an interest sightseer and I, in my unacademic way, a beauty sightseer. John and Jack often preferred to settle in a pub over a drink. In the course of some talk or other I had confessed to vestiges of East Anglian Puritanism. 'I'm not a Puritan,' said John truthfully. 'Ah,' said Jack, 'I knew I had recognized a brother.'

The Priestleys still came to Mill House. After dinner on one of their visits, Jack announced: 'I've got something I specially want to read to you.' So we settled in front of a wood fire, and Jack read us an account of his recent dream. It had made him feel quite extra-ordinarily happy; this was 'The Happy Dream':

> It was perfect weather, the Maytime of some mysterious dimension. I was moving about in a group of young people, and felt my body as that of a young man again, though I was still my present self. What came through was not simply pleasure, but a rich breadth and depth of happiness I never remember feeling before, awake or in dreams . . . there were no striking events . . . just this glorious atmosphere radiating happiness so memorable that I could not forget it if I tried. What that Happy Dream celebrated so richly was the defeat of Time.

The group appeared to be drifting around Cambridge. Why Cambridge? Jack had never liked it when he was there, but there was a clue – Jacquetta – born and brought up there, 'a Cambridge girl if ever there was one'. They passed an enormous kind of shed, where an orchestra was rehearsing just inside the entrance, and there were sounds of distant music. And then it wasn't Cambridge, it was the Isle of Wight, and a different group climbing up a hill to a castle. 'There was a girl in front, no particular girl, just Woman, essential femininity

On vacation in Dorset, 1983, at the holiday house of Jack's daughter, Sylvia Goaman

bringing a new and extra glow of happiness. . . . We never reached that castle on some Isle of Wight in an unknown dimension. (You take the symbolism; I pass.) This one brief dream towered above and outshone all the recent events of my old age. It has been the greatest gift that has lately come my way.'

There were other compensations of old age:

> Heart-warming love, hardly known to my younger self, of sky, scenery, sunsets, gathering storm-clouds, those palest and clearest blues that belong to the Kingdom of Heaven. Constant dialogues with Death, of whom I am not afraid. . . . Finally, something I never knew in earlier years, the blessed feeling coming through occasionally like some snatch of a heavenly song, the blessed feeling of *conscious* love. What a prize for fumbling and bewildered old age!

We do indeed learn, in Shakespeare's words, 'To love that well that thou must leave ere long.'

Jacquetta had been cherishing a somewhat dreamlike idea for a book. She wanted to write of woman's relationship with man throughout the ages. The outcome was *A Quest of Love*. The woman we meet in these different ages and in different situations of the book is Jacquetta herself, drawing on her personal experience, and imaginatively acting and feeling as she herself might have done. Her gift for making the past live for us is brilliantly evident, and she handles her theme so skilfully that a number of readers have believed that she was genuinely recalling scenes and experiences from previous incarnations. In the final chapter she becomes openly autobiographical, and describes briefly her childhood, her marriage and her relationship and marriage to Jack. I gave *A Quest of Love* to a number of friends. Most found it enthralling, others had reservations, and some were worried by the autobiographical ending. After reading Jacquetta's writings, I think that her key-word is imagination.

Jacquetta's last major book was the biography she was asked to write of her old friend and admirer, Sir Mortimer Wheeler. Good as the book is, Jacquetta did not much enjoy writing it; she was not, she found, a natural biographer.

Jacquetta as a character tends to be self-absorbed, not at all the same as selfish or self-centred, which Jacquetta is not. Her rich and imaginative inner life emerges in her writing, but not immediately in human relations. This, combined with her natural shyness and compulsive honesty, is why some people find her intimidating, and why others not immediately attracted by her can feel an adverse reaction. But Jacquetta is quickly self-critical. If she feels she has been in any way at fault she hastens to make amends. With all her talent and brilliance she is essentially very modest. She has many friends who are devoted to her.

In his eighties Jack wrote *Over the Long High Wall: Some Reflections on Life, Death and Time*, a summing-up of much that he had thought and written over the years, familiar material, but pulled together and freshly presented. He still wrote essays and novels and one 'Final Chapter of Autobiography', quoting:

> Men must endure
> Their going hence, even as their coming hither:
> Ripeness is all.

The book was called *Instead of the Trees*, he explained, because he had intended to write such a work in or near the giant redwood trees of

Time moves on. Jack is pictured in the garden of Kissing Tree House (photograph by Stephen Hyde)

California, 'tranquil ancients to which I had taken a great fancy'. But the war had come and put an end to travels, and it was long before Jack returned to complete his trilogy.

Then at last came the sad time when Jack realized that he could not write any more: he had said it all. He found this deeply distressing. 'I'm a creative man', he said, 'or I'm nothing.' His distress slowly subsided into a gentle melancholy, and he seemed to withdraw into himself. He also became rather deaf and unable to take part in general conversation. As with so many of us, his memory too began to fail. Jacquetta was wonderful with him, quietly patient, and sensitively preserving the difficult balance between caring and fussing. When I told her how much I admired this, she simply replied: 'But I do still love him.'

Our own lives were changing. At the end of November 1981 John retired as Canon of St Paul's Cathedral. The last, and in many ways, the best dinner party that we gave in Amen Court was for Jacquetta's birthday on 5 August. We wanted to have her close friends from all or most of her life. John and Marghanita Howard, Jacquetta's first publishers, were away, but Norah Smallwood of Chatto was able to come, and so was her Newnham friend Peggy Lamert. Iris and John Bayley were away, but happily Denis and Helen Forman were free. It was a good evening. Jacquetta wrote that it was one of the nicest birthday presents she had ever had, and Helen wrote that the love flowing through it was palpable.

John was the first of us to go. He died very suddenly from a heart attack on 31 December 1982. Jack was beginning to fail by then, and had to have one or two hospital sessions. But there were still flashes of the old Jack, and he was fine in a one-to-one conversation. 'Now nature's got no more use for me,' he said, 'she keeps giving me nasty little jabs, as much as to say we're tired of you, off you go.'

By 1984 plans were made for Jack's ninetieth birthday on 13 September. He wouldn't want to move far, so there was to be a birthday lunch at a good hotel in the neighbourhood. Barbara and Sylvia planned a joint visit to Kissing Tree House in the second week or so of August, but Jack suddenly fell ill, and by the time they arrived he was clearly dying. Two nurses were now needed, and in between the nursing shifts one or other of the family would sit with him. Jack knew that he was dying, and said goodbye very sweetly to his two dear daughters. He was calm and unafraid throughout.

On the night of 13 August Jack was much worse. Jacquetta, with Barbara, Sylvia and Miss Pudduck, took turns to sit with him. It was

Believed to be one of the last photographs of Jack, taken by Granville Davies in June 1984

late into the night; the duty nurse had gone downstairs, and Jacquetta stayed on with Jack. She held his hand, and then held him in her arms as quietly and very peacefully he slipped away forever.

Barbara and Sylvia remember the owls in the trees outside Jack's bedroom, and their mournful chorus of long melancholy hootings. There is an age-old belief in the relationship of owls and death. Strange – perhaps not really so strange. As Jack would have said, 'it is all a mystery', and 'far more is happening than we can know or understand'.

TWENTY-ONE

TIME TO GO ON

Long obituaries appeared almost immediately. That in *The Times* was, as always, factual and anonymous, but the writer also spoke of Jack's 'independence of mind, egalitarian, non-conformist, together with a temperament innately romantic . . . that is the constant element in his work. . . . He expressed it in a prose of such sinew and liveliness that it is possible to say of him that he never wrote a dull sentence.' The *Sunday Times* printed a long obituary from Jack Lambert, who knew Jack well, and who wrote of 'this amazing, exasperating, loveable man, this unstoppable, stimulating, disappointing, provocative writer. His place in English literature and in the English theatre will sort itself out in time,' and he ended:

Capable of shatteringly disagreeable ungraciousness when required to go through his formal paces, especially on special occasions, he was in relaxation the embodiment of a delicious spirit of mischief, his little eyes glinting, his pipe-laden lower lip as expressive as his wrinkled brow, his cavernous mumbles as gleeful as his well of absurd similes (his publishers might do worse than put out an anthology of these illuminating delights). Take him for all in all, a man not to be underrated or a writer to be forgotten.'

Anthony Burgess, who had only met Jack occasionally, wrote sympathetically:

I remember J.B. Priestley denying to me that he was a genuius, but claiming that he had 'a hell of a lot of talent'. He was not being just to himself. Talent is a small fiddling capacity for producing the conventional and the well-shaped. It rarely means volcanic ebullience.

Priestley was volcanic, fertile, often careless, but never dull. It was said that he wrote too much, but that was said of everybody who was not a costive product of Bloomsbury. I think Priestley had genius, and that it was never sufficiently appreciated. . . . My generation had been warned off him by the intellectuals, who derided or patronised him. . . . The fact is that Priestley was an intellectual himself, a man of wide erudition, the width of whose reading and understanding of what he read can be seen in his admirable *Literature and Western Man*. He knew what the avant-garde novel was all about, but he preferred to work in the tradition of Smollett and Fielding. . . .

Of course, he was always more subtle than he usually wished to appear. If he scorned experiment in his novels, he produced in the 1930s a series of plays which brought something wholly original to the theatre. His plays always had ideas in them, though some of the ideas have dated like most ideas. . . . I don't think he'd want to be remembered anyway as an ideas man. When he was didactic, it was in the blunt manner of a popular, secular preacher who wanted us to use our common sense, not to be taken in by the spurious, to cherish the beef and pudding tradition of an old England he looked at with the ambiguous eyes of a George Orwell. . . . He was perhaps the last of the literary men willing to spill out of the confines of his study and dare to be a public figure revered for what he stood for, and not just for what he wrote. What he wrote, at least a good half of it, ought to survive . . . the young seem to be rediscovering him. He can do them nothing but good. I've read nearly everything he wrote, and not for one moment did I ever think I was wasting my time.

As he had grown old, Jack had seemed to shrink; he finally appeared a small, short man, yet his personality filled the house. When I first returned to Kissing Tree House after his death, the house seemed suddenly so large and so empty. I couldn't go to Jack's funeral in Stratford-on-Avon, as I had arranged with a cousin to escort her elderly mother to Dubrovnik for two weeks. But since we flew from Birmingham, I was able to visit Jacquetta on my way, and on my return.

After a death there is much to be done, and much to be decided; one operates in a state of numbed unreality. All I can say is that I knew from my own experience, and was able to share a little in Jacquetta's sense of overwhelming loss. For someone like Jack, there had to be a memorial service in London, and Westminster Abbey seemed the right place, especially as in the Very Reverend Edward Carpenter it had a particularly sympathetic dean. Jacquetta and I went to spend a night or two with Denis and Helen Forman, and then came on to Mill House. Jacquetta didn't know much about church services, and wanted suggestions for hymns and music. Also she had asked me to give the address, the hardest assignment that had ever faced me, and I needed her help in this.

We chose that celebration of the natural world, the paraphrase of Francis of Assisi's 'Hymn to the Sun', and Addison's 'Eternal Ruler of the Ceaseless Round', that would reflect Jack's abiding interest in astronomy and cosmology. The anthem was a beautiful setting of 'Many Waters Cannot Quench Love'.

Jacquetta chose the readings and the readers. Denis Forman read from one of Jack's favourite bits of the Bible, Ecclesiastes: 'or ever the silver cord be loosed, and the golden bowl be broken . . .'; it is well known, and is pure poetry. Charles Pick read an extract from *Margin Released* about music on a summer's evening in Bradford. Jack's friend of more than fifty years, lovely Peggy Ashcroft, gave a marvellous reading from Jack's long essay 'Whatever Happened to Falstaff?', Jack's favourite Shakespearian character. And then Richard Pascoe moved us all by the last speech from *Johnson Over Jordan*. The final hymn was one that Jack loved and that expressed his hopes for England – Blake's 'Jerusalem'.

I really sweated over that address. Of course, one had to recognize the public man and writer, and I did. Once I had got over the inevitable nerves, I could begin: 'J.B. Priestley, OM. Few people during the last seven weeks can have failed to be aware of the passing of a great man. Jack was a great writer, a great Englishman, and perhaps transcending even these, a great man. . . .' But somehow I wanted to convey that other essential Jack, the man beneath the confident, pugnacious, apparently conceited public persona that he had built up to protect that other self that he described as 'Amiable, indulgent, affectionate, shy and rather timid at heart'. I wanted to speak of the man of compassion and understanding, the dreamer and visionary, the seeker after wisdom and of magic, which he found in nature, art and love, yet who was still looking for 'something more', who wrote of 'the hunger of the heart', 'the secret dream', 'the delight that never was', the desire for something more than all the delights, far 'better bread than was ever made with wheat'. I spent a long time reading and thinking about this remarkable many-talented man. I thought of his honesty and self-knowledge, the way he dealt with negative emotions, the attention he paid to his friends, his insight. I remembered how I had been considerably shaken in the early days of our acquaintance when he told me – very kindly – things about myself that I suppose I might have half known, but now had to recognize as true. 'How do you know all this?' I asked. 'I'm a novelist,' he replied, 'I have to observe other people'. But, of course, it was not just observation; much of it was that intuitive insight.

I remembered one of his favourite quotations from Jung: 'A man at peace with himself, who accepts himself, contributes an infinitesimal amount to the good of the universe. Attend to your own private and personal conflicts, and you will be reducing by one millionth millionth the world conflict.' That was true of Jack by the time John and I knew him, so that, while it was interesting, stimulating, sometimes uproariously funny to be with him, it was also, at the same time, a relaxation.

Jacquetta was a great help, and I felt that as long as I could please her and Jack's family, it would be all right, and thankfully it was. Perhaps I might just quote my ending:

> At the conclusion of that giant of a book *Literature and Western Man* Jack wrote, 'we live under God in a great mystery'. And that is where we must leave him in the final and greatest mystery, the mystery of death. We leave him with those qualities that he most valued, with admiration, with hope and with love. He helped and taught us to admire so much, and he gave us so much of his own for our delight and admiration. We can share his hope for the kind of England in which he believed, the vision he never abandoned . . . and for that other hope of personal survival, the great question mark we can believe or disbelieve, we cannot know. Jack was open-minded, believing or doubting in his own highly individual fashion. I, for one, have a hope, and want to leave Jack with it.
>
> And love — well love is easy. Jack was a man who gave and received much love. He wrote 'to create and sustain *conscious* love against heavy odds, may be what this universe is all about'. Maybe it is, maybe Blake 'who understood so much' — Jack's words — is right that
>
> > We are put on earth a little while
> > that we may learn to bear the beams of love.
>
> But last words should be personal not general, the words of one of the young nurses who cared for Jack throughout his final illness. She wrote: 'He died peacefully, with dignity and surrounded by love.'

Jacquetta unveiling the fine statue of Jack made by Ian Judd, located near the
Alhambra Theatre in Bradford, 31 October 1986 (Picture House)

After a year, always with the invaluable support of Miss Pudduck, Jacquetta sold Kissing Tree House and bought Littlecote at the north end of the long and attractive high street of Chipping Campden. Stephen and Amy Pratt had already retired there and were enthusiastically helpful in finding Jacquetta this suitable and delightful house. The town was a good place to be, far enough from Alveston and all its associations, but not too far to cut her off from her friends and local interests.

After the death of a husband there is an inner loneliness that we now always carry with us, but that apart, Jacquetta has been happy in Chipping Campden, and has made many new friends. She and I are the survivors, and we have continued to go on holidays together. First to Morocco, where we were joined in Taroudant by Tom Priestley, and since then we have explored much of southern France together. Now we both feel that travel and long car journeys have become somewhat daunting so we stay at home.

After a few years, Jack the public man was properly honoured in his home town of Bradford. A young man, Ian Judd, then working in Leeds, was commissioned to produce a statue. This was to stand in the centre of the city, between the Central Library and the National Museum of Photography, Film and Television, with the library on one hand, and the refurbished and extended Alhambra Theatre on the other. It was a wonderfully commanding and appropriate site. Ian Judd is a very talented young man. 'All I heard about J.B. Priestley', he said, 'seemed to point to a rather difficult gentleman, but reading his books convinced me otherwise. Those who knew him described a shy, humorous and amiable character, who nevertheless wasn't afraid to speak his mind. It was that Priestley that I wanted to convey.' The result is a triumph. This statue is the best and most satisfying likeness of the Jack we all knew. Alfred Robinson, writing to W.R. Mitchell, who edited a delightful anthology *J.B. Priestley's Yorkshire*, pointed out that Vera Brittain, writing in 1940 about possible literary tourists in Yorkshire, had suggested that 'Perhaps they will first visit the stocky, pugnacious statue of J.B. Priestley, which will then stand before the Alhambra Theatre'. What a piece of literary prescience! This large bronze statue doesn't look stocky or pugnacious; it stands 9 ft high on a stone pedestal 7 ft high, and Jack, pipe in hand, looks out in a contemplative and protective mood over and beyond the city of his birth. He is wearing a long greatcoat which billows out behind him as if blown by a great wind from the moors and dales that he loved. Jacquetta was invited to unveil the statue, and there was a grand civic lunch in her honour. This was a gathering of the Priestley family, along with a few friendly hangers-on like me.

Jack wrote a great deal about, and in praise of, Bradford, thinly disguised as Bruddersford, in his novels, but that is not where I want to leave him. Jacquetta wanted Jack's ashes to be buried in Hubberholme, the small remote place in the Dales that they both loved. She also wanted a modest memorial tablet in the church. So when, after going through all the bureaucratic machinery of acquiring a legal faculty, all was in order, the Priestley family, together with a few friends and a number of local people from Bradford and around, assembled at Hubberholme on Saturday 19 April 1986 for a short ceremony.

Spring comes late up here, and it was a grey, rather chilly day at the end of the lambing season, so lambs and their mothers were perpetually bleating and calling to each other. Hubberholme Church is solid and unwavering, with no lofty spire – that would have been damaged by winter winds sweeping down the valley – just a square, grey stone tower. It is an ancient church, with a fine old 'rood' loft, and its pews were made by Robert Thompson, 'the mouse man of Kilburn', a well-known wood carver who liked to put his signature on his work, so that here and there on the pew-ends you can find carved into the wood little squiggly brown mice! The river, the Wharfe, runs close by and just over the bridge is the pub. The

A brief memorial service for Jack was held here, at Hubberholme Church, on 19 April 1986 (Yorkshire Post Newspapers)

memorial tablet on the wall facing the entrance to the church was waiting to be unveiled by Jacquetta.

The service was short and simple, and Tom Priestley gave the address, with a text from the poet, George Herbert:

> A man that looks on glass,
> On that may stay his eye,
> Or if he pleaseth through it pass,
> And then the heavens espy.

How right for Jack, who always saw beneath and beyond the surface of things! Tom referred to one of Jack's short stories 'The Other Place': a man has a vision of paradise, a glimpse of a magical landscape inhabited by friendly and generous people, but he can only get into it when in the right frame of mind, at certain special times; trying to find it again, he comes to look for it here in Hubberholme – 'a good place to look', said Jack. Tom continued:

> This concern with the feeling of otherness is a recurring theme in much of his writing. . . . Behind the sense of otherness is the feeling that it represents a glimpse of something permanent, but the permanence gets swamped by the everyday. However, one should aim at a balance between the two, as between the outer man and the inner man. . . . For him the easiest way to that other, inner world was through the creative imagination. . . . I feel now, that if we could find our way round some magical corner . . . there he would be with his wide-brimmed hat and his walking-stick, pointing at the heights, dabbing at the clouds with his finger – indicating 'the beyond'.

There were three readings from Jack's writings. Peter Wykeham read about going to Hubberholme in autumn, from *English Journey*.

> The morning was on fire. The dry bracken and the heather burnished the hilltops; and all the thick woods beside the Wharfe were a blaze of autumn. The trees dripped gold upon us. We would look down russet vistas to the green river. We would look up, dazzled, to see the moorland heights a burning purple. If we had been ten years in a dark cell and newly released, we could not have stared at a world that seemed more extravagantly but exquisitely dyed. I have never seen Bolton Woods looking like

that before, and hardly dare hope to see them like that again. It was their grand carnival; and it will riot and glow in my memory as long as I live. . . . Hubberholme is sheer magic, not quite in this world.

A local girl read a piece from *Delight*: 'Blossom – apple, pear, cherry, plum, almond blossom . . . once every spring on a fine morning . . . we stare again at the blossom and are back in Eden. We complain and complain, but we have lived and have seen the blossom – in the sun; and the best among us cannot pretend they deserve – or could contrive – anything better.' And then I was especially happy to read the dream that meant so much to Jack, the dream of the birds.

Jacquetta unveiled the memorial tablet, which reads:

Remember
J.B. PRIESTLEY, O.M.
1894–1984

Author and Dramatist whose ashes
are buried nearby

He loved the Dales and found
'Hubberholme, one of the smallest
and pleasantest places in the World'

We all stayed in the church while Jacquetta went out alone and buried Jack's ashes.

Then we drove down the valley to Buckden to a warm and welcoming pub, 'a notable goal for Bradfordians who have emptied the barrels at the inn there many a time', Jack had written. Here we were entertained by Jack's sister Winnie to a splendid, slap-up Yorkshire tea.

So now that small, remote place Hubberholme is linked forever with the name of J.B. Priestley: this place, Jack had written, 'where there is space and beauty. The elements seem to be balanced; the earth seems to touch the sky'; where he could gaze on 'those high remote skylines, stern enough and yet still suggesting a brooding tenderness'; where he could find perpetually renewed

The silence that is in the starry sky
The peace that is among the lonely hills.

Soon there would be increasing cascades of song from the nesting larks, and flutings and pipings from the woods; the valleys would echo with calls of returning cuckoos; and, in the background, wild moorland birds would be crying and calling. Perhaps Jacquetta's favourite bird, the busy little dipper, would dart backwards and forwards from beneath the old stone bridge. All this singing and mating and building would subside into the warmth of summer and the drowsy hum of insects, before the blaze of autumn, the howling of the winter winds, and finally the still silence of fallen snow.

The year would turn, and once again would come the rush of new green, fields and hillsides in flower, flutings, pipings, trillings and carollings – all the bursting energy of creation and procreation, freshly and joyously repeated over and over and over again. . . .

> Lo! for there among the flowers and grasses
> Only the mightier movement turns and passes
> Only winds and rivers, life and death.

INDEX

J.B. Priestley is abbreviated to JBP, and Jacquetta Hawkes to Jacquetta. Page numbers in italics indicate illustrations.

Acland, Lady (Anne), 93, 94
Acland, Sir Richard, 92–5 *passim*
Adrian, 1st Baron, 118
Aitken, Janet, 17
Akhenaton, Pharaoh, 215
Alveston, *see* Kissing Tree House
Ames, Evie, 230
Ashcroft, Dame Peggy, 20, 66, 170, 222, 241
Attlee, Clement, *later* 1st Earl Attlee, 1
Augustine of Hippo, St, 194

Bacon, Francis, 222
Balogh, Thomas, *later* Baron Balogh, 92
Bannerman, David, 180, 183
Bayley, John, 210, 224
Billingham Manor, *66*: Priestley family at, 64, *87*; new study built, 74; *Rain Upon Godshill*, 79; Army commandeers, 88; depredations by Army, 98; sold, 99
Birkett, Miles, 122, 126
Blackett, Patrick, *later* Baron Blackett, 14
Bliss, Sir Arthur, *50*, 164
Blunden, Edmund, 46
Bradford: Priestley family, 37; JBP's youth in, 41, 68; JBP's affection for, 43, 245; social hierarchy, 45; JPB marries in, 47; Great War reunion dinner, 72–3; JBP's statue, *243*, 244
Breuil, Abbé, 135
Britten, Benjamin, *later* Baron Britten, 85
Brogan, Denis, *later* Sir Denis, 135
Brogan, Olwen, *later* Lady Brogan, 135
Brooke Hill, *25*: Collinses at, 24, 186; position and interior, 24; gardens,

24–5; daily routine, 25; walks from, 26; a happy house, 32; JBP rents, 99; Jacquetta at, 178; Denisons at, 180; JBP and Jacquetta live at, 186; Iris Murdoch at, 210
Breughel, Pieter the Elder, 82
Bullett, Gerald, 50, *51*
Bullet, Rosemary, 50
Burgess, Anthony, 239
Butler, R.A., *later* Baron Butler, 154

Calder, Ritchie, *later* Baron Ritchie-Calder, 16, 93
Cambridge: JBP and Pat, 47; 71 Grange Road, 108, 109, 113, 118; Nicolas with grandparents in, 143
Cambridge University: JBP 46, *47*; Parliamentary candidates, 95; Hopkins, 106, 107–8, 115–16; Trinity College statutes, 110; Newnham, 122, 123; C.P. Hawkes, 130
Campaign for Nuclear Disarmament: Collinses, ix; British nuclear policy, 11; JBP and, 16; founded, 16; public launching, 17; women, 17–21 *passim*; Aldermaston marches, 21–2, *21*
Carpenter, Very Revd Edward, 240
Casson, Lewis, *later* Sir Lewis, 164
Cervantes, Saavedra, Miguel de, 197
Chadwick, Sonia (Mrs Christopher Hawkes), 186
Chamberlain, Neville, 1
Chekov, Anton, 70, 214, 222
Chipping Camden, 244

Church, Richard, 230
Church Harborough, College House, 56, 57
Churchill, Winston, *later* Sir Winston, 1–2, 8
Collins, Diana: CND, ix, 19; happy marriage, xi; JBP's broadcasts, 2; and Priestleys, 14, 16, 214, 227, *231*, 233; Aldermaston marches, 22; at Brooke Hill, 24–6, 33, 186; and Aclands, 94; and Peggy Lamert, 125; mystery of ourselves and our species, 189; at Kissing Tree House, 192, 203, 232, 240; *Saturn Over the Water*, 206; on JBP's prose, 219–20; Mill House, 233, 241; and death of JBP, 240; memorial address, 241
Collins, L. John: and Priestleys, vii–viii, ix, 14, 16, 214, 227, *231*; CND, ix, 16; happy marriage, xi; JBP's broadcasts, 2; RAF chaplain, 3; priest, 11; 2 Amen Court, 14; JBP and, 23, 26, 61, 233; at Brooke Hill, 24, 186; and Aclands, 94; at Kissing Tree House, 192, 203; *Saturn Over the Water*, 206; Homosexual Law Reform Campaign, 207–8; Hubberholme, 228; retirement and death, 237
Cooper, Susan, 230–31, *233*
Council for the Preservation of Rural England, 207

Davison, Edward, 48, 49, 55, 74
Davison, Natalie, 74
Davison, Peter, 173
De la Mare, Walter, 49
Denison, Michael, 86, *176*, 178, 180
Duff, Peggy, 12, 14, 16, 17
Dunne, J.W.: JBP and, vii, 79, 84, 212; *An Experiment in Time*, 77–8; Turner and, 149

Elgar, Sir Edward, 165
Engels, Friedrich, 198, 200
excavations, 126, 127, 135, 141–2

First World War, 22, 44–6, 115
Foot, Michael, 17
Forester, C.S., 49
Forman, Denis, *later* Sir Denis: and Helen Mouilpied, 154, 170; and Collinses, 214; Jacquetta's birthday party, 237; Jacquetta and Diana Collins stay with, 240; JBP's memorial service, 241
Foster, Sir Michael, 106
France (*see also* Paris), 135

Garrod, Tony, 214
Gauntlett, Raymond, 93
Gertrude: at Brooke Hill, 25–6, 180, 186; 'Priestley nurseries', 89; at Kissing Tree House, 192, 203; to Florida, 227; retirement, 232
Goaman, Michael, 172, 232
Goaman, Vicky, 232
Gollancz, Victor, *later*, Sir Victor, 11, 92
Good, Alan, 92
Goss, Arthur, 12
Gosse, Edmund, *later* Sir Edmund, 47
Gowland, James, 105, 106, 112
Graves, Robert, 46
Gray, Dulcie, 86, *176*, 178
Greene, Graham, 49
Greenwood, Arthur, 1
Gurdjieff, George Ivanovitch, vii

Hales the gardener, 204, 233
Halifax, 1st Earl of, 1
Hansford-Johnson, Pamela (Lady Snow), 229
Harris, Wilson, 95
Hawkes, Charles Pascoe, 130, 133, 134, 182, 184
Hawkes, Christopher: reputation, 126; appearance, 126; Jacquetta and, 126, 127, 129, 133, 134, 162, 170, 181–2; brilliant and gifted, 129–30; personality, 130, 143, 162, 170; broken engagements, 130; wedding, 131; honeymoon, *133*; British Museum, 134, 138, 162; and Jacquetta's parents, 135, 139; Clermont-Ferrand excavation, 135;

Lascaux caves, 135; 'workaholic', 137–8, 142; Scandinavia, 138; moves to Primrose Hill, 139; and his mother, 139–41; outbreak of war, 143; *The Prehistoric Foundations of Europe*, 145; Professor of European Archaeology, 162; and Wheeler, 170; divorce, 182, 183, 184; and his father, 183; writes to Nicolas, 184; second marriage, 186; writes to Sonia, 186–7

Hawkes, Eleanora, *née* Davison, 130, 131, 134, 139, 183

Hawkes, Jacquetta (Jacquetta Priestley): archaeology, vii, 18–19, 113–14, 122, 125, 205–6; writer, vii, 18; marriage with JBP, xi, 185, 186; background, 11; religion, 11, 208–9; Priestley/Hawkes divorces, 11; CND, 14, 17–21 *passim*, 23, 207; appearance, 15; Aldermaston marches, *21*, 22; scholarly mind, 26; hostess, 26; poetry, 43, 129, 149; UNESCO, 101, 154, 162; birth, 106; and her father, 106–7, 116; and her mother, 106, *115*; early memories, 108, 109–10, *109*; childhood, 110–14, *111*, 116–19, *117*; honesty, 111, 159, 183, 236; courage, 112–13; Perse School, 119; ornithology, 120–21, 126; Newnham College, 122–3, 124; and King of Sweden, 124; and Peggy Lamert, 125; rugby football match, 125–6; excavations, 126, 127, 135, 141–2; and Christopher Hawkes, 126, 129, 145, 162, 170, 181, 182; in Palestine, 127–9; wedding arrangements, 131; honeymoon, *132*, 133, *133*; early married life, 134; Lascaux caves, 135–7; Scandinavia, 138; pregnancy, 139; birth of son, 139; move to Primrose Hill, 139; Fellow of Society of Antiquaries, 142; her marriage with Hawkes, 142–3; outbreak of war, 143, 144; homosexual passion, 143; civil servant, 145, 153; and Turner, 145–6, 149, 152–5 *passim*, 162, 171; her fascination, 150; and Helen de Mouilpied, 154; and JBP, 154, 155, 237; love affair with JBP, 159–60, 162; and Nicolas, 152, 180, 184, 185, 208; book dedications, 169, 188, 208, 209; divorce, 182–3; and Hawkes's second marriage, *185*, 186; humanist, 190; Kissing Tree House, 192, *205*, *216*, 244; *Literature and Western Man*, 202; archaeological correspondent of *Sunday Times*, 206; involvement in community affairs, 207; views on education, 207; Collinses' guest, 214; John Danz lecture, 215–17; influenced by *Beyond Reductionism*, 216; JBP refuses CH, 219; Johnson's sketch of Kissing Tree House, 222; and Marghanita Laski, 224; and JBP's OM, 224; attitude to royalty, 224; and Barbara, 227; holidays, 227, 232; Priestley exhibition, 232; staff problems, 232–3; personality, 235–6; birthday party, 237; JBP's death, 237–8; memorial service, 240–41, 242; unveils JBP's statue, *243*, 244; JBP's memorial tablet, 245–6, 247

works:

articles: 'Art in a Crystalline Society', 166; 'The Proper Study of Mankind', 205

books: *The Archaeology of Jersey*, 138, 139; *Dawn of the Gods*, 215; *Early Britain*, 148; *Fables*, 208; *The First Great Civilization*, 215; *Guide to Prehistoric and Roman Monuments*, 170; *Journey Down a Rainbow* (with JBP), 26–32; *A Land*, 14, 166–9, *167*; *Man on Earth*, 129, 136, 188–91; *Man and the Sun*, 110, 208; *Man of Two Worlds*, 215; *Providence Island*, 208; *A Quest of Love*, 235

plays (with JBP): *Dragon's Mouth*, 175–8, 180; *The White Countess*, 180, 181 poetry: 'Man in Time', 129; *Symbols and Speculations*, 152–3

Hawkes, Nicolas: birth, 139; his father and, 139, 180; holiday with parents, 142; with grandparents, *140*, 143, 145; and his mother, 150; unaware of tension, 162; Bryanston, 180; and his parents' divorce, 184–5; *Fables* dedicated to, 208; CND, 232

Hawkes, Penelope, 134

Heinemann, publishers, 229, *231, 232*

Herbert, Evelyn, 118

Hitler, Adolf, 90

Hodgkin, Dorothy, 21

Homosexual Law Reform Campaign, 207

Hopkins, Barbara, 106, 112, *113*, 119, 122

Hopkins, Frederick Edward, 106, 112, *113*

Hopkins, Sir Frederick Gowland, *113, 140*: history, 105–6, 108; personality, 106; Grange Road house, 108; powers of concentration, 108; agnosticism, 110; death of his mother, 112; First World War, 115–16; and Jacquetta, 116, 118; honours, 124, 131; Hawkes and, 127, 135; at pinnacle of his profession, 130–31; *Symbols and Speculations*, 152

Hopkins, Jessie Ann, née Stevens, *107, 113*: history, 106; marriage, 106; Jacquetta and, 106, 110, 111, 114, 122, 131; appearance and personality, 107; and her husband, 107; First World War, 115; and Barbara, 119; and Hawkes, 135; stays with Hawkeses, 139; Nicolas and, 145

Howard, John Eldred, 109, 222, 237

Hulton, Edward, 92

Ireland, 141–2

Isle of Wight, *see* Billingham Manor *and* Brooke Hill

Jameson, Storm, 17

Japan, 181, 182

Jersey, 139

John, Rosamund, *176*, 178

Johnson, Marigold, 222

Johnson, Paul, 222

Judd, Ian, *243*, 244

Jung, Carl Gustav: JBP and, vii, viii, 99, 174–5, 212; influence on Priestleys, 17; *Journey Down a Rainbow*, 26; JBP on, 200; quoted 242

Kendon, Frank, 50

Kendrick, Tom, *later* Sir Thomas, 127, 142

Kennan, George Frost, 14

King Edward VI Grammar School, Stratford on Avon, 207

King-Hall, Sir Stephen, *later* Baron King-Hall, 14

Kissing Tree House, *193, 204*: Priestleys' hospitality, viii; description of, 192; Priestleys at, 192; weekends at, 203, 222, *223*, 224; gardens, 203–4; Paul Johnson's sketch of, 222; JBP dies at, 237–8; sold, 244

Lambert, Catherine, 222

Lambert, Jack, 222, 239

Lamert, Peggy, 124–5, 145–6, 237

Lane, John, 49

Lane, Margaret, *later* Countess of Huntingdon, 17

Laski, Marghanita (Mrs John Howard), 237: CND, 17; *The Offshore Island*, 23; Admass, 30; atheism, 209; personality, 222–4

Laughton, Charles, 175

Laval, M., 135

Leigh-Hunt, Barbara, 96

Littlewood, Mark, 172

London: Highgate, 3, 63–4, 88; Blitz, 6, 88; Collins and St Paul's, 6; 2 Amen Court, 14, 16, 214, 230, 237; Albany, 14, *15*, 19, 88, 192, 214, 229; Central Hall, Westminster, 17; Festival Hall, 22; JBP to, 48, 49; Scarsdale Villas, 55; Hampstead, 57; Cleveland Gardens, 134; British Museum, 134, 142, 162; Primrose Hill, 139, 145; St Pancras Town

Hall, 178; Wimbledon picture gallery, 232; Buckingham Palace, 224; Westminster Abbey, 240
Lonsdale, Dame Kathleen, 21
Lynd, Robert, 49

Mackereth, James A., 43
Macmillan, Harold, *later* 1st Earl of Stockton, 20, 21, *160*
Mahr, Adolf, 141
Martin, Kingsley, 13, *13*, 14, 92, 147
Marx, Karl, 198, 200
Maud, Sir John, 154–5
Meredith, George, 54–5
Mexico, 156, 159
Meynell, Dame Alix, 21
Montaigne, Michel Eyquem de, 196
Moore, Henry, 168
Morris, Henry, 153
Moseley, Sir Oswald, 90
Mouilpied, Helen de, *later* Mrs Denis Forman: Jacquetta and, 154; lovers, 154; JBP and, 155; marries, 170; and Collinses, 214; Jacquetta's birthday party, 237; Jacquetta and Diana Collins guests of, 240
Murdoch, Iris, *later* Dame Iris: and Priestleys, vii-ix, 210, *211*; *A Severed Head*, viii, 209–10; CND, 20; reviews *The Image Men*, 218; at Kissing Tree House, 224; JBP's seventy-fifth birthday, 230, *232*
Mussolini, Benito, 1, 90

New Statesman, 12–13
New Zealand, 227
Nicholls, Maurice, 173, 174
1941 Committee, 92, 93, 94
Norfolk, 120, 121

Orloff, Count Sergei, 133
Ouspensky, Peter: JBP and, vii, 79, 84, 173, 174, 212; *New Model of the Universe*, 78

Palestine, 127
Paris: UNESCO meeting, 155; evidence for JBP's divorce, 183

Pascoe, Richard, 96, 241
Pick, Charles, 229, 241
Pickthorn, Kenneth, *later* Sir Kenneth, 95
Pinney, Betty, 143
Pirie, Antoinette, 17, 19
Poland, 227
Post, Ingaret van der, 15
Powys, John Cowper, vii, 80
Pratt, Amy, 207, 244
Pratt, Stephen, 207, 244
Previn, André, 227
Priestley, Amy, née Fletcher, 39, 41, 48
Priestley, Barbara: birth, 49; and her grandmother, *51*, 53, 57; unhappy childhood, 64; as adult, 64; in Arizona, 76; marries, 172; her husband, 227; her father and stepmother and, 227; artist, 232; death of JBP, 237, 238
Priestley, Emily Jane, née Tempest, *see* Priestley, Pat
Priestley, Emma, née Holt, 37–9, *38*
Priestley, Jacquetta, *see* Hawkes, Jacquetta
Priestley, Jane, *later* Mrs David Bannerman: JBP and, 53, *56*, 61, *89*, 161, 170, 173, 178, 183; Mary's birth, 53, 55; marriage, 56; appearance, 56; personality, 56–7; and her stepdaughters, 57; capability, 64; problems, 64; dedications to, 74; unexplained illnesses, 74, 173; winters in Arizona, 74, *76*; JBP discusses his work with, 82; *When We Are Married*, 83; French cuisine, 88; organizes 'Priestley nurseries', 88–90, *89*; OBE, 90; visits Soviet Union, 98; invests in farmland, 98–9; 'flu, 162; and Tom, 180; divorce, 180; and Bannerman, 180, 185–6; JBP's generosity, 183
Priestley, John Boynton (1894–1984): broadcaster, vii, 2–8, *4*, 88; painting, vii, 24, 210, 214–15, *215*, 222, 227, 228, 232; Christianity, vii; Time Plays, viii, 84; religion, 11, 31; divorce, 11, 182; voice, 2,

64; CND, 14, 17, 20, 21, 22, 23;
appearance, 15, 240; Diana Collins
and, 15, 16; philosophy, 17–18,
76–81; Aldermaston marches, 21–2;
First World War, 22, 44, 45, *45*;
personal conflict, 22; *Stars in Your
Eyes*, 22; and Collinses, 24, 230,
233; music, 24, 44, 85; at Brooke
Hill, 25–6, *100*, 210; *Admass*, 29;
Yorkshire and family background,
37–9; birth, 37–8; stepmother, 39;
boyhood home, 39, 42; and his
father, 40, 48, 53; on Liberalism,
41; youth, 42; poetry, 43; European
holiday, 44; Cambridge, 46, 47, *47*;
and Pat, 46, 47, 48, 50, 53, *54*;
degree, 47; moves to London, 48,
49; freelance work, 49; birth of his
children, 49; to Chinnor, 50;
financial problems, 53; and Jane, 53,
56, *89*, 170, 173, 180; Church
Harbour, 56; Hampstead, 57;
literary output, 57, 219; Walpole
and, 57, *58*, 59; The Grove,
Highgate, 63–4, *65*; Billingham
Manor, 64, *79*, *80*; taxation, 64;
promiscuity, 64; and Ashcroft,
66–7; theatre, 67, 68–9, 83–4, 86,
209; attitude to Chekhov, 70;
winters in Arizona, 74, *75*, *76*;
critic, 75, 77; dreams, 81, 234–5;
Denison on, 86; and Richardson,
84; World War II, 88; moves to
Albany, 88; politics, 90–91, 93–94,
95; 1941 Committee, 92–5; stands
for Parliament, 95, 170; visits Soviet
Union, *97*, 98, *213*; buys farms, 99;
convalescence 99; UNESCO, 101,
154, 155, 156, *160*; Jacquetta's *Man
on Earth*, 129; *New Statesman*, 148;
and Mary, 155–6, 161, 170,
220–21, 222; and Hawkes, 182;
judge attacks, 183; at Kissing Tree
House, 192, *199*, *233*, *236*; and Iris
Murdoch, 210, *211*, *232*; accused
of failure to create evil, 212;
humour, 214; Collinses' guest, 214;
tries different forms of writing, 217;

declines honours, 219; science
fiction, 221; on failure and success,
222; and Marghanita Laski, 223;
clown, 224; Order of Merit, 224;
attitude to royalty, 224; attitude to
censorship, 225; 'The Moments',
226–7; and Barbara, 227, 237;
Yorkshire Dales, 228; Savoy Hotel
celebratory dinners, 229; birthdays,
229, *231*, *232*; old age, 230, 235,
237, *238*; death, 237–8;
obituaries, 239; memorial service,
241; statue, *243*, 244; burial of
ashes at Hubberholme, *245*, 247

and Jacquetta: ix; happy marriage, xi,
32; his divorce, 11, 183; letters to,
149, 150, 160–61, 163, 171, 173–5,
178–9; on her poetry, 152; love
affair, 159–60, 162; they marry,
185, *185*; his refusal of CH, 219;
holidays, 227, *234*; in his old age,
237; his death, 238

personality: charm, vii–viii; dogged
determination, 48; entertaining,
162; extrovert, 26, 192; family man,
64–6, 76, 87; generosity, 55, 183,
207; grumbler, 11, 227, 228, 229;
grumpiness, 11, 67; human
understanding, 171; indolence, 74;
intuition, 23; as Jacquetta's husband,
186; loyalty, 229; moodiness, 67;
pessimism, 228; responsibility, 55;
romantic, 86; self-knowledge, 171;
stimulating, 162; sympathetic
insight, 155; tempter, 173;
unaffectedness, 59; unforgetting of
kindness, 59; warmhearted, 86;
wide-ranging mind, 26; Davison
on, 173; Diana Collins on, 241–2;
Dulcie Gray on, 86; Walpole on,
59, 61

works:

books: *Adam in Moonshine*, 57; *Angel
Pavement*, vii, 62–3, *62*; *Benighted*,
57; *Brief Diversions*, 47; *Bright Day*,
99–100; *Delight*, 39–40, 65, 174,
247; *The Doomsday Men*, 23, 206;
English Journey, 71–3, *72*, 74, 90,

246; *Farthing Hall* (with Walpole), *58*, 59; *Festival at Fairbridge*, 172–3; *George Meredith*, 53, 54; *The Good Companions*, vii, 59, *60*, 61–2, *61*, 64, 82, 172; *The Image Men*, vii, 217–18; *Instead of the Trees*, 236–7; *Journey Down a Rainbow* (with Jacquetta), 26–32; *Lost Empires*, vii, 212; *Literature and Western Man*, viii, 193–202, *195*, 240, 242; *Over the Long High Wall*, 236; *Man and Time*, 210–12; *Margin Released*, 46; *Midnight on the Desert*, 75, 76, 77; *Out of the People*, 93; *Papers from Lilliput*, 48; *Rain Upon Godshill*, 76, 79, 80, 82; *Saturn Over the Water*, 206–7; *Snoggle*, 221; *They Walk in the City*, 188; *Thoughts in the Wilderness*, 225–7; *A Visit to New Zealand*, 227

essays: 'Britain and the Nuclear Bomb', 12; 'Eros and Logos', 17

libretto: *The Olympians*, 164

plays: *Cornelius*, 84; *Dangerous Corner*, 68; *Doomsday for Dyson*, 22; *Dragon's Mouth* (with Jacquetta), 175–8, *176*, 180; *Eden End*, 70, *71*, 74, 84, 164; *Home is Tomorrow*, 162, 165; *I have Been Here Before*, 84; *An Inspector Calls*, vii, 95–6, *96*, 98, 164; *Johnson Over Jordan*, 85–6, 147, 230, 241; *Laburnum Grove*, 69; *The Linden Tree*, 162, 164, *164*, 165; *Music at Night*, 86; *A Severed Head* (with Iris Murdoch), 209–10; *Summer Day's Dream*, 165; *Time and the Conways*, 84, 85, 165; *When We Are Married*, 83–4, *83*; *The White Countess* (with Jacquetta), 180, 181, *181*

Priestley, Jonathan: education, 37; marriages, 37, *38*, 39; houses, 39; personality, 40–41; play reader, 41; socialist, 41; and JBP, 42, 48; book dedication to, 48; death, 53

Priestley, Mary: birth, 53; name, 55; and her mother, 64; as a child, *63*, 88; breakdown, 155–6; JBP and, *76*,

87, 161, 170, 220, 222; marriage, 172; later history, 220; pen-and-ink drawings, 232; music, 232

Priestley, Pat: and JBP, 46, 47, *52*; pregnancies, 48, 49; birth of daughters, 49, 50; personality, 49, 55; illness, 50; appearance, 53; death, 55

Priestley, Rachel, 63, *63*, 76, 98, 172, 232

Priestley, Sylvia: birth, 50, *51*; flourishes, 50; her stepmother and, 57; at Rachel's christening, *63*; unhappy childhood, 64; in Arizona, 76; as adult, 64; marries, 172; artist, 232; flautist, 232; death of her father, 237, 238

Priestley, Thomas: birth, 63; sweetness of nature, 67; *Eden End* dedication, 74; in Arizona, 76; school, 98, 170, 180; and his parents' divorce, 180; drawings and paintings, 232; funeral address, 246

Priestley, Winifred, 39, 41, 48, 247

Puddock, Ann, 214: cook-housekeeper, 25, 88; to Highgate, 89; 'Priestley nurseries', 89; BEM, 90; Brooke Hill, 180; after Priestley divorce, 186; at Kissing Tree House, 192, 203, 224; to Florida, 227; high standards, 233; death of JBP, 237; and Jacquetta, 244

Rabelais, François, 195–6

Richardson, Ralph, *later* Sir Ralph: JBP and, 84–5, 227; *Johnson Over Jordan*, 85, 86, 230; *An Inspector Calls*, 96, 164; Savoy Hotel dinner speech, 229

Robinson, Josephine, 224

Robinson, Robert, 224, 230

Russell, 3rd Earl, 12, 16, 23

Sandys, Duncan, *later* Baron Duncan-Sandys, 11–12

Sassoon, Siegfried, 46

Scandinavia, 124, 138

Scotland: JBP in Highlands, 99; Jacquetta in Orkneys, 154

Second World War: Churchill's oratory, 1–2; Dunkirk, 1; JBP's broadcast 'postscripts', 2–8, *4*; Priestleys, 88; 'Priestley nurseries', 89, *89*; war declared, 143; Hawkses, 143–4, 145

Shakespeare, William, 196–7

Shaw, George Bernard, 84, 175

Smallwood, Norah, 237

Snow, Sir Charles, 229–30

Soviet Union, 96, 98

Squire, J.C., *later* Sir John, 47, 49, *50*

Stalin, Joseph, 98

Strachey, Joan Pernel, 123

Suffolk, 126

Sweden, Crown Prince Frederick, *later* Frederick IX, King of, 124

Swift, Jonathan, 198

Taylor, A.J.P., 17

Tempest, Granny, 50, *51*, 53, 57

Thompson, Robert, 245

Thorndike, Sybil, *later* Dame Sybil, 164, *164*

Turner, Delphine, 145

Turner, Emma, 120

Turner, Kitty, 117–18

Turner, Walter, *146*: and Jacquetta, 145–6, 149, 152, 154, 162, 171; history, 146–7; critic, 147; and JBP, 147–8; personality, 148; poet, 149; death, 150; *Fossils of a Future Time?*, 150–52; dedication of *A Land*, 169

Tynan, Kenneth, 178

UNESCO, 101, 154, 155, 156, *160*, 215

USA: *Journey Down a Rainbow*, 26–32; Priestley family in Arizona, 74; *Eden End* in New York, 74; JBP in New York, 161, 175; Jacquetta lectures in, 175, 215–16; Florida International Music Festival, 227

USSR, *see* Soviet Union

Vernon-Jones, Esther, 116

Walpole, Hugh, *later* Sir Hugh, 57, *58*, 59, 61, *63*

Wheeler, Mortimer, *later* Sir Mortimer, 170, 235

Wilkinson, Ellen, *later* Dame Ellen, 154

Wilson, Angus, *later* Sir Angus, 214, 229

Wilson, Harold, *later* Baron Wilson, 219

Wooland, Norman, *176*, 178

Wykeham, Peter, *later* Sir Peter, 172, 227, 246

Wyndham-Lewis, Angela, 53, 56, 66, 76, 88, 172

Wyndham-Lewis, Jane, *see* Priestley, Jane

Wyndham-Lewis, Mary, *see* Priestley, Mary

Yeats, W.B., 149

Yorkshire (*see also* Bradford): Dales, 227–8; Arncliffe, 228; Hubberholme, 228, 245–7, *245*

Zimmerman, G.D., 149